THE TRUTH

THE TRUTH OF ŽIŽEK

EDITED BY

PAUL BOWMAN AND RICHARD STAMP

continuum

Continuum International Publishing Group
The Tower Building   80 Maiden Lane
11 York Road   Suite 704
London SE1 7NX   New York, NY 10038

British Library Cataloguing-in-Publication Data
A catalogue record for this book is available from the British Library.

ISBN-10: HB: 0-8264-9060-3
         PB: 0-8264-9061-1
ISBN-13: HB: 978-0-8264-9060-5
         PB: 978-0-8264-9061-2

Library of Congress Cataloguing-in-Publication Data
A catalog record for this book is available from the Library of Congress.

Typeset by Servis Filmsetting Ltd, Manchester
Printed and bound in Great Britain by
Antony Rowe Ltd, Chippenham, Wiltshire

CONTENTS

CONTENTS

NOTES ON CONTRIBUTORS

Simon Critchley is Professor of Philosophy at the New School for Social Research, New York, and at the University of Essex, UK. During 2006–07 he is a Getty Scholar at the Getty Research Institute, Los Angeles. He is author and editor of many books, most recently *Things Merely Are* (Routledge, 2005). His new book, *Infinitely Demanding*, is forthcoming from Verso in 2007.

Leigh Claire La Berge is a doctoral candidate in the American Studies Program at New York University. She is writing her dissertation on representations of finance in twentieth-century American Literature.

Paul Bowman is Senior Lecturer in Media and Cultural Studies at Roehampton University, London. He has written for numerous academic journals and books, and is the author of *Post-Marxism versus Cultural Studies: Theory, Politics and Intervention* (Edinburgh University Press, 2007), editor of *Interrogating Cultural Studies: Theory, Politics and Practice* (Pluto Press, 2003) and is currently preparing a book on the politics of popular culture.

Mark Devenney teaches political philosophy at the School of Historical and Critical Studies at the University of Brighton. He recently published *Ethics and Politics in Contemporary Theory: Between Critical Theory and Post-Marxism* (2004) with Routledge, and is completing a book on political philosophy and death. He graduated from Essex University, England where Ernesto Laclau was his supervisor. His research interests include continental political philosophy, psychoanalysis, conceptualizing death and the novels of J.M. Coetzee.

Jeremy Gilbert teaches cultural studies at the University of East London. He is co-author (with Ewan Pearson) of *Discographies: Dance Music, Politics and the Culture of Sound* (Routledge, 1999) and co-editor (with Timothy Bewes) of *Cultural Capitalism: Politics After New Labour* (Lawrence and Wishart, 2000). He is currently working on *Anti-Capitalism and Culture* (Berg, forthcoming) and *Common Ground: Democracy and Collectivity in an Age of Individualism* (Pluto, forthcoming).

Iain Hamilton Grant is the author of several essays on contemporary philosophy and German Idealism, including *Philosophies of Nature after Schelling* (Continuum, 2006), and teaches at the University of the West of England, where he is Director of Philosophical Studies.

Oliver Marchart teaches cultural studies at the University of Basel and political theory at the University of Vienna. His recent books include *Laclau: A Critical Reader* (Routledge, 2004), edited with Simon Critchley; *Techno-Colonialism: Theory and Imaginary Cartography of Culture and the Media* (Löcker, 2004, in German); and the forthcoming (in English) *Beginning Anew: Hannah Arendt On Revolution and Globalization* (Turia & Kant 2005, in German).

John Mowitt is Professor in the departments of Cultural Studies and Comparative Literature, and English at the University of Minnesota. Author of numerous texts on the topics of culture, theory and politics his most recent book, *Re-Takes: Postcoloniality and Foreign Film Languages*, appeared in 2005 from the University of Minnesota Press. He is also a co-editor of the journal, *Cultural Critique*. His current research concerns radio as an object of scholarly inquiry.

Ian Parker is Professor of Psychology in the Discourse Unit at Manchester Metropolitan University. He is a psychoanalyst in Manchester, where he is secretary of Manchester Psychoanalytic Matrix. He is a member of the Centre for Freudian Analysis and Research, the London Society of the New Lacanian School and the College of Psychoanalysts. His books include *Psychoanalytic Culture: Psychoanalytic Discourse in Western Society* (Sage, 1997) and *Slavoj Žižek: A Critical Introduction* (Pluto, 2004).

Richard Stamp is Lecturer in Cultural Studies at Bath Spa University. He has published work in books such as *Theoretical Interpretations of the Holocaust*, *Dying Words: The Last Moments of Writers and Philosophers* and *Monsters and the Monstrous: Myths and Metaphors of Enduring Evil* (all Rodopi). He has also written on Žižek and film theory for *Film-Philosophy.com*.

Jeremy Valentine teaches cultural studies at Queen Margaret University College, Edinburgh. He is co-author (with Benjamin Arditi) of *Polemicization: The Contingency of the Commonplace* (Edinburgh University Press, 1999) co-editor (with Alan Finlayson) of *Politics and Poststructuralism: An Introduction* (Edinburgh University Press, 2002), and co-editor of the Edinburgh University book series *Taking on the Political*.

Slavoj Žižek is a philosopher and psychoanalyst who was born in Ljubljana in 1949. He is currently Senior Researcher at the Department of Philosophy, University of Ljubljana, and Co-Director of the International Center for Humanities, Birkbeck College, University of London. He is the author of many books, the most recent of which are *The Parallax View* (MIT Press 2006) and *How to Read Lacan* (Granta 2006).

FOREWORD: WHY ŽIŽEK MUST BE DEFENDED

Simon Critchley

Leaving aside the considerable implications for fist-fucking that Žižek so eloquently describes, let us get straight into his metaphysics as it is expressed in the central concept of his recent work: the parallax.[1] The concept of parallax and the parallax view is a way of giving expression to, at its deepest, the radical non-coincidence of thinking and being. If Parmenides and the entire onto-theological tradition that follows him, famously recovered by Heidegger, claims that it is the same thing to think and to be, then Žižek disagrees. Between thinking and being, between, in his parlance, the ticklish subject and the tickling object, there exists a radical non-coincidence, a constitutive lack of identity. That is, there is no sameness, no oneness, to thinking and being. In Lacanese, and this is something that Žižek has been teaching us since *The Sublime Object of Ideology* in 1989 – which, to my mind, is still an amazingly rich and, more importantly, *effective* book – the parallax view is the expression of the not-all, the *pas-tout*, that circles around the traumatic kernel of the real.

Žižek's metaphysical claim is that there is a gap at the heart of ontological difference. In Heideggerian terms, to which Žižek constantly refers – and his engagement with Heidegger on questions of ontology and politics is one of the most compelling aspects of his recent work – there is an irreducible break between the ontological and the ontic. It is precisely this gap that Heidegger sought to cover up in his political commitment to National Socialism and his pathetic attachment to life in the provinces by claiming to find an instantiation of the ontological in the ontic, of being's historicity in the German people, say. Žižek's methodological claim is that this non-coincidence between thought and being requires a *dialectical* articulation. To avoid misunderstandings, this dialectic is not positive, that is, it does not culminate in a higher positivity, synthesis or reconciliation of opposites. It is rather characterized by what Žižek calls *Versagung*, a denial, privation or failure, in a word a *not* that expresses the *knot* at the core of that which is, namely its traumatic kernel. As Žižek insists, this 'that which is' is materiality itself, and therefore his method is a dialectical materialism understood in a very new sense. That is, not the ossified stupidities of *Diamat*, nor the aestheticized resignation of Adornian negative dialectics (although there are often unspoken proximities to Adorno and maybe they sometimes live in neighbouring houses in the same theoretical *cul-de-sac*), but something rather novel, a fusion of Lacan, of Hegel *à la Slovène* and Marx very much *à la Slovène*. It is a dialectic that forces us to face an insurmountable parallax gap at the heart of that which is.

Žižek explores this parallax view, this radical non-coincidence of thought and being, in three main areas: philosophy, science and politics, which correspond to the three main sections of *The Parallax View*, complete with their charming extended interludes on Henry James and the impasses of what is called 'anti-anti-Semitism'. What is most novel in Žižek's recent work is his extended engagement with the brain sciences and debates in the philosophy of mind. Although I have second (and, to be frank, some third) thoughts about Žižek's views on philosophy and science, I would like to raise a specific question with regard to the third parallax, namely politics.

In the conclusion to *The Parallax View*, although it is suggested throughout the book, Žižek claims that the parallax view opens onto a subtractive politics, expressed in the figure of Melville's Bartleby, who is Žižek's heroic anti-hero. What interests Žižek in Bartleby is his insistent 'I would prefer not to', where Žižek places the emphasis on the 'not to' or the 'not to do', on Bartleby's impassive, inert and insistent being, which hovers uncertainly somewhere between passivity and a vague threat of violence. Žižek's closing fantasy is a movie version of Bartleby, with a Norman Batesesque Anthony Perkins playing the psychotic lead. So, at the level of politics, it is ultimately the politics of Bartleby's smile, of his 'not' that Žižek wants to oppose to other forms of political theorization. Which other forms? Well, mine for example. So, enough about Žižek, let's talk about me.

There are a series of vicious remarks about me at the beginning of the final chapter of *The Parallax View*, 'The Obscene Knot of

Ideology, and How to Untie It'. Žižek compares my position to that of an academic *Rumspringa*, the Amish practice of letting their children run wild for a couple of years of sex, drugs and rock 'n' roll with the 'English' before either deciding to return to their community or preferring not to. Basically, Žižek accuses me of engaging in an academic *Rumspringa* in my recent writings on politics, where I allegedly engage in a series of hysterical political provocations based on the dim memory of some radical past.[2] After a series of quotations and comments from me, Žižek writes:

> Does not Critchley's position, then, function as a kind of ideal supplement to the Third Way Left: a 'revolt' which poses no effective threat, since it endorses in advance the logic of hysterical provocation, bombarding the Power with impossible demands, demands which are not meant to be met? Critchley is therefore logical in his assertion of the primacy of the Ethical over the Political: the ultimate motivating force of the type of political interventions he advocates is the experience of injustice, of the ethical unacceptability of the state of things. (Žižek 2006: 333–34)

For Žižek, my position is too determinate, too 'coarse', and risks losing sight of the irreducibly antinomical structure of the parallax view. That is, I end up in a theoretical position of opposition that loses any possibility of being heard by the capitalist globalization that it seeks to undermine. He goes on to call my position and the position of people like me a 'fake' (Žižek 2006: 334), a false idea of resistance that fails to adopt the parallax view.

Now, of course, it goes without saying that this is an awful calumny and a horrible distortion of my entirely coherent and well-conceived position, but – perverse as it may seem – that is what I like about Žižek, what we might call the narcissism of big differences. We do not agree and perhaps we should not agree. In many ways what is needed at the present theoretical conjuncture are big differences, although slightly less narcissism, if that is not a performative contradiction. According to this slightly counter-intuitive logic, the chapters in the present book, often by way of attack, might also be seen as defending Žižek. And I should make a confession: the text to which Žižek makes allusion above also contains some vicious remarks about him, about his political views and in particular what

I would see as his utterly mannerist attachment to the tatters of Leninism and Stalinism. We are dealing here with an economy of viciousness, which I think is both intellectually healthy, has sharp philosophical edges, and is even sometimes entertaining. We do not all agree and the dreadful thing about so much of American academic life is the sentimental belief that we do. So, it is despite these vicious remarks, or rather because of them that I think Žižek, like society in Foucault, must be defended.

This brings me, of course, to my vicious question: how can we conceive of *action* in relation to Žižek's account of the parallax view? I am not just thinking about political action, but also psychoanalytic action, scientific action or even philosophical action. What we seem to be left with is the passivity and inertia of Bartleby's smile and some rather vague threats of violence. I always find and have found Žižek's work diagnostically brilliant in its perspicuous and counter-intuitive analyses of philosophical or sophistical *doxai*, political orthodoxies and cultural objects, but weak at the level of prescription, action and the old Chernyshevskyan–Leninist question, 'What is to be done?' Žižek's work is littered, cluttered even, with the most spectacular reversals, inversions, surprises and concatenation of objects that one would usually consider as opposed, moving in one paragraph from Hegel to cannibalism to Kafka to action movies and so on and on and on in splendidly obsessional ranting. But it sometimes seems to me that all these spectacular dialectical inversions serve to illustrate is the extent of our capture by the mirror games of ideological fantasy, where any seeming transgression is instantly recuperated as just a new form of normalization.

With this in mind, let us take up Žižek's basic argument about ideological fantasy that one finds all over his early work and which has been constantly reiterated in his later writings. Ideology is not an illusion, a dream, it is rather that which structures our effective, really existing social relations, masking what the early Žižek – at the time much closer to Laclau than at present – saw as the basic antagonism that structures society. The nature of ideological fantasy is expressed in Marx's dictum, 'they know not what they do, but they do it'. That is, ideology is not in a state of epistemic deficit or deception. We *know* very well that our lives are structured by fantasies, but we still *believe* in those fantasies. This is the deep, abiding truth of Marx's analysis of commodity fetishism: we know that there is nothing magical about commodities or indeed about the money that is needed to buy them, yet we act as if there were. To use an example obviously not drawn from personal experience, the punter knows that the dominatrix that is trampling his balls is doing it for the money, yet he believes in the fantasy nonetheless. We are fetishists in practice, not in theory. Reality is structured by belief, by a faith in fantasy that we know to be a fantasy yet we believe nonetheless. This is a stunning diagnostic insight, yet my question is and always has been: what does one *do* with this insight? What follows for action from this argument for the constitutive nature of ideological fantasy? Are we not eternally doomed to an unending plague of more fantasies that can in turn be criticized by Žižek and by generations of future Žižeks? Sometimes, I wonder. To use the word that Žižek uses against me, is there not something fake about this position, something fraudulent and fraudulently powerless about its hysterical provocations?

Let me return to *The Parallax View* and take another political example. Žižek offers a very powerful critique of Alain Badiou's conception of politics based on the notion of the truth-event. Žižek's point is that Badiou's insistence that politics be thought and practised around the notion of event as that which exceeds what he calls the 'situation' and which takes place without regard for any structural support in that situation, ends up in what might be called a pure politics. Such a position has no way of thinking the question of economy, of the critique of political economy. Again, Žižek is not arguing for a return to a reductive Second International economism, but against pure politics and in favour of a parallax view of the relation between politics and the economy. That is, we need to account for both the political event or the formation of subjectivity in relation to the event *and* the socio-economic determinations of that subjectivity, which together form what a quasi-Gramscian like me would call a 'historical bloc'. Now, this critical insight strikes me as powerfully right and a strong critique of pure politics or what some have called 'disco-Marxism', the reduction of Marxism to discourse and discursive articulation. But my question is: what does one *do* with this insight at the level of prescription, action and the rest? This is left absolutely vague.

For me, diagnostically powerful as it is, Žižek's work and the central concept of the parallax is the expression of a *deadlock*, both a transcendental-philosophical deadlock and a practical-political deadlock. The only way of unblocking that deadlock for Žižek is by vague apocalyptic allusions to violence and utopian allusions to future structural antagonisms in capitalism that will have possibly dramatic political consequences. Yet, I think this is so much whistling in the dark. Read in a certain light, Žižek's work is very dark indeed.

I remember asking Žižek years ago about the implications of his work for political action and he answered, characteristically, 'I have a hat, but I do not have a rabbit'. My question is: where is the rabbit? We need at least one rabbit, maybe more if we want them to breed. Let us just say that I do not think Bartleby is that rabbit.

NOTES

1 Slavoj Žižek, *The Parallax View* (2006: 13). For reasons of economy and clarity, I will focus my comments on this book, Žižek's *magnum opus*, according to the publisher's blurb, although Žižek expressed some doubts about that particular choice of words the last time I spoke with him.

2 The paper that Žižek refers to can be found online at <http:/www.politicaltheory.info/essays/critchley.htm>. A greatly revised version of this paper will appear in *Infinitely Demanding* (forthcoming).

EDITORS' INTRODUCTION: IS THIS NOT PRECISELY. . . THE TRUTH OF ŽIŽEK?

Paul Bowman and Richard Stamp

A blurred contour, a stain, becomes a clear entity *if we look at it from a certain 'biased' standpoint* – and is this not one of the succinct formulas of ideology?

(Žižek, *Did Somebody Say Totalitarianism?*)

Is this not the very logic of melancholic identification, in which the object is overpresent in its very unconditional and irretrievable loss?

(Žižek, *Did Somebody Say Totalitarianism?*)

Is this not the supreme proof of the emotional abstraction, of Hegel's idea that emotions are *abstract*, an escape from the concrete sociopolitical network accessible only to *thinking*.

(Žižek, *Revolution at the Gates*)

Is this not the most radical expression of Marx's notion of the general intellect regulating all social life in a transparent way, of the postpolitical world in which 'administration of people' is supplanted by the 'administration of things'?

(Žižek, *Revolution at the Gates*)

And is not Alfred Hitchcock in such a position of exception with regard to this standard Hollywood narrative? Is he not the very embodiment of Hollywood 'as such' precisely insofar as he occupies the place of exception with regard to it?

(Žižek, *The Fright of Real Tears*)

And, to go a step further, is the practice of fist-fucking not the exemplary case of what Deleuze called the 'expansion of a concept'?

(Žižek, *Organs Without Bodies*)

At the time of writing this introduction, in the never-quite-sultry first weeks of July 2006, British television has been broadcasting nightly bulletins promising a 'pervert's guide to cinema', presented by pervert-in-chief, Slavoj Žižek (2006a). The programmes' presenter is billed as 'philosopher and psychoanalyst', professions that do not often appear in TV schedules – except perhaps in the same popular films that Žižek takes for his examples. Indeed, the three hour-long instalments of *The Pervert's Guide to Cinema* appear to be a striking and timely historical conjunction between a particular form of intellectual celebrity and the niche market diversification of broadcast media.[1] How Žižek and we have arrived at this conjunction might provide the opening for any one of the contributors to this present volume of chapters – not least for Žižek himself.

Žižek first came to the notice of international intellectual and academic communities outside of his native Slovenia in the late 1980s, with his engagement with the post-Marxist political theory of Ernesto Laclau, who – reciprocally – wrote the preface to *The Sublime Object of Ideology* (1989), Žižek's first book in English. The ensuing critical debates with Laclau and Mouffe, and later also Judith Butler, drew Žižek into the forefront of critical and cultural theory, where he has remained, developing his unique position as instigator and mediator between various theoretical traditions, ever since.

In some sense, this 'success' clearly relates to Žižek's now-signature use of examples from popular culture, particularly the cinema, to illuminate and explicate the finer points of Lacanian theory and the speculative reflexivity of Hegelian ontology. This was developed most acutely in a trio of publications that introduced Žižek to the fields of cultural studies and film studies: *Looking Awry: An Introduction to Jacques Lacan Through Popular Culture* (1991), *Enjoy Your Symptom! Jacques Lacan in Hollywood and Out* (1991a) and the edited volume, *Everything You Always Wanted to Know About Lacan (But Were Afraid to Ask Hitchcock)* (1992). He has not stopped, or even slowed down, since then. Indeed, since 1992, Žižek has published over twenty further authored and edited volumes, and there are currently (as always) many more in preparation.

However, in the face of such prolific productivity, sustained scholarly reception of his work has actually been rather belated. The sole exceptions to this absence have been two volumes edited by Elizabeth and Edmond Wright: first, their themed collection of Žižek's writings, *The Žižek Reader* (1999); and second, a Žižek-themed issue of

Paragraph (24 [2001]). Only in the last few years has Žižek's growing international and multidisciplinary influence and public media profile been met with a rush of publications: Sarah Kay's *Žižek: A Critical Introduction* (2003), Tony Myers' *Slavoj Žižek* (2003), Ian Parker's *Slavoj Žižek: A Critical Introduction* (2004), Slavoj Žižek & Glyn Daly's *Conversations with Žižek* (2004), Matthew Sharpe's *Slavoj Žižek: A Little Piece of The Real* (2004) and Rex Butler's *Slavoj Žižek – Live Theory* (2005). Further introductory texts on Žižek are also 'currently in preparation'.

The most immediately striking fact about these books is that they have been preoccupied with *introducing* Žižek to a wider specialist and non-specialist audience. This is of course understandable, given the need to become acclimatized with Žižek's often complex and elliptical explications of Lacan and Hegel. However, in the majority of cases, these 'critical introductions' have been rather more 'introductory' than 'critical'. (It is perhaps significant that Kay, Daly and Butler all acknowledge the direct involvement of Žižek in their books' production.)[2] Quite distinct from this, *The Truth of Žižek* is aimed at readers for whom these introductions, and Žižek's own texts, have left them with the desire for a more challenging range of critical responses to his work. This is the key contribution of this book. Whereas already existing 'introductory' scholarship has in many cases been produced with some degree of 'authorization' or even 'correction' by Žižek – as mentioned: Kay (2003), Žižek and Daly (2004), Butler (2005); even Parker (2004), with which Žižek seems content 'to agree to differ' – *The Truth of Žižek* offers a series of independent and thought-provoking assessments of Žižek's work, which challenge and recast Žižekian scholarship, in order to develop it and move it further along.

Of course, although this book was conceived to be as free as possible from such 'authorization' or 'correction', it seemed not only fair but also *potentially* eventful to provide Žižek with a platform to respond directly to his critics. This right to respond seemed particularly appropriate given both the provocative nature of Žižek's own work and the highly engaged critique of his work and its intellectual and political contexts undertaken in this present collection. For, the aim of this book is to make a series of interventions: to intervene by assessing, pressuring, redirecting, reorientating and developing not only Žižek's work, but also the future of Žižek-affiliated or Žižek-informed theory and practice. This strikes us as a particularly important and timely task because Žižek's work has made such a dramatic contribution to the reinvention and revivification of key theoretical and political debates in many academic fields and cultural contexts today. The unmistakable influence of Žižek's work has been and continues to be felt increasingly in the fields of media studies, film studies, political theory and cultural studies of all kinds, as well as directly and indirectly in both 'continental' and 'analytical' philosophy, as it is in anthropology, sociology and indeed in any of the wide array of fields that incorporate Freudian and Lacanian psychoanalysis and Marxist and post-Marxist political theory.

Moreover, as the TV broadcast of his *Pervert's Guide to Cinema* demonstrates, Žižek's work now overflows the confines of specific disciplines and academic debates. Žižek has not remained confined to the circuits of academic publishing and colloquia, and has begun to establish himself as a globally identifiable public intellectual: from his regular appearances on BBC Radio 4 and many high-profile public-speaking engagements, newspaper articles, and beyond, to his current role as International Director of the Centre for Public Intellectuals at Birkbeck. He is perhaps in the process of becoming 'the intellectual's Public Intellectual'. Certainly, the first documentary film made about him (with the arresting title of *Žižek!*), not only sold out at its premiere in San Francisco, but queues of people are regularly turned away at the door of all manner of invariably sold-out Žižek events.

Clearly, Žižek's work has intervened into a very wide array of intellectual, cultural and political contexts. Yet it is remarkable that Žižek has achieved this far-reaching intervention by staunchly claiming the *necessity* of capital-P 'Philosophy' and 'High Theory', and by developing – in the era of supposed 'dumbing down' – an unashamedly and polemically theoretical approach to *all* subjects. Whether it is making sense of the reality-TV phenomenon or discussing moral hypocrisy in debates about torture, the NATO bombing of Sarajevo or global terrorism, Iraq, re-interpreting Hitchcock, or identifying and diagnosing contemporary fantasies and phobias, Žižek is always involved in a bold, philosophically charged retheorization of concepts of subjectivity, politics, truth, authenticity and action. In the process, his work can be playful and provocative, polemical and aggressive, even knowingly belligerent – *all at the same time*.

Consequently, the important question seems to be: what is the intellectual status of Žižek's work? Or, indeed, 'when the hurly burly's done', what is the *truth* of Žižek? In posing this question, this book picks up a gauntlet thrown down by Žižek himself, in the name of a certain 'truthfulness' or 'fidelity'. For, in a dedication to Joan Copjec at the start of *Organs Without Bodies* (2004a), Žižek pledges what could be characterized as a 'hyper-Kantian' mode of *respect*: namely, responding to another thinker with what he calls 'the coldness and cruelty of a true friendship'. This was a role played in Kant's own life by J.G. Hamann, whose own idea of friendship might be read as the obverse of Kant's doctrine of virtue: 'I'm not one of your listeners. Instead I'm your prosecutor who contradicts you'.[3] *The Truth of Žižek* should be read as just such a paradoxical expression of friendly, respectful fidelity. For what all of the chapters in this book share is the recognition that Žižek's impact on an ever-widening range of disciplines (and beyond) demands the seriousness and coldness of critical examination. Anything less would, according to Žižek's own declaration, be *disrespectful*. To borrow a phrase from Ernesto Laclau: 'any intellectual intervention worth the name will be "heterodox"' (Laclau 2000: 65).

But in terms of this very hyper-Kantian framework, since his arrival on the intellectual scene Žižek's work has largely been greeted in one of two equally 'disrespectful' ways. The first is a tendency towards uncritical hagiography. (This is perhaps best exemplified by Eagleton's oft-cited remark about Žižek being 'the most formidably brilliant'.) The second is the disparaging dismissal of his work as either 'pop philosophy' or as critical theory 'for the TV generation'.[4] Quite distinct from either of these impulses, *The Truth of Žižek* is entirely concerned with taking Žižek seriously. Even at their most critical (and some of the chapters in this book are fiercely critical) all of the contributors share a conviction that – to borrow Simon Critchley's apt Foucauldian formula – 'Žižek must be defended'.

Perhaps this is especially so even if one seeks to *refute* Žižek, because getting the measure of his work – for whatever reason: whether to explicate it or to challenge it – demands serious intellectual effort. In intellectual and academic contexts, hagiography and vitriol must both give way (at some point) to *thought* and *analysis*. Even if one wished to argue that Žižek does not theorize, philosophize or analyse 'thoroughly' or 'correctly', the fact is that Žižek's retheorization of the human and inhuman world is thrown down as a challenge. What such intellectual provocation *obliges* is a reciprocal form of intellectual radicalization on the part of his readership, which is inseparable from serious scholarship and critical scrutiny.

Whether or not Žižek himself achieves his much-touted political aim of acting in such a radical way as to 'shift the terrain' and 'alter the coordinates' of the terms of intellectual debate is surely, well, debatable. Indeed, even whether such an achievement itself would be at all 'radical' is equally debatable. For it is a question of whether such an *academic* achievement would be of any *political* conse-quence, radical or otherwise. In this regard, it seems prudent to bear in mind that academics in particular are quick to reach for such adverbs as 'radical,' and that all too often such words are used pre-cisely when their radicality is most questionable, even doubtful. Too often, it seems, academics forget (or pretend to forget) that they speak and write from a position that is already situated within a complex set of apparatuses, which are not merely disciplinary and institutional but bound up with commercial and market-driven imperatives. So: what could possibly be radical about such speech and writing?

As a public intellectual and (at least something of) a celebrity who claims radical political credentials at the same time as declaiming academics for deluding themselves that they somehow hold radical credentials, Žižek inevitably raises eyebrows. However, before meting out judgments about whether Žižek's position involves a performative contradiction, or even some kind of hypocrisy, there is virtue in *considering* Žižek, as an example or case study. For Žižek's own 'public position' foregrounds what may otherwise remain below many radars: namely, the complex imbrication of intellectual production in academic and commercial institutions, forces and imperatives. Intentionally or inadvertently, Žižek's very success – or his plight – demands an intellectual interrogation. It promises to teach us a great deal about our own 'position' or loca-tion, and as such, about the limits and possibilities of the imbrica-tion and reticulation of academic intellectual life with society, culture and politics.

So where does Žižek stand with respect to this dilemma of the 'intellectual as celebrity'? On the one hand, his work seems to trample across all institutional and disciplinary borders, just as his global intellectual fame takes him across geopolitical ones. On the other hand, however, Žižek very rarely takes cognizance of the institutional and commercial forces that act upon him and make his interventions possible. Such 'facts' as these, often moving in apparently contrary directions (sometimes even at the same time), call out for further study and analysis; a rigorous engagement not just with Žižek, but with the institutions, mechanisms, forces and fault-lines of culture and politics. These questions should not be 'mere' inquiries about Žižek the person, for they have a direct bearing on the question of the ethical, political and cultural status of academic intellectual work.

Thus, *The Truth of Žižek* assesses the international, multidisciplinary, motivated 'event' of Žižek's work and its effects. This is a body of high theory that has sought to foster radical political engagement, to respond to – and even to *induce* – important shifts, jolts and mutations of intellectual and political practices. Moving from philosophy to political activism, from cultural and political theory to theology and science studies, Žižek's work seeks to intervene, to alter, and *to make a difference*. What is that difference? *The Truth of Žižek* offers a thorough first engagement with the sizeable yet still unclear impact of Žižek's work. The overarching question of the book is: what is the nature and what are the effects of Žižek's intervention? The chapters address this in diverse yet abutting and often overlapping ways: from those which chiefly 'psychoanalyse' and historicize Žižek's position itself, in the sense of bringing both history and Žižek's own preferred psychoanalytic categories to bear on his own efforts and orientations (La Berge, Parker, Mowitt); to those which focus on assessing the philosophical grounds, underpinnings, and political stakes and consequences of his work (Hamilton Grant, Marchart, Devenney); to those which problematize and deconstruct his use of categories and examples (Bowman, Stamp); to those which question the validity of his methods and the credibility of his scholarship itself (Gilbert, Valentine).

Such a brief list is, of course, violently reductive in the face of the complexity and subtlety of the contributions to this book. A great deal more ought to be said about each one. They all rigorously engage with the breadth and richness of Žižek's formidable body of work, from distinct disciplinary and intellectual perspectives. However, this Introduction is not intended as the place to 'sum up' or pass some kind of anachronistic definitive 'first and last word' on the works that follow – as if the issues and questions raised here are now closed and resolved.[5] Instead, we would prefer simply to extend our sincere thanks to all of the contributors to this book, each of whom has intervened invaluably and engagingly in the important theoretical and practical debate with, on, about, around and far beyond the work of Slavoj Žižek. Needless to say, without them, this book would not have been as it is. We would also like to thank Sarah Douglas and Continuum not only for publishing but also for making some very helpful suggestions about this book, from the first stages of our discussions about it. Thanks are also due to Adrian Rifkin and Kristin Ross, whose tangential involvements also added to the book. We thank Simon Critchley for providing his helpful and enlightening Foreword. And finally, but not least, we would like to thank Slavoj Žižek for generously rising to the important challenge of responding to his critics.

NOTES

1   The three instalments of *A Pervert's Guide to Cinema* were transmitted on the free-to-air digital channel, More4 (3–5 July 2006). Marketed at its launch in 2005 as 'the new adult entertainment channel', More4 is a subsidiary channel of Channel 4, focusing it's output on documentaries (the new 'new rock 'n' roll', apparently) and 'high-quality' US imports, such as *The West Wing*, *Sopranos* and *NYPD Blue*. Pound for pound, and dollar for dollar, it has one of the most import-heavy schedules of the main UK free-to-air channels. Needless to say, it is the perfect outlet for a highly marketable international intellectual commodity.

2   Even the forthcoming *International Journal of Žižek Studies* features Žižek as the most prominent member of its editorial board. The notable exception in this respect is Parker (2004), which has nonetheless received praise from its subject (on the back cover), 'despite obvious differences'.

3   Hamann to Kant, dated December 1759 – cited in Morgan 2000: 215.

4   This entrenched perspective is fuelled by a noxious mixture of theoretical puritanism – 'too much popular culture'; 'you don't mix *this* with *that*' – and (as Ian Parker notes in his *Critical Introduction* (2004) to Žižek) an intra-European mythologization – 'the mad monk of Ljubljana'.

5   Indeed, in the spirit of open-ended and ongoing intellectual debate, this 'Editors' Introduction' itself was written before Žižek composed his Afterword, and it was shown to him along with all of the chapters. Apart from this final added footnote and some slight copy-editing corrections, we have not subsequently revised this text.

THE WRITING CURE: SLAVOJ ŽIŽEK, ANALYSAND OF MODERNITY[1]

Leigh Claire La Berge

For a companion philosopher, the only sign of real respect is envious hatred – how is it that I did not come upon what the author is saying? Would it not be nice if the author had dropped dead prior to writing this, so that her results would not disturb my self-complacent peace?

(Žižek 2000b: xiii)

WHAT'S YOUR FANTASY?

Readers of Slavoj Žižek's critical theory cannot fail to be impressed by his prolific oeuvre. His first English-language book, *The Sublime Object of Ideology*, published by Verso in 1989, has given way to a career of bountiful and frenetic academic writing if ever there was one: a total of 24 monographs in the last 15 years, as well as several edited and co-authored volumes.[2] There is a temporal regularity to Žižek's approach, a constant stream of intellectual production that is momentarily focused and epiphanic, though often repetitive, circuitous, and diffuse. Regardless of the content, whether Žižek is making a singular point or explaining to us yet again that the Lacanian real is 'that which resists symbolization absolutely', he is an entertaining writer, as one of his titles 'Postmodernism or Class Struggle? Yes Please!' (2000a, 90–135) demonstrates. His style is dogged, engaged and frequently humorous as he juxtaposes the most banal of popular and commercial culture with the history of philosophy, critical theory and psychoanalytic theory in order to critique Althusser's theory of ideology, Kant's notion of a regulative idea, Marx's theory of commodity fetishism, and, always, how any of these, and many more, modern epistemic problematics fare in the face of a Lacanian critique.

9

Žižek uses the capaciousness and breadth of his philosophical repertoire to pursue a rearticulation of the great utopian combination that has eluded so many attempts at synthesis from the 1920s through to our own day: Marxism and psychoanalysis.[3] Žižek has simply updated the bibliographic references for our time. Instead of Marx's critique of industrial capitalism, Žižek engages with what Marxist economist Ernest Mandel has theorized as 'late capitalism', what others have called a globalized or post-industrial economy;[4] within psychoanalysis Freud has been replaced by Jacques Lacan, Žižek's strongest influence. Žižek himself has described his animating question as being: 'Is it still possible to pursue the Enlightenment goal of knowledge under conditions of late capitalism?'[5] He has also suggested that 'the core of [his] entire work is to use Lacan as a privileged intellectual tool to reactualize German Idealism. From [his] perspective, the celebrated post-modern displacement of subjectivity rather exhibits the unreadiness to come to terms with the truly traumatic core of the modern subject' (Wright & Wright 1999: ix). Thus Žižek's is a restorative project, a philosophical excavation that longs to reaffirm – not displace – the modern. His stated period of inquiry, 'late capitalism', has certain postmodern overtones but, as Žižek intimates above, for him the postmodern is but a symptom of the modern. In this sense the student of modernity resembles the Freudian analysand as one who is always 'ready to be content with an incomplete solution' (Freud 1964: 231).

For his exposition of the traumatic core of modernity – what will figure as his own unconscious – it is unsurprising that Žižek would attempt to combine aspects of Marxism and psychoanalysis. Each offers a sweeping revision of modernity by focusing on what is repressed/denied by most narratives of the modern: Marxism theorizes the progress of capitalist accumulation through capital's attendant destruction/enslavement of much of the world's populace in its pursuit of surplus value; psychoanalysis investigates subject formation by focusing on the psychosexual sublimation and repression necessary to produce the modern individual. Žižek attempts to revamp these paradigms of modernity, to construct a critical theory based on the insights of Lacanian structural analysis, and, in doing so, to produce what many have claimed Marxism is no longer capable of: an ideological critique of contemporary global capitalism.[6]

Although Žižek repeatedly emphasizes that to dismiss Marxism by neglecting analyses of capital formation and accumulation is tantamount to 'naturalizing capitalism', Žižek himself rarely ventures into the political economy of Marx's work. He stays close to the commodity fetish and the analysis of the forms of value (both from *Capital* vol. I, ch. I: Marx 1992). In fact, Žižek's primary engagement with Marxism is rhetorical and polemical; it is the utopian act of simply positing a horizon beyond capitalism, a hope for its defeat somewhere, at sometime, as a political gesture. His most consistent use of the Marxist canon is through the theory of commodity fetishism, which he uses to construct various homologies to psychoanalytic fetishism, so that fetishism becomes the transubstantiating category between psychoanalysis and Marxism. As capital reproduces itself over time under the dictates of the law of value, expressed by the human commodity fetish, human beings live according to the repetition compulsion, repeating infantile fantasies. Marxism attempts to expose the first by applying dialectical thinking to political economy; psychoanalysis attempts to expose the second by making the unconscious conscious through verbalization.[7] We see, then, that while Žižek claims an allegiance to Marxist political economy, his more dominant interest is in the construction of a Lacanian critical theory, and Lacanian reformulation of the modern philosophical canon (including Marx himself).

Despite the fact that Žižek's oeuvre is copious and ambitious, a systematic consideration of his work is possible precisely through his consistency, repetition and rhetorical style. The clearest route through Žižek's prodigious content is via its form, and for that reason I engage in a stylistic consideration of his work. What is so attractive, even seductive, about Žižek's prose? On what is his style modelled? Hegel's dialectic density? Marx's empirical-to-abstract systematicity? Lacan's sinuous, obscurantist lectures? To an extent, Žižek adopts all of these. But the form of his writing, his prose style itself, is fashioned around a psychoanalytic session in the context of an extended course of analysis. Žižek's prolific, repetitive, regularized oeuvre should be understood as a writing cure. Žižek is the ultimate analysand of modernity itself – doubting, disobeying, perverting and demanding in an attempt to cure, not exactly the patient, but that with which the patient identifies most strongly: the modern. This chapter will explore exactly how Žižek constructs his (over-)identification with modernity, and why he chooses a discursive simulacrum of a course of psychoanalysis in order to sustain this relationship, what I refer to as Žižek's readership-as-analyst construction. We should remember from Lacan that while the real resists symbolization or experience, the most proximity we may ever develop to it is in the relationship between analyst and analysand. It is this ethic that animates Žižek's style. He will never produce a monolithic architectonic like Kant's *Critiques*, nor will he ever produce a systemic appraisal like Marx's *Capital*. Rather he will continue, month after month, year after year, to write slim books, to revisit the same narrative, to tell us the same epistemological stories with only slight variation, and occasionally there will be a breakthrough – but he will not abandon the analysis! 'Keep talking' is the analytic dictum; 'Keep writing/publishing' is Žižek's. Any associations? Let's go back. These are the injunctions from analyst to analysand, and this is the relationship Žižek has constructed between himself and his readership.

We can use psychoanalysis, both an individual session and the duration of a course of analysis, as an optic to analyse Žižek's style at the level of paragraph, monograph and oeuvre. What is the analytic style? On the most basic level, it is frequent. Analysands see their analysts multiple times per week for years. The duration and frequency fosters dependence, intimacy and, most importantly, transference, that unique relationship which develops between analyst and analysand. If the form of analysis is regular and planned, the content is anything but. In the sessions themselves, free-associative speech on the part of the analysand is demanded. The classic analytic spatial arrangement renders the analyst out of sight of the analysand, the latter of whom is reclining comfortably on a couch; the analyst observes the analysand but is free from his gaze.[8] The two may address each other face to face only in the few moments of daily arrival and departure. The analysand, unburdened by eye contact or reactive facial expressions on the part of the analyst, lying supine and feeling loquacious, begins to respond to the analyst's seemingly facile command: 'Tell me what's on your mind'.

ANY ASSOCIATIONS?

The fundamental process of psychoanalysis relies on the development of a transferential relationship on the part of the analysand towards the analyst.[9] In this section we will explore how the transference is represented in both classical and contemporary psychoanalytic theory, locate a possible characterological profile of Žižek as an analysand, and finally describe the transference that Žižek has developed between himself and his readership-as-analyst. Thus our discussion of transference, a topic that Freud himself describes as 'almost inexhaustible' (Freud in Esman 1990: 28), is done in the exclusive service of locating what I refer to as Žižek's writing-as-transference, a rather awkward exercise in which we must discern how Žižek relates to his readership, what he demands, what he represses, and how this manifests transferentially in his texts.

Freud theorizes the transference as a relationship that develops under controlled conditions in the 'laboratory' of an analysis, but which will nonetheless recapitulate the dominant tendencies of the analysand's relationships:

> The transference thus creates an intermediate region between illness and real life, through which the transition from one to the other is made. The new condition has taken over all the features of the illness; but it represents an artificial illness which is at every point accessible to our intervention. It is a piece of real experience. (Freud 1990: 411)

During the course of an analysis, the analyst will represent lovers, parents and so on; the analysand expresses these relations by re-enacting the infantile desires and fears that structured his early life.[10] The analytic relationship is further determined by a lack of correspondence between object of transference and object of desire. This constitutive gap becomes the breeding ground for fantasy, and eventually for cure. 'What I really want is to sleep with you', the analysand says to the analyst. 'If only you were my mother, then I would be content', he continues. These are, of course, transference demands, and the analyst will avoid gratifying them. As Žižek explains, the analyst knows that the analysand is 'demanding this of you, but what I'm really demanding is for you to refute my demand because this is not it!' (1999: 112).

The process of deciphering the question of what 'it' is is the narrative of a course of analysis, and should be understood as the patient demanding of the analyst that the analyst inform him of the basic fears and desires that structure his psychic reality. According to Lacan, 'the subject is looking for his certainty' (1979: 129).[11] The answer can only come through the verbalization of the analysand himself, by way of the abstinent and ascetic persistence of a course of analysis. The kernel of the analysand's fantasy life will manifest in the transference as long-repressed loves and fears emerge and take the analyst as their object, a process which transpires through repetition and becomes the central vehicle for analytic progress. Thus transference is simultaneously a condition for and an object of the analysis, but it is also 'the most powerful resistance to treatment' (Freud in Esman 1990: 29). It is resistance *and* progress, and it is the province of the analyst to interpret whether the transference has manifested in a resistive or progressive fashion.[12] More simply, 'transference is the greatest ally of analysis when understood, and the greatest obstacle when unnoticed' (Rioch in Esman 1990: 253).

Freud explains the contingencies of transference interpretation:

> We find in the end that we cannot understand the employment of transference as resistance as long as we think simply of 'transference'. We must make up our minds to distinguish between a 'positive' transference and a 'negative' one, the transference of affectionate feelings from that of hostile ones, and to treat the two sorts of transference to the doctor separately. Positive transference is then further divisible into friendly or affectionate feelings which are admissible to consciousness and prolongations of those feelings into the unconscious. (Freud 1990: 32)

Thus for Freud resistive transference may itself be manifest in a seemingly positive fashion, much as negative transference may be progressive.

Beginning in the 1960s, and following the work of analysts Elizabeth R. Zetzel and Ralph R. Greenson, what some analysts had previously identified as positive transference came to be described as a 'therapeutic alliance' or a 'working alliance', respectively. This alliance is defined as a certain maintained identification from analysand to analyst which facilitates the beginning and continuation of an analysis on the most basic and functional level. According to its proponents, the 'therapeutic [or working] alliance precedes analysis' (Brenner in Esman 1990: 173). A working alliance is what enables the analysand to feel comfortable and trusting enough of the analyst that he initially attends his appointments, speaks to the analyst, etc. Some members of the psychoanalytic community, however, have been quite critical of the working-alliance theory. After all, they ask, is not the working alliance simply part of the transference? They remind us that when the transference is passively accepted and not analysed is precisely when it becomes an obstacle.[13] At this juncture, when the question of positive transference or working alliance emerges, we are in a position to return to Žižek and to question where he and his writing-as-transference fall in relation to the above continuum. Should we consider Žižek's written texts as positive transference manifestations or are they instead a form of 'working alliance', in this case the sustenance needed to be a productive, employed, quasi-public intellectual? Is Žižek merely a repetitive writer or is he operating under what Lacan calls the 'vanity of repetition' in the transference? (Lacan 1979: 128).

Analyst Martin H. Stein investigates the difficulty in distinguishing positive transference from working alliance in his article, 'The Unobjectionable Part of the Transference', which we can use to develop a characterological portrait of Žižek.[14] In what we will see is a situation uncannily similar to the one that Žižek has presented us with, Stein describes an analytic situation in which what appears to be a basic working alliance is itself a resistance in the form of positive transference. He uses a 'special' group of patients to exemplify this dynamic: 'intelligent, highly articulate' patients who charm the analyst with 'intelligence, warmth and humor', and who finally 'demonstrate the characteristics of brilliant, charming and precocious children who on a superficial level appear very mature' (Stein 1990: 384–85). These analysands conjure a pleasant countertransferential reaction in their analyst, producing 'a tendency to fall into a comfortable situation dominated by mutual teasing, appreciation and intellectual competition' (1990: 387). This appears to be an unproblematic, if not enjoyable, state of affairs. And yet, as Stein suggests, this particular dynamic leads to a situation in which the analysand's 'underlying sexuality and hatred are so effectively disguised' that they cannot be analysed or rendered conscious. In the meantime, however, both parties are gratified without having to recognize the fundamental fantasy/transference demand. 'One of the risks [of not analysing the positive] is that the patient and analyst may find themselves in a state of mutual narcissistic regression, a kind of near-erotic mutual sleep' (1990: 397). This situation is allowed to transpire precisely because these analysands' intense transference-love for their analyst is 'readily concealed by what looks like the unobjectionable part of the transference and is manifested by their devotion to analysis or to what some would call the working alliance' (1990: 385). Finally, Stein concludes that 'even the most essential and finely constructed instruments [rationality and intelligence] are double-edged. . .sadly therefore we must confront and analyze those traits we are most likely to admire' (1990: 387).

Now that we have an understanding of the transference and a possible characterological profile of our analysand, we can ask our most basic question: what is 'it'? What is our analysand really demanding? Why is Žižek writing and publishing books so desperately and impulsively? Is he remembering or simply repeating? Is the writing cure progressing or are we trapped in an analytic stalemate controlled by Žižek's repetitive monograph production? It is here that we turn to Lacan, and specifically to Žižek's reading of Lacan, for it is Lacan who supplies the key clinical-theoretical construct of moving beyond regressive analytic gratification in order to free the analysand from his dependence upon the Other. This is the process of 'traversing the fantasy', the ultimate analytic pinnacle. Which fantasy? Whichever fantasy sustains the analysand and 'lets him falsely believe that there is something in me more than myself, some special unique substance which makes me worthy of the Other's desire' (Žižek 1999: 296). In Lacanian parlance this experience is explained by the *objet petit a*, (defined by Jacques-Alain Miller as 'in-itself which is for us')[15] which will come to be embodied in the analyst, and then traversed through the process of an analysis. 'The traversing of fantasy involves the subject's assumption of a new position with respect to the Other as language and as desire. . . There where it – the Other's discourse, ridden with the Other's desire – was, the subject is able to say "I" ' (Fink 1995: 62). Here we find Lacan's structuralist, linguistic version of Freud's *Wo es war, soll Ich werden*: where it (Other/Id) was, I (ego) shall come into being.

Žižek describes the traversal as such:

> what is the analysand to do when he reaches the end of the analytic cure. . .? Lacan. . .insists that. . .there is a desire that remains even after we have traversed our fundamental fantasy. . .and this desire, of course, is *the desire of the analyst* – not the desire to become an analyst, but the desire that fits the subjective position of the analyst, the desire of someone who has undergone 'subjective destitution' and accepted the role of the excremental abject, desire delivered of the phantasmic notion

that 'there is something in me more than myself', a secret treasure which makes me worthy of the Other's desire. (1999: 296)

In Žižek's case, his perceived 'secret treasure' that makes him worthy of the Other's desire is his ability to write/publish rather continually while incorporating ever-newer current events and popular cultural phenomena into his humorous, Lacanian critical theoretical apparatus. Whether his object of critique is the design of toilet bowls, habits of feminine pubic-hair grooming in different countries (both in *The Plague of Fantasies*), the events of 11 September 2001 (in *Welcome to the Desert of the Real*), or whatever else enters his gaze, Žižek will provide the discourse. Is there not some special substance motivating him, telling him to go ahead and turn that five-minute conversation into another book? Some nudging, encouraging Other reminding him that he has more to write and that his readership wants him to write it? 'Remembering, Repeating and Working-Through', Freud's description of the therapeutic trajectory of psychoanalysis, is for Žižek a professional modus operandi.

But because Žižek has interpellated us, his readership, into his readership-as-analyst – that is, because the Other's desire is represented by the analyst and his analyst is his readership – we are now in a position to have to respond, and therefore to interpret his writing-as-transference. And now that we understand the process by which Žižek will be extricated from his dependence on his readership-as-analyst, we can approach his texts with some amount of specificity. What is Žižek's most basic transference demand, and is it progressive or resistant? Is he asking that we understand the ideological disposition of late capitalism? By engaging with Žižek on this level, will we enable him to traverse the fantasy? Or are we 'charmed by intelligence, warmth and humour', trapped in an analytic stalemate with him? Is Žižek really on his way to realizing himself as 'excremental abject', as Lacan would have it?

A recount before we move into a close reading of Žižek's transference as it manifests in specific texts: Žižek has constructed a transferential relationship by positioning his readership as his readership-as-analyst. His doing so has not been recognized as such, mistaken instead for a working alliance, a misdiagnosis that frequently happens with loquacious, intelligent, precocious analysands. Yet now that we have diagnosed his prodigious prose as writing-as-transference, we can interpret his work in hopes of him eventually traversing the fantasy. As Lacan himself says, 'the analyst must await the transference before beginning to give his interpretation' (Lacan 1979: 130). In the next section we will locate Žižek's structuring fantasy through his symptomatology as it manifests in his compulsive attacks on the postmodern and his consequent identification with the modern.

CAN YOU SAY MORE ABOUT THAT?

To what do we owe Žižek's systematic denigration of what he alternately refers to as political correctness, multiculturalism and postmodernism? Although Žižek's terminology differs, there is a single object of his critique, and the fact that this discourse is repeated and that it indeed exhibits a repetition compulsion necessitates that we analyse it.[16] Through an examination of this repetition, which takes the form of attacks on political correctness, multiculturalism, postmodernism and identity politics somewhat indiscriminately, we will trace the emergence of the symptom which Žižek's writing cure must confront. We will use his own definition: 'A symptom . . . is an element which – although the non-realization of the universal principle in it appears to hinge on contingent circumstances – *has* to remain an exception, that is the point of suspension of the universal principle' (1997: 46). We will see how this symptomatic mistaking of the rule for an exception is the form of Žižek's demand that we stop trifling with political correctness in order to reorient ourselves towards political economy. And it is through this understanding of Žižek's conception of the philosophical postmodern and its various institutional accompaniments that his symptom will be transferentially replicated and revealed.

Žižek narrates this fundamental part of his written case-history:

> today's 'postmodern' political thought [is] against the spectre of the (transcendental) Subject. . .[in order] to assert the liberating proliferation of the multiple forms of subjectivity – feminine, gay, ethnic. . . According to this orientation, one should abandon the impossible goal of global social transformation and, instead, focus on. . .asserting one's particular subjectivity in our complex and dispersed postmodern universe, in which cultural recognition matters more than socioeconomic struggle – that is to say, in which cultural studies have replaced the critique of political economy. (Žižek 1999: 3)

This passage is representative of much of Žižek's writing on the 'postmodern'. He begins by vaguely locating postmodern political thought against Enlightenment political thought and then moves on to the political manifestations of that thought wherein anyone, it would seem, who is not a straight white male is given the pedestrian branding of 'particular' as against the unmentioned/repressed 'universal'. These agents of the particular advocate their own cultural recognition as a political platform, thus fracturing any possibility of collective praxis; they have furthermore succeeded in usurping institutional academic attention by shifting our critical focus away from the study of the forces and relations of production and onto themselves via the discipline of cultural studies. Here we see an important rhetorical move on Žižek's part: the equating of being a minority with the proliferation of the postmodern in the form of cultural studies, and the equating of global capitalism with multiculturalism. The ethos that enforces this project *en toto* is 'the PC' or politically correct one, as it manifests in affirmative-action programmes, institutional-diversity campaigns, and public recognitions of the value of ethnic plurality. In order to challenge this postmodern, politically correct hegemony, Žižek informs us that he is engaged in a 'political intervention, addressing the burning question of how we are to reformulate a leftist, anti-capitalist political project in our era of global capitalism and its ideological supplement, liberal-democratic multiculturalism' (1999: 4).

I have said that Žižek's critique of postmodernism will help us to locate his symptom, and now we see that Žižek himself has located postmodernism as a symptom, a key symptom of late capitalism, what he calls 'Multiculturalism, Or, the Cultural Logic of Multi-national Capitalism'. And because he understands multiculturalism to be a symptom of capitalism, he bases his critique of that capitalism on it. His most basic criticism is relatively straightforward: that the focus on race, gender, sexuality and ethnicity within socio-cultural criticism has obscured the focus on class. Thus for Žižek the primary motor of social oppression is elided and even naturalized in the process. This includes, 'a theoretical retreat from the problem of domination within capitalism . . . an exemplary case of the mechanism of ideological displacement . . . when class antagonism is disavowed other markers of social difference may come to bear an inordinate weight' (Žižek 2000: 97). More specifically, demands for political recognition within a liberal framework are always already 'grounded in a depoliticization of the economy' (2000: 98); class becomes 'named but rarely theorized', while 'the global dimension of capitalism is sustained in today's multicultural progressive politics' (2000: 96).

Žižek has told us that he is trying to formulate an ideological critique of late capitalism that reorients our attention to political economy, but he cannot quite complete the formulation because his associations seem always to drift back to what he calls the 'ideological supplement' of liberal multiculturalism. He concludes that the institutional, academic attention paid to Others is the problem, one that is furthered by their uncanny ability to design an episteme (postmodernism) that advances their own recognition. Like an analysand who tries once again to convince his analyst that *this* complaint is not the transference, that *this* problem really does concern the person of the analyst herself, that *this* demand is exceptional, Žižek leaves the terrain of potential political economy in order to dissect the particular struggles themselves. But even when the analysand succeeds in seducing the analyst into actualizing a transferential demand, it is *still* transference.[17] That is, even if Žižek has a formula for moving beyond the tired dichotomy of cultural studies versus political economy, he is *still* engaged in a transferential relationship with the former.

It is this fact that leads Žižek to explain repeatedly not only that minority political demands structurally sustain late capitalism, but that the demands themselves are frequently conceived and executed in a state of aporia. Thus the problem with queer demands of social/legal acceptance, Žižek concludes, is that what they *really* want is the exclusiveness/radicality that goes with social stigma and that on some level, queers enjoy making demands and positioning themselves as alterity more than they want reconciliation/recognition (1999: 225). Through this optic, apartheid becomes a kind of anti-racism (1993: 226), feminism does not adequately understand Lacan's injunction that woman is but a symptom of man (1994: 142), and so on. From his reading of Lacan's claim that 'there is no sexual relationship', or no sex without a third term, Žižek argues that we can find a logical fallacy in sexual-harassment legislation, for 'there is no sex without an element of "harassment"' (1999: 285). We can fairly easily deconstruct any one of Žižek's complaints. To take the last one, Žižek conflates sexual harassment (unwanted sexual attention) with the impossible desire for a love object, a distance that can never be entirely subsumed and thus creates a space for the desire itself (sexual tension). Thus, there can be no sex without desire manifest as tension, but no sex without harassment? However, to deconstruct any one of his missives is already to miss the point of the demand and subsequently to gratify instead of to analyse Žižek. We are not interested in the particular problems of social movements but in Žižek's effort to resuscitate political economic critique.

Žižek uses a similar logic to seduce us into criticizing the contradictions of consciousness-raising groups: when does the pleasure of talking about one's exclusion and denigration overtake any attempt at praxis?[18] This criticism provides a clue because we know that the unconscious temptation to accept stasis while gratifying oneself with minimal, verbal progress is hardly confined to liberal politics: we witness it in analysis too. And where Žižek advises us to look at the structures of liberal-democratic multiculturalism to understand the lack of political economic critique, we might instead look at Žižek's writing-as-transference. We do get something from Žižek's books, and he does get something from their publication, but is it enough? Or are we (in collusion with publishers, and especially Verso) continuing to gratify Žižek without any hope of a writing cure?

Let us take his most consistent demand: that we must look beyond capitalism, that we must continue to envision a Marxist and revolutionary agenda and possibility, a demand which we have already seen is deeply and dialectically intertwined with a critique of liberal politics through the pejorative optic of 'political correctness'. Ernesto Laclau has, quite properly, called Žižek on this. Laclau explains that he knew what Lenin and Trotsky meant when they issued calls for revolutionary seizures of state power, but Žižek? Does 'he have a secret plan of which he is careful not to inform anyone?' Laclau asks (2000: 206). Of course not, we can easily respond. Nonetheless it is pleasurable and possibly even germane for Žižek to demand revolutionary social transformation. So, then, is this what Žižek really wants, socialism? Would a decisive, historical reconciliation between the forces of production and the relations of production satisfy him? Or is this a classic example of a resistive transference demand that is itself symptomatic? Is Žižek confusing his criticism of marginalized political Others with his demands on the big Other? And, more problematic still, has his readership-as-analyst slipped into a stage of 'mutual, narcissistic regression', with him, where he is gratified that we continue to buy his monographs and we are gratified that he continues to publish them?

We now understand that despite his frequent rhetorical endorse-ments of the struggles of various subaltern constituents (women, gays, racial minorities), Žižek is critical of most, if not all, of the programmes that elevated and/or assisted their minimal social ascent: consciousness-raising groups, affirmative action, queer liti-gation, feminism and so on. He is further critical of any attempt at theorization of such praxis, whether realized as Laclau and Mouffe's 'chain of equivalences', or larger discourses like queer theory. Taken together these dramatic refusals by Žižek reveal a symptom. Is his constant denigrating of political Others not the intellectual equiva-lent of the infamous analysand who cannot make progress in his analysis because he cannot quit complaining about the state of the analyst's office? 'If only your couch were more comfortable, then I might be able to free associate'. 'If only you had better magazines in your waiting room, then I wouldn't be so angry and disappointed'. What Žižek is essentially saying, pleading is: if only we did not have political correctness, then we might have a proper revolution. If only we did not have liberalism, then we might have socialism. But within the transference, these claims should be read as: if only I [Žižek] was not busy attacking postmodernism, then I might very well be able to formulate a political economic critique.

One deduction that Žižek could not phantasmatically make, however, is: 'if only the Others didn't get so much recognition, then I might get more'. Quite the opposite, in fact; if the Others and their postmodern episteme were to vanish, Žižek would get less recogni-tion, not more. 'Everyone's analysis unearths a central fantasy', one analyst has claimed, and now we come to the object of our writing cure, the fundamental traumata.[19] Žižek, through his transference, is revealing to us his symptom: namely that the ascent of identity pol-itics and the symbolic redress of grievances from the white-male establishment is in fact sustaining his very own subjectivity. This is the fantasy that Žižek must traverse for the writing cure to be salu-tary. Žižek keeps obsessively, repetitively, desperately writing of the various problems of political correctness precisely to make sure that they will still be thought of as problems, problems designed for him to address – exactly what he accuses its proponents of doing, which is the surest indication of a symptom.

The PC [politically correct] attitude is an exemplary case of the Sartrean *mauvaise foi* of the intellectuals: it provides new and newer answers in order to keep the problem alive. What this attitude really fears is that the problem will disappear, i.e., that the white male heterosexual form of subjectivity will actually cease to exert its hegemony. . . The PC attitude is the form of appearance of its exact opposite: it bears witness to the inflexible will to stick to the white-male-heterosexual form of subjectivity. (Žižek 1993: 214)

This is perhaps the clearest transference manifestation thus far during the course of Žižek's writing cure.[20] He, a white heterosexual male who is neurotically invested in the criticism of political correctness, has accused the liberal, politically correct establishment of being fearful that he himself might disappear. That establishment, the very demographic that purchases Žižek's more-than-annual Verso monographs and showers adulation upon him when he frequently descends upon the university lecture circuit, is being accused of hating him so much that it secretly loves him; of wanting him gone so desperately that it cannot resist regularly attending his engagements. And yet this precise dynamic is but another projection: for it is Žižek himself who is caught in a dialectic of love–hate recognition with his object of study. It is he who has claimed that the Others are preventing the realization of the proper study of political economy, and it is he who is trying to offer a criticism thereof in order to move the object of critique from superstructure to base. But it is also he who is limited in his critical scope because his recognition is tied to theirs.

One of the most prominent fears that Žižek has so astutely diagnosed between competing inter-ethnic, inter-cultural or inter-racial factions is the fear of loss of pleasure, or theft of enjoyment. 'They [the Others] are stealing my enjoyment, taking what is properly mine' (1993: 203–204). Žižek cites the pleasure that Marxists have long taken from pointing out with amazement the failure of the working classes to see the light. We now see that in addition to trading Freud for Lacan, Žižek has updated and personalized this Marxian pleasure/frustration as well. While the paternalistic Marxist of yore could enjoy his exasperation by understanding that proletarians were operating under the sway of false-consciousness, Žižek has a different approach. Instead of 'I can see the light and you can't!' Žižek offers his readership/analyst: I can't see the light because you are blocking it! I can't provide the political economic

critique that we all so desperately need because I have to keep pointing out that what you Others are doing is not political economy –
which destroys my chance to do political economy.

At the same time, the Others' postmodern, politically correct platform has been internalized and transformed by Žižek into a
symptom, *his symptom*, that which is pleasurable and pathological
simultaneously, that which serves as the base of his neurotic control.
Žižek entitles one of his monographs *Enjoy Your Symptom!* (1991a)
and we can see now that he certainly does. Of course he resents the
Others' myriad political demands; at the same time, his resentment
has become the most stable part of him, the part which allows him
to ground his intellectual work. And now, like most analysands,
Žižek is reluctant to forgo his symptom which, after all, is the base
for his clarion and utopian call of Marxist revolution, and for his
career as well.

To keep reading/critiquing Žižek is to be trapped in this dichotomy, which has all the structure of a stalemated threat: either you
destroy the analysis or I will, is always, in a sense, the analysand's
ultimate threat. The discursive analysis he has constructed between
himself and his readership provides the circuit for sustaining this
dialectic: his projective assaults on the postmodern serve to reaffirm
his own ego (unconscious) as modern. Once this interpretation has
been offered in the service of his writing cure, it seems we should
then rest with a classically modern response: analytic silence.

NOTES

1 Thanks to Dehlia Hannah, Kristin Ross, Ann La Berge and Mary
  Poovey for their comments on an early version of this chapter. Thanks
  also to New York University's Marx Reading Group (Wol-san Leim,
  Michael Palm, Maggie Clinton, Quinn Slobodian, Steve Fletcher, Max
  Ward, Descha Daemgen and Osamu Nakano) for additional feedback.
2 See www.lacan.com for an updated, complete bibliography.
3 Members of the Frankfurt School inaugurated this tradition and it
  again was attempted in the 1960s and 1970s with the rise of the New
  Left. See also Fredric Jameson's 'Imaginary and Symbolic in Lacan:
  Marxism, Psychoanalytic Criticism, and the Problem of Subject' (1978)
  for a review of attempts to combine the Marxist category of the social
  with the psychoanalytic category of the subject, a gap which Jameson
  argues that Lacan may help us bridge.
4 The concept of 'late capitalism' was made famous in cultural studies
  circles by Jameson's 1984 essay, 'Postmodernism, or the Cultural Logic
  of Late Capitalism'. Yet for Ernest Mandel in his book *Late Capitalism*,

from which Jameson took the title (thus forever conflating the two in the minds of many cultural critics), late capitalism is in no way post-industrial. Far from it, Mandel discusses the massive automation and computerization of previously manual trades like agriculture (see Mandel 1975). Žižek's use of the term 'late capitalism', is thus rather vague. He seems to be referring to Jameson's interpretation of Mandel. Jameson himself has updated this figuration in his *The Cultural Turn* (1998) in which he does offer a much more political economic focus.

5 Taken from the preface to his own edited *Wo es War* series from Verso.

6 Žižek refers to the political economic object of his critique in various terms: late capitalism, multinational capitalism, and global capitalism are his most common. These correlate to a superstructure of postmodernism, political correctness and multiculturalism, again, all used somewhat interchangeably throughout his oeuvre.

7 In both cases, the biblical claim that 'they know not what they do' applies. See Slavoj Žižek's *For They Know Not What They Do* (1991b). Marx's famous description of those acting under the influence of capitalist ideology is, more precisely, 'they do not know it, but they are doing it'. See Marx's *Capital* vol. I, ch. 1 (1992). Freud's description of a similar dynamic is that 'man is not the master of his house'.

8 To refer to the analysand I have chosen to use the male pronoun; the analyst will be characterized as 'she'.

9 The feelings that the analyst develops towards the analysand are characterized as 'countertransference'.

10 'Transference-love consists of new editions of old traits . . . and it repeats infantile reactions. There is no such transference state which does not reproduce infantile prototypes' (Freud 1990: 29).

11 One can see, as Žižek does time and time again, how easily consumer capitalism can answer this question, and how futile any answer would be. One of Žižek's most entertaining and insightful combinatory uses of psychoanalysis and Marxism to investigate late capitalist society comes in his slender volume *The Fragile Absolute* (2000) which demonstrates how one of the most successful capitalist enterprises of all time answers this precise question: What is 'it'? The analyst knows that the analysand will gradually come to understand this himself, through the abstinent and ascetic persistence of a course of analysis. Coca-Cola, on the other hand, is more than happy to answer this most existential question: '*Coke is it*', is the infamous company's slogan. 'Coke is what?' any reasonable interlocutor might reply. According to Žižek 'it' is 'the mysterious and elusive X we are all after in our compulsive consumption of merchandise' (2000: 22). The X is that which both forms and ensures the continuation of our desire. Much like the answer to the analysand will only disappoint him and at the same time encourage him to ask for more to ameliorate his new lack, the beverage Coke actually makes one thirsty. The more you drink, the more you want.

12 'Freud regarded transference manifestations as a major problem of the resistance. However [he also said], it must not be forgotten that [transference], and [transference] only, renders the invaluable service of

making the patient's buried and forgotten love-emotions actual and manifest' (Rioch 1990: 253).

13 The debate over the working alliance is in many ways a debate about the boundaries and beginnings of an analysis, and it consumed the analytic community for some 30 years, in most cases being settled in favour of the working-alliance theory with only strands of traditionalists still supporting the ascetic, analytic neutrality that accompanies those who reject the working-alliance theory. For a lengthy recapitulation of the debate, see Esman's *Essential Papers on Transference* (1990).

14 Stein, who published this article in 1981, has subsequently lost his licence to practise. 'In September 2001, Stein agreed to $200,000 to settle a lawsuit alleging medical malpractice, sexual battery and fraud'. For the story of Stein's banishment from the analytic/psychiatric community, see *The Washington Post*'s exposé on 28 September 2003 (p. A21).

15 See footnote 42, p. 245, of *Tarrying with the Negative* (Žižek 1993).

16 Freud describes the repetition compulsion as it manifests in analysis by claiming that the analysand is 'obliged to repeat the repressed material as a contemporary experience instead of, as the physician would prefer to see, remembering something as belonging to the past' (Freud in Schafer 1990: 404).

17 See Schafer 1990: 410–11.

18 This point in its particular formulation is taken from a paper that Henry Krips circulated at the University of Melbourne entitled 'New Politics, Feminism and Science', in 10 October 2001.

19 See Janet Malcolm *Psychoanalysis: The Impossible Profession* (1981), p. 61.

20 It is also repeated often in Žižek's prose. For example, 'the conclusion to be drawn is thus that the problematic of multiculturalism. . .which imposes itself today is the form of appearance of its opposite, of the massive presence of capitalism as a *universal* world system: it bears witness to the unprecedented homogenization of the contemporary world' (1997: 29).

THE TAO OF ŽIŽEK

Paul Bowman

Like a sword that cuts, but cannot cut itself;
Like an eye that sees, but cannot see itself.
(Zenrin Poem)

THE TAO OF IDEOLOGY

The list of contemporary books whose titles begin with the phrase
'The Tao Of. . .' is extensive, and growing. These books range from
scholarly works to business manuals, via all kinds of self-help and pop
psychology to clearly New Age publications. In fact, the list of topics
that allegedly have a Tao of their own now encompasses virtually
every mainstream and marginal academic discipline as well as multiple (and – apparently – multiplying) cultural practices. There are Taos
on topics that extend from the predictable to the preposterous, from
the esoteric to the exoteric, and from the sublime to the ridiculous.

Apparently everything can be made into a book propounding this
or that Tao: from the nooks of philosophy to the crannies of science
(Watts 1995; Siu 1957), and from individual subsets of science to the
relationships between 'modern physics and eastern mysticism'
(Capra 1985), and beyond. Prominent are books on the Taos of this
or that kind of human selfhood: from the Tao of the psychological
subject (Bolen 1982) to Taos of the genders (Metz & Tobin 1996);
from the Taos of competitive subjects (Landsberg 1996) to those of
getting motivated (Landsberg 2000); from the health-focused subject
(Blate 1978) to Taos of work: there are Taos of business (Autry &
Mitchell 1998), management (Messing 1989), and sales (Behr & Lao
1997). There are Taos of icons like Bruce Lee (Miller 2000) as well as
Taos *by* them (selections from Bruce Lee's notebooks have been

posthumously published under the titles *The Tao of Jeet Kune Do* [Lee 1975] and *The Tao of Gung Fu* [Lee & Little 1997]). There is also a *Tao of Muhammad Ali* (Miller 1997), and even a *Tao of Islam* (Murata 1992). There is also, of course, a *Tao of Pooh* (Hoff 1982).

As J.J. Clarke points out, the original and central text of Taoism, the *Tao te Ching* (a title that is usually taken to mean *The Way of Virtue*) has recently become 'one of the most frequently translated of all the world's classic texts, with over two hundred versions in seventeen different languages' (2000: 56). As the *Tao te Ching* itself might say, from this original Tao 'the ten thousand things have sprung': myriad translations, offshoots, books, manuals, practices and worldviews each characterized by some relation to Taoism have emerged. What is more, this does not even scratch the surface of the vast and immeasurable sea of publications and practices that entail strong Taoist-sounding orientations and pretensions yet without explicitly shouting 'Tao' in their titles. Once more, prominent among these is the veritable torrent of management self-help books all heavily reliant on pseudo-Taoist tropes, of which *Who Moved My Cheese?: An Amazing Way to Deal With Change in Your Work and in Your Life* is but one exemplary example (Johnson 1998).[1]

Quite why there is such a contemporary proliferation both of the 'original' *Tao* and of new Taos is debatable.[2] But Slavoj Žižek's interpretation is unequivocal: the emergence of Taoist and Buddhist worldviews is, he contends, a 'spontaneous ideology' (2001: 216), an ideological response to the 'new conditions', in two crucial realms: that of *science* and that of the *economy*. That is, Žižek regards 'Western Buddhism' chiefly as *a non-scientific response to science* (a 'supplement'), and 'Western Taoism' chiefly as a straightforwardly ideological response to the chaos caused by contemporary economic processes. This is the root of Žižek's very obvious disdain for all things 'New Age' (2000a; 2001; 2001a; 2005).

In fact, it is crucial to note that Žižek's disdain for all things 'New Age' is much more than a '*mere*' distaste. It is not any old distaste. Rather, to Žižek, *this* taste – the taste for all things New Age – is exemplarily ideological, in the most pejorative sense. Indeed, Žižek actually argues that the contemporary Western interest in and turn to 'New Age "Asiatic"' thought. . .in its different guises, from "Western Buddhism". . .to different "Taos", is establishing itself as the hegemonic ideology of global capitalism' (2001a: 12). In other words, for Žižek, the contemporary 'Western' engagement with the 'mystical Oriental Other' is far from an innocuous or insignificant matter. Rather, *it is the exemplary ideological – and therefore fundamentally intellectual and political – problem of our time and place.* This is because, to Žižek's mind, the contemporary 'Western' recourse to Buddhism and Taoism is simply the perfect way to *avoid* intellectual, political and economic problems, by taking recourse to a fetishistic supplement:

> 'Western Buddhism' is such a fetish: it enables you to fully participate in the frantic pace of the capitalist game while sustaining the belief that you are not really in it, that you are well aware of how worthless the spectacle is – what really matters is the peace of the inner Self to which you know you can always withdraw. . . as in the case of a Western Buddhist unaware that the 'truth' of his existence is the social involvement which he tends to dismiss as a mere game. (2001a: 15)

THE TAOIST ETHIC AND THE SPIRIT OF GLOBAL CAPITALISM

Above, not a tile to cover the head;
Below, not an inch of ground for the foot.
                    (Zenrin Poem)

All that is solid melts into air, all that is sacred is profaned.
                    (Marx and Engels 1967: 83)

Žižek offers the image of a meditating yuppie in order to claim that there is a widespread cultural growth of a vaguely Taoist-sounding 'acceptance of change' as the dominant 'ideological attitude'. To Žižek's mind, this arises because the contemporary experience of global capitalism tends to be that of 'being thrown around by market forces' (2001a: 116). He takes this to be definitive of the form of life under contemporary capitalism, owing to the turbulent effects of deregulated markets and chaotic international flows of capital. Because of this, Žižek argues that there is now a growing ideological injunction not to 'cling' to old forms and values. In these conditions, he suggests, other than a retreat into defensive fundamentalisms, a Taoist ethic presents itself as an ideal ideological option. However, Žižek's point is that this 'Western Taoist' attitude is no *solution* to the problems of capitalism. In fact, for Žižek, this 'celebration' or resigned acceptance of unfixity, flow and non-clinging, is *nothing but the problem itself in inverted form, masquerading as (if) the solution*. It is an active misrecognition of a problem as (if) a solution, one that presumably, to Žižek's mind (although this is never really spelt out), facilitates the intensification of everyone's exploitation.

The very high incidence of business-management or performative-capitalist titles in the list of books entitled *The Tao of. . .* (management, sales, motivation, competition, performance: *results!*), as well as the immediately palpable sense in which Taoism is very often taken to mean *individualist laissez faire passivity* passed off as enlightened empowerment, certainly bolsters the Žižekian position (see Johnson 1998; Bowman 2003). As such, Žižek's argument recasts contemporary interest in all things 'New Age' and 'Oriental' in a provocative new light. But what is the source of that light? And what are the implications of this particular perspective?

The answer is simple. Žižek's entire argument is specifically designed to refute every other contemporary approach to understanding culture, society, politics and ideology than his own. The argument about New Age Taoism as ideology is primarily a key part in Žižek's ongoing critique of 'postmodernist relativism', 'deconstructionism', identity politics, multiculturalism and cultural studies (among others, as we will see). For, in recasting something so *apparently* innocuous, gentle, naturalistic, sweet and innocent as Taoism as *ideological*, Žižek seeks reciprocally to implicate any approach that might regard it as an interesting or beneficial 'multicultural' development or 'encounter'. For Žižek, both the practice and any intellectual interest in it or approval of it are *strictly ideological* (2001). Against this, rather than running with the multiculturalists, postmodernists or post-Marxists who might view the contemporary articulation of East and West as truly new, Žižek sees himself as remaining courageously faithful to the truth of Marxism (2001a: 33; 2002a: 308). Thus, he begins his argument about Western Buddhism and Taoism by finding a precedent in the work of Max Weber.

For Weber, Žižek reminds us, Protestantism was a necessary ideology of industrial-stage capitalism. By the same token, proposes Žižek, Taoism, Buddhism and New Age mysticism are to be regarded as the necessary ideology of contemporary 'postmodern' capitalism. This is because, for Žižek, it's like this: according to

Weber, during the 'industrial stage', the religiously informed work ethic of Protestantism (suffer now for rewards in the hereafter) guaranteed the discipline and active participation of the workforce. So, Žižek argues, Taoism and mysticism function in a similar way today: 'If Max Weber were alive today', he declares, 'he would definitely write a second, supplementary volume to his *Protestant Ethic*, entitled *The Taoist Ethic and the Spirit of Global Capitalism*' (2001a: 13). What defines the new spirit of capitalism is no longer the former need to embrace frugality, moderation, hardship and a sedulous work ethic as virtues (as was the case during the 'industrial stage'). Rather, today sees the new 'need' to actively embrace ceaseless change and rootlessness, because 'being thrown around by market forces' (Žižek 2001a: 116) is definitive of the contemporary era. Thus, not clinging to stable forms becomes a 'virtue', because it is the current way of capitalism. The way of ideology is the emergence of value systems produced to enable us to cope with – *by in some sense 'avoiding' the truth of* – real conditions.

For Žižek, the embracing of Taoism is recourse to an ideological 'supplement'. It becomes a kind of fetish. Thus, in his signature psychoanalytic idiom, Žižek classes 'Western Buddhism' as a perfect example of a *'fetishist* mode of ideology', in which the fetishistic attachment functions as 'the embodiment of the Lie which enables us to sustain the unbearable truth'. It remains a kind of avoidance of the truth even though 'fetishists are not dreamers lost in their private worlds, they are thoroughly "realists", able to accept the way things effectively are – since they have their fetish to which they can cling in order to cancel the full impact of reality' (Žižek 2001a: 13–14).

Of course, there may be no 'problem' with such a crutch in itself. Surely, finding ways to cope with the contexts into which one is flung and within which one finds oneself is not only a necessary but also a good thing. But, implicitly at least, Žižek is concerned that in this ideological attitude the problem itself returns as (if) both virtue and solution. Also, it is expressed through the sentiments of it being a 'good thing' not to cling, and instead to move with the times, go with the flow, not expect stability, and just change with changes. Ultimately, 'clinging' itself is couched as a *personal* failing, a shortcoming, a psychological problem and is rearticulated as if irrational (Johnson 1998; Bowman 2003). As Žižek formulates this: when 'you can no longer rely on the standard health insurance and retirement plan, so that you have to opt for additional coverage for which you have to pay', the ideological injunction has become one in which you must 'perceive it as an additional opportunity to choose: either better life now or long-term security? And if this predicament causes you anxiety', he concludes, you are likely to be accused 'of being unable to assume full freedom . . . of the immature sticking to old stable forms' (2001a: 116). So, Žižek implies, 'Taoist' tropes help facilitate the re-presentation of what are in truth collective socio-economic and political problems as if they are individual and subjective matters.

In this regard, 'Taoism' could be said to facilitate the ethically and politically debilitating ideology of *individualism*. For, overall, Žižek's argument is that the contemporary logic of capitalism demands that change become a virtue. (And *Tao te Ching* is mostly translated as *Way of Virtue*.) The necessary ideology is one that valorizes change, makes it a virtue. But crucial here is that this is not *active* change. An ideology of the value of *active* change could lead to group action and fundamental socio-political change. Rather, *passive* change is what is demanded: passivity in the face of unquestioned change; rudderless change. (Again, Johnson 1998 is an exemplary case.) As Žižek concludes, when this is combined with 'the ideology of the subject as the psychological individual pregnant with natural abilities and tendencies', then everyone will tend to 'automatically interpret all these changes as the result of my personality, not as the result of me being thrown around by market forces' (2001a: 116). (Hence the utility of so many Taos about this or that essence of human selfhood. The ultimate Tao 'to come' would surely be best entitled *The Tao of Sacking and Being Sacked*.)

That is, Taoism becomes the order of the day not because it is true but simply because the virtually global advocation of free-market capitalism means, as Marx and Engels prophesied, that:

> [a]ll fixed, fast-frozen relations, with their train of ancient and venerable prejudices and opinions are swept away, [that] all new-formed ones become antiquated before they can ossify [and that] [a]ll that is solid melts into air, all that is sacred is profaned. (Marx & Engels 1967: 83)

In contexts 'outside' of working life – and ironically particularly in contexts specifically intended to offer ways of escaping the stresses of working life – this New Age mysticism and spirituality arises as offering a very effective way of appearing to cope with working life. One may engage in t'ai chi-ch'uan, chi-gung, yoga or meditative practices as escape, release, or respite. But, says Žižek, 'the "Western Buddhist" meditative stance is arguably the most efficient way, for us, to fully participate in the capitalist dynamic while retaining the appearance of mental sanity' (2001a: 13). So, even though ' "Western Buddhism" presents itself as the remedy against the stressful tension of the capitalist dynamics, allowing us to uncouple and retain inner peace and *Gelassenheit*, it actually functions as its perfect ideological supplement' (2001a: 12). For Žižek, the way of capitalist ideology is the way of the fetishistic and mystificatory ideological supplement, which closes down the possibility for sustained thought and collective political action.

THE WAY OF THE SUPPLEMENT

As Žižek sees it, this mystificatory supplement springs up everywhere – even where one would expect it least, and where it should be least welcome: namely, in putatively rational intellectual and academic contexts, contexts that explicitly champion *science*. In the scientific realm, he contends, such radical developments as quantum physics and astrophysics introduce a deeply disturbing ontological complexity and undecidability into traditional notions of reality. This is so much so that what he calls the 'dominant', 'traditional', 'positivist' and 'cognitivist' approaches *cannot* grasp contemporary science's transformed notions of reality. Thus, he claims, vaguely Buddhist 'spiritualist' interpretations have sprung up to supplement conventional rationality's lack of ability to interpret current scientific theory, practice and findings.

Žižek claims that the problem is that 'the moment one wants to provide an ontological account of quantum physics (what notion of reality fits its results), paradoxes emerge which undermine standard common-sense scientistic objectivism' (2001: 217). As a consequence, 'contemporary cognitivism often produce[s] formulations that sound uncannily familiar to those who are acquainted with different versions of ancient and modern philosophy, from the Buddhist notion of the Void, and the German Idealist notion of "being-in-the-world", [to] the deconstructionist notion of *différance*' (2001: 200), and ultimately to the situation wherein:

From David Bohm to Fritjof Capra, examples abound of different versions of 'dancing Wu Li masters', teaching us about the Tao of physics, the 'end of the Cartesian paradigm', the significance of the anthropic principle and the holistic approach, and so on. To avoid any misunderstanding: as an old fashioned dialectical materialist, I am opposed as ferociously as possible to these obscurantist appropriations of quantum physics and astronomy; all I claim is that these obscurantist shoots are not simply imposed from outside, but function as what Louis Althusser would have called a 'spontaneous ideology' of scientists themselves, as a kind of spiritualist supplement to the predominant reductionist-proceduralist attitude of 'only what can be precisely measured counts'. (Žižek 2001: 216)

So, Žižek claims that the 'standard common-sense scientistic objectivism' of mainstream scholarship resists acknowledging the fact that its own central ontological premises and tenets about reality are 'naïve', and have been demonstrably undermined by science itself. Because such developments as quantum mechanics *cannot* be translated into the 'dominant' ways of understanding what counts as reality, Žižek's argument is that 'obscurantist' 'spiritualist' interpretations spring up to supplement them at their points of failure and inadequacy. These supplements are attempts to plug the holes in a dominant paradigm that really should be rejected *tout court*. But the 'spiritualist supplement' supports – maintains – the dominant view by fudging over or obscuring its limitations, its failures. Žižek's claim, then, is that because *the spiritual* is of an entirely different order to *the rational* or *scientific*, and indeed to *knowledge per se*, then recourse to the 'spiritualist supplement' is utterly at odds with knowledge as such. Any recourse to 'spiritualist' accounts of ontology by avowedly 'rational' thinkers is, for Žižek, deeply self-contradictory. It has happened because common-sense rationality *cannot* comprehend the truth approached by science, so it hides its inability by making a pathetic recourse to a spiritualist mumbo-jumbo. This is why he claims: 'obscurantist New Age ideology is *an immanent outgrowth of modern science itself*' (2001: 216).

So, Žižek regards any unscientific supplement to science to be evidence of a (dominant) form of rationality transgressing its own central (Enlightenment) premises. Recourse to a 'spiritualist supplement' means, for Žižek, that any 'interpretations' made on the strength of this supplement are actually *anti*-intellectual *non*-interpretations. The spiritualist supplement not only *answers nothing*, it actually works to close down rigorous ontological inquiry. It is also, once again, the return of the problem as if a solution. Accordingly, as Žižek implies, any such supplement that operates like this, to close down thinking and analysis, is to be identified *and rejected*.[3]

For, Žižek, the supplement is that which *seems* to stabilize something, *seems* to answer a question, *seems* to fix a problem, fill a hole, etc.; but which *actually* subverts the entire system that it initially seemed to support. In this, Žižek *directly* appropriates and form(ulaic)ally applies Derrida's trailblazing analysis and account of the work of *supplements* (Derrida 1976). Here, Žižek identifies the 'Western Buddhist' ideological supplement in the realm of academia as a 'red herring' that actually operates to *close down* thinking and analysis, and the vaguely 'Taoist' stance as the general contemporary ideological supplement, which operates to close down thinking and anti-capitalist politics. Because of this, Žižek claims to be explicitly opposed to anything that functions as a '*denkverbot*', an implicit or explicit 'prohibition' against thought (Žižek 2001: 3). Indeed, Žižek claims to be opposed to *any and all* 'obscurantism'. So it must also be asked whether Žižek is exempt from doing anything as suspect as operating in a way that might close down thinking and analysis, or from any obscurantist supplements.

THE TAO OF HEGEMONY

One obvious way to broach this question is merely to ask: is Žižek's argument *correct*? At times it seems persuasive, but on what model of causality is it premised, and is this model or paradigm *sound*? Does it *think* and *analyse* everything, or does it rely on any unthought or even obscurantist supplements?

The first thing that must be made clear is that Žižek's account hinges on a very particular conception of ideology. It also bundles heterogeneous practices together, claims that they constitute a coherent entity or collection of equivalent entities, and claims that this object or field *is* the 'hegemonic ideology of global capitalism'. Already there may be much to doubt here. One might merely ask, for instance, what grounds there are for accepting that there *is* 'ideology', or that 'it' is what Žižek says it is, or that 'this' is 'it'. But we are not all at sea here. These are not 'abstract' questions to be subjected to supposedly context-free, value-free interrogation. For Žižek speaks of 'hegemonic ideology', and makes reference and appeal to some ostensibly legitimating truth of Marxism. Now, it is unquestionably the case that *any* academic or intellectual usage of the term 'hegemonic' necessarily evokes Antonio Gramsci's seminal theorization of culture and society (Gramsci 1971). This is never more so than when the term 'hegemonic' arises in a Marxist text. Indeed, here, the passage through Gramsci is overdetermined. Thus, we ought to tarry a while, and unpack Žižek's phrase 'hegemonic ideology'.

In the wake of Gramsci, whatever is called hegemonic (from the Greek *hegemon*, meaning prince, leader or guide) is to be regarded as being of both ethical and political significance and consequence. This is because, in Gramsci's paradigm, the discourses and practices that permeate and constitute society, culture and politics, are involved in 'discursive' (i.e., open-ended, contingent, quasi-'conversational', institutional) processes, wherein parties and ideologies:

> come into confrontation and conflict, until one of them or at least a combination of them tends to prevail, to gain the upper hand, to propagate itself throughout society – bringing about not only a unison of economic and political aims, but also intellectual and moral unity, a 'universal' plane, and thus creating the hegemony of a fundamental group over a series of subordinate groups. (Gramsci 1971: 181–82)

This does not sit entirely comfortably with Žižek's use of the term 'hegemonic ideology'. For, a key point that the avowedly Gramscian theorists Laclau and Mouffe (1985) extracted from Gramsci's perspective is the insight that *therefore* culture and society are thoroughly contingent and *political achievements* in and of themselves. They are not passive expressions of the 'economic infrastructure' or indeed the 'economic base' (which is what Žižek's theory of Taoism-as-ideology implies). Indeed, in Gramsci and in Laclau and Mouffe (and beyond), 'hegemony' is clearly at odds with the paradigm that Žižek uses to make his claim about 'ideology'. This is because Žižek uses a paradigm that is now often termed 'crude' or 'vulgar' Marxism. Its central claim is that the 'economic base' (capitalism) *determines* the 'ideological superstructure' (the beliefs and practices of culture and society). The problematic difference between Žižek's and the Gramscian (and Laclauian) understandings of hegemony is that, for Žižek, hegemony is something that *is simply ideological*, in the sense that it all 'grows out from' and sits on top of the economic base, which is the driving force of everything.

In contrast to Žižek's usage, Laclau and Mouffe argue that the *economic cannot be divorced from the political*. What this means becomes apparent when one translates Laclau and Mouffe's terms back into those of the crude Marxism that they reject. In this retranslation, any transformation in the 'ideological superstructure' may well have effects on the 'economic base', because base and superstructure are no longer conceived of as separable, but rather as contingent political establishments and constellations in the larger discursive movements of history. In other words, the notion of hegemony *subverts* the 'ideology' (and paradigm) of crude Marxism, in which the superstructure is regarded as distinct from, yet determined by, the economic base. In the post-Marxist theory of hegemony, in fact, there is no fundamentally distinct base and superstructure, only contingent political establishments, which will take the form of different forms of socio-political arrangements. Human life is not a passive reflection of economic dictates. It can and does intervene decisively into 'the economic system'.[4]

THE WAY OF CHANGELESS CHANGE: ŽIŽEK'S LIMIT PROBLEM

But Žižek does not accept the Laclauian argument about hegemony, nor does he accept the efficacy or even the reality of politics construed as changes in legislation, inter-institutional organization, or anything 'pragmatic' like that. Indeed, he refers to every such kind of non-revolutionary politics as proof of 'the sad predicament of today's Left'. This he says is characterized by 'the acceptance of the Cultural Wars (feminist, gay, anti-racist, etc., multiculturalist struggles) as the dominant terrain of emancipatory politics; [and] the purely defensive stance of protecting the achievements of the Welfare State' (Žižek 2002a: 308). To this impulse in Žižek's work, Laclau replies: because Žižek 'refuses to accept the aims of all contestatory movements in the name of pure anti-capitalist struggle, one is left wondering: who for him are the agents of a historical transformation? Martians, perhaps?' (Laclau 2004: 327).

The point here is that the theory of hegemony construes society (including the economy) as consisting of contingent political constructs which can be intervened into and altered to effect significant alteration. Žižek, on the contrary, regards such change as 'intra-systemic', as obscuring and preserving 'a certain limit' (Žižek 2002: 170; Laclau 2000: 205). Thus, he argues, even efforts 'like *Médecins sans frontières*, Greenpeace, feminist and anti-racist campaigns ... are all not only tolerated but even supported by the media, even if they seemingly encroach on economic territory (for example, denouncing and boycotting companies which do not respect ecological conditions, or use child labour) – they are tolerated and supported as long as they do not get too close to a certain limit' (2002: 170). What is this 'limit'? Žižek explains:

> This kind of activity provides the perfect example of interpassivity: of doing things not in order to achieve something, but to prevent something from really happening, really changing. All this frenetic humanitarian, Politically Correct, etc., activity fits the formula of 'Let's go on changing something all the time so that, globally, things will remain the same!' (2002: 170)

This 'formula' is Žižek's interpretation of politics under capitalism. Thus, what 'invisibly' remains the same is *the way of capital* per se. Žižek calls this the unseen 'backdrop', the unacknowledged 'horizon', the unapproachable 'limit'. He has even argued that there is a 'silent prohibition' against *even talking about* anti-capitalism or undertaking class analysis in the contemporary university. (The fact that this is *demonstrably* false, especially for UK universities, does not stop him from regularly making this polemical claim. He makes it mainly to try to provoke American intellectuals to start to construe 'capitalism' as 'the problem itself'.) In other words, quite against Laclau who exemplifies the tendency to regard the organization of culture and society as the result of fundamentally consequential socio-political 'battles', Žižek regards all of this as the simple *imposition* of a particular ideology determined by an agenda set by the requirements of 'global capitalism', in an automatic process. This is what leads him to regard all politics (other than globally revolutionary anti-capitalist 'class' politics) as blind to their own 'context' – what he calls the 'backdrop' or 'horizon': The Capitalist System. For 'backdrop' and 'horizon' one cannot but read 'economic base' (Laclau 2005: 205). Thus, ultimately, Žižek's vision of Taoism as/and ideology has been produced by a crude base/superstructure model of the world. In this, the *hegemon* that guides ideology is not a prince but a straightforward *henchman*; not a leader or guide in any sense, but a collaborator, in the service of the capitalist 'economic infrastructure' (Žižek 2001a: 12).

That being said, what nevertheless makes Žižek's rejection of politics strangely consistent and apparently (paradoxically) 'valid' is the fact that he does *not* actually think that the majority of the world *are* subjugated and controlled by *actual* groups or classes. Or, that is: even if people *are* subjugated by other people, by *particular* groups, the buck does not stop there. On the contrary, for Žižek, the problem is strictly 'systemic'. The problem with capitalism is not *capitalists*. The true problem is the *system*. His conviction is that what is leading and guiding and controlling all of us today is the invisible hand of the capitalist *system* itself. So, for Žižek, the universal/class enemy is not some actual or fixed class or group of *people* 'in control'. Rather, what Žižek deems to be 'in control' is a machinic *system* (Žižek 2001: 1–2). This is why Žižek can claim simultaneously that 'the fundamental antagonism' is 'the class antagonism' *and* that there is no 'authentic working class' (2002: 308). That is, because the problem is systemic or structural, then every actual instance of its realization is asymptotic to the real of the structure that it (never quite) exemplifies.

This 'system' or 'structure', construed through an ultra-formalist perspective is the problem for Žižek (2002: 308). It is also the problem *of* Žižek, in the sense that his hyperbolically 'consistent' ultra-political stance must paradoxically reject all forms of politics other than something he conceives of as complete 'systemic' global anti-capitalist revolution (2002: 170). His polemical target is a perceived contemporary 'consensus' (that he regards as 'resigned and cynical') that capitalism is 'the only game in town' (2000: 95). From this perspective, all non-revolutionary or non-anti-capitalist theory and practice cannot see the changeless 'backdrop' to its own activity: capitalism, the horizon within which all actually existing politics drone on, but always avoiding '*the* problem itself'. This is why Žižek accuses contemporary cultural, intellectual and political life of having fallen all but entirely under the sway of capitalism. He portrays 'capitalism' and its liberal or neo-liberal ideology as the total and universal backdrop against or within which things *appear* to change but fundamentally remain the same.

But, just to be clear, the basic problem here remains that this very position arises only through the optic of what Laclau calls a very 'crude version of the base/superstructure model' (Laclau 2000: 205).

Adopted in the name of furthering *radical* politics, it paradoxically *rejects* all politics, because none could possibly hope to measure up to the impossibly total demands generated by such a caricatural and hyperbolic paradigm. It 'totalizes' everything ('*the* global capitalist system'), and so precludes the value of specific action. In insisting on inferred fundamental ('ontological' or 'real') structures it refuses even to look at any significant aspect of actually existing ('ontic') reality. In insisting on radical politics, it even prohibits working out *what* valid political action might be. (It merely evokes some enigmatic kind of universal spontaneous political combustion.) In fact, Žižek's totalizing leads to a *prohibition of any analysis*.

This is because Žižek's polemical gestures levy a very heavy rhetorical and analytical toll. In order to make them, Žižek cannot analyse or question his own central categories (the notions he champions or denounces). This is so much the case that, rather than treating 'neoliberalism' (for example) as a complex, historically real, deliberately implemented geopolitical economic 'experiment' of ongoing, piecemeal, pragmatic, legislative violence (Kingsnorth 2003), Žižek merely picks up some familiar emotive terms – 'capitalism', 'the system' – and deploys them *as if they are already fully understood* and as if they simply *must* be taken to be millenarian signifiers of pure evil. In short, 'capitalism', 'liberalism', etc. function within Žižek's discourse *purely as emotive rhetorical devices*, whilst being analytically empty (not to mention often categorically dubious). That is, on the one hand, these terms are *irreducible, central* to his discourse: they actually overdetermine, constitute, and orientate the shape and form of his intellectual production through and through. But, on the other hand (and unfortunately for anyone concerned with knowledge, analysis, or politics), they also signal the *limit* of his thought. 'Capitalism' is the central, fundamental point beyond which Žižek cannot or will not go; something that a Rortyan perspective might regard as Žižek's 'final vocabulary': the tautological start and endpoint of his discourse; as if the entire political dimension of the work of Žižek consists in the repetition of the following mantra or koan: '*What is the problem? Capitalism. What is capitalism? The problem.*'

THE TAO OF HOLDING THE PLACE

The reasons for Žižek's refusal to analyse are certainly multiple. But they hinge on his avowed aim of 'holding the place' (Žižek 2000). He sees it as his intellectual responsibility to keep 'radical' theoretical and political themes on the table of public intellectual debate. As we have seen, in the cultural and political dimension, for Žižek this basically means maintaining a crude Marxian mantra. This is because, as he sees it, he is actually being courageous by *resolutely not losing his nerve*, 'in a time of continuous rapid changes' when 'the retreat of old social forms' means that 'thought is more than ever exposed to the temptation of "losing its nerve", of precociously abandoning the old conceptual coordinates' (Žižek 2001a). As he rather surprisingly alleges, even 'the media constantly bombards us with the need to abandon the "old paradigms"'.[5] But, he counters: 'Against this temptation, one should rather follow the unsurpassed model of Pascal and ask the difficult question: how are we to remain faithful to the Old in the new conditions? *Only* in this way can we generate something effectively New' (2001a: 32–33). *This* is Žižek's wager, Žižek's act: rejection of the way of capitalism; holding the place of the old against 'today's twin brothers of deconstructionist sophistry and New Age obscurantism' (1998: 1,007), and against 'capitulation itself' (2002: 308), the position of 'Third Way' ideologues, like Giddens or Beck, and all who do not vociferously oppose capitalism.

What is particularly striking, however, is the way that the rhetorical *'points de caption'* that structure Žižek's texts – signifiers like 'capitalism', 'the system', 'anti-capitalism', 'revolution' – are *entirely hypostasized place-holders*. That is, they are never specified further. Indeed, one might say, within Žižek's discourse, his key categories are *supplements*, in an almost exemplary sense.[6] And they do exactly the same kind of work as the recourse to spiritualism that he criticizes in his object of critique. His key categories are uninterrogated 'pegs'; 'pins', whose removal would cause his text to unravel entirely. But, furthermore, these place-holders are actually elevated to something very like the status of the figure of 'the eternal Tao' in the *Tao te Ching*. In deconstructive terms, this means that the central categories of Žižek's system are actually radically external to it, strangely excluded from it. They are there on full show, yet concealed from inspection. Placing them on full show is actually the way Žižek conceals them from inspection. To echo Žižek's 'formula' of the non-politics of politics, his approach is thus: 'Let's go on talking about something all the time so as to avoid talking about it' (see Žižek 2002: 170, quoted above). This rhetorical (anti-)analytical strategy puts Žižek's entire approach on a par with the very style of mystificatory (non)engagement and intellectual failure that he critiques as being *the* move of the 'hegemonic ideology of global capitalism'.

Does this mean that the way of Žižek is somehow a manifestation of the hegemonic ideology of global capitalism? This would be the deepest irony, given Žižek's explicit declaration to try to 'remain faithful to the Old in the new conditions'. The problem is that his (e)very effort to move involves tying his laces together. Every possible theoretical or political move meets one of his own unnecessary self-imposed puritanical 'prohibitions' (Žižek 2001: 204–205, 220). The most striking is perhaps the refusal to question the supposedly 'old' *paradigm itself*, in the name of 'remaining faithful' to it. This amounts to the advocation of an anti-theoretical and straight-forwardly anti-intellectual, quasi-religious or spiritualist '*denkverbot*' or 'prohibition against thinking' (Žižek 2001: 3).

Of course, such a strangely paranoid defensive reaction *might* – *possibly* – but only tentatively, and forever only tenuously – *sometimes* – be *strategically* justifiable in the context of Žižek's claim that he sees his role and intellectual contribution to be that of 'holding the place', of keeping traditional radical political questions and perspectives on the agenda, so to speak, *lest we forget*. But there are many other, more honest, intellectually open ways to do this than simply *refusing* to think, theorize or analyse. But, *even if* as an intellectual, philosopher, theorist or academic one could possibly decide something like 'it's not how crude it is but what you do with it that counts', the problem remains that Žižek refuses to do *anything* with his crude paradigm. He refuses to question, interrogate or analyse anything to do with the supposedly determinant 'base' at all. This refusal begs a question of the *point* of analysing *anything*, especially anything in or of the superstructure. In other words, Žižek does not do with the paradigm the very thing that the paradigm is supposedly set up to do, the very thing it seems to demand and that he implicitly most advocates. That is, as 'the economy' is placed in a determinant position, one might expect some analysis of it – perhaps of consequential moments, movements, acts, interventions or events that have taken place in the determinant realm. But this never appears. This is because any attempt at such analysis would reveal the economic system to be contingently and politically instituted and modifiable, thus revealing the inadequacy and untenability of his paradigm and his entire position (Laclau & Mouffe 1985; Laclau 2004).[7]

Thus, Žižek's own position is strictly fetishistic. According to his own argument, this makes Žižek entirely consistent with the logic of contemporary capitalism. As a 'position', Žižek's work straightforwardly relies upon the logic of the supplement. It falls apart according to that same logic too. But Žižek does not care, because although he relies upon the deconstructive supplement, his work proceeds according to the psychoanalytic logic of the fetish. Thus, his mantras enable him to 'fully participate in the frantic pace of the capitalist game while sustaining the belief that [he is] not really in it, that [he is] well aware of how worthless the spectacle is. . .unaware that the "truth" of his existence is the social involvement which he tends to dismiss as a mere game' (Žižek 2001a: 15).

For Žižek, the name of the game is 'holding the place'. This relies on 'place holders': repeated evocations of the *names* of problematics as if naming them is everything. Naming is both to gesture to and yet *thereby* bracket off, silence, close down analysis, *in the same gesture*. This is a structure of foreclosure and denial in which what *apparently* holds the structure in place *actually* lacks any possible content. Were the supplements – the place holders – engaged, fleshed out, the structure would collapse. Žižek joyously ignores this untenable incoherence because he obeys his fetish: '*I know very well* [that what I am saying is untenable and empty], *but nevertheless* [I will continue to say it – because I enjoy it/it enables me to "face" things]'. *So what? Who cares?* The issue here, as Žižek so completely demonstrates, is that this gesture is *anti*-theoretical, *anti*-intellectual, *anti*-philosophical, *anti*-analytical and *anti*-political – indeed, arguably exemplifying the very ideological, intellectual and political problem of our time and place.

NOTES

1 For an engagement with *Who Moved My Cheese?* and the discourse it typifies, see Bowman 2003.

2 According to Clarke, 'there are various possible reasons for its wide appeal. One is the protean quality of the text, namely its readiness, as one writer puts it somewhat cynically, to "furnish whatever the reader needs", a factor which gives it "an immense advantage over books written so clearly that they have only one meaning"' (2000: 56). Of course, *no* text will ever 'have only one meaning'. The endless proliferation of translations of the *Tao te Ching* may merely testify to the fact that the Tao that can and will be translated is never going to be the final translation, because 'translation' is one version of the question of

'interpretation', and no interpretation of any text is ever going to be the final interpretation. Texts are read in contexts, and contexts cannot be exactly the same twice. Pragmatic problems of *translation* can themselves be referred back to the fundamental problem of *interpretation* (Zhang 1992; Derrida 1992; Mowitt 1992).

3   His ultimate argument, of course, is that 'standard common-sense scientistic objectivism' needs to be replaced, because it is intellectually naïve and ideologically unsound – because it cannot handle 'the Real'. To his mind, his own Lacanian paradigm is the answer, the solution, the best candidate for the job of understanding all realms and registers of reality (from the 'impossible real' which cannot be directly apprehended, to the failed attempts to approach it in the 'symbolic order'; to, in fact, *all* other aspects of the human condition).

4   As Laclau puts it, in response to Žižek's criticisms of post-structuralism and post-Marxism: 'Nobody seriously denies [the centrality of economic processes in capitalist societies]. The difficulties come when [Žižek] transforms "the economy" into a self-defined homogeneous instance operating as the ground of society – when, that is, he reduces it to a Hegelian explanatory model. The truth of the economy is, like anything else in society, the locus of an overdetermination of social logics, and its centrality is the result of the obvious fact that the material reproduction of society has more repercussions for social processes than do other instances. This does not mean that capitalist reproduction can be reduced to a single, self-defining mechanism' (Laclau 2005: 237).

5   Quite *which* media it is that 'constantly bombards' Žižek with such intellectually stimulating provocations is – regrettably – left unsaid. If he had named them, I for one would be tuning in.

6   Indeed, more than Žižek's *use* of the deconstructive notion of the supplement, his fundamental *reliance on* it should be noted. For, he both *relies on* the supplement in many of his arguments, and yet *disavows deconstruction*. This means that, here, *deconstruction is literally Žižek's own supplement*. In Derrida's analyses, this is *precisely* what a supplement is: that which is simultaneously central *and* excluded; something apparently only 'added on' but actually fundamental, constitutive; something disavowed yet relied upon. What becomes apparent in reading Žižek is that deconstruction is subordinated or even excluded by his own avowed position, yet nevertheless central to it. Furthermore, the very fact that he always deploys the notion of the supplement so *formalistically* and *formulaically* (and without any actual 'reading') actually means that Žižek himself seems to be the best example of a 'deconstructionist' – or the sort of proponent of *formulaic* deconstruction that he regularly denounces – to be found.

7   Žižek's argument in his analysis of Lenin is a case in point (Žižek 2002). Here Žižek effectively argues for the primacy of the *political* intervention over the 'economic system'.

ŽIŽEK'S PASSION FOR THE REAL: THE REAL OF TERROR, THE TERROR OF THE REAL

Mark Devenney

TERROR OF THE REAL

In an article titled 'The Revolution against Capital' (written in 1917) Antonio Gramsci celebrates the event of October 1917. He writes:

> The Capital that this event is a revolution against is not just Capitalism as an economic and political system: it is Marx's Capital, *which has been overtaken by an event outside of history so to speak, yet which alters the coordinates by which we understand that history.* Henceforth Marxists will have to account for that excess which transcends the strict correlation between class position and potential action. (Gramsci 1977: 31, emphasis added)

Gramsci neither denies the hegemony of capitalism, nor denounces Marx's analysis of capital. He points instead to an excess which no history can predict or domesticate, anticipating his own account of hegemony as a politics which exceeds determination by economic coordinates.[1] He links this excess to an act which changes the coordinates of history, an act which henceforth must be considered an ever present possibility, a possibility which inhabits any established order. Almost a century after Gramsci's optimistic salute to this revolution against capital, Žižek defends the possibility of a radical act which in Gramsci's words *alters the coordinates by which we understand that history.* Žižek writes: 'an act is neither a strategic intervention *in* the existing order, nor its "crazy" destructive negation; an act is an "excessive", trans-strategic intervention which redefines the rules and contours of the existing order' (2004: 81).

Žižek is all too aware of the perfidious 'passions for the real'[2] that marked the politics of the twentieth century. He condemns the ruthless ambition to strip away all appearances in search of the real, and the consequent attempts to purify the body politic of its infirmities (Žižek 2002: 5–12). A progressive passion for the real, a progressive act, does not seek reality below its immediate appearance, but recognizes this as the ultimate shadow game. Yet Žižek also refuses Burke's conservatism which holds that democracy is weighed down, and anchored, by the dead, and thus condemns the presumption of the new (Burke 1982). Žižek rejects the modern version of this argument, a form of liberal blackmail, which insists that because we can never know the real we should reject all passionate political attachments, and resign ourselves to a pragmatism which does not challenge the existing order. He contends that the *faux* radicalism of multi-cultural politics, the deconstructive ethics of *différance*, and the post-Marxist account of hegemony all neuter the possibility of a radical revolutionary act, and indirectly affirm the hegemony of capitalism in defending an empty neutrality which mimics the false abstraction of the commodity form.[3]

His insistence that the Left requires a renewed critique of political economy is nothing new (even though Žižek himself has not developed such a critique). More interesting is his linking of this to a radical (revolutionary) act, an act which may be deemed authentic, in contrast to the many false acts of the twentieth century. This discrimination between acts is not mere prejudice: he contends that the authentic act 'traverses the fundamental fantasy' in treating the social symptom. Žižek is, in one sense, trying to rescue Gramsci's notion of the act, whilst avoiding two dangers: the first of simply validating the terroristic act, the second of refusing to act for fear of becoming or being labelled a terrorist. Everything hinges on the claim that the authentic act traverses the fantasy, and both sides of the copula are important here. First we should be able to diagnose the fundamental fantasy, even if only by reading the symptoms – this is a hermeneutic exercise whose model is the analytic session. Second the act which traverses the fantasy must be an im/possible act, in appealing to the sediment of the impossible which is the disavowed real of contemporary societies. The contours of what such an act might be are already apparent in Žižek's work: if traversing the fundamental fantasy is a requirement for an authentic act, then this act will have to treat what Žižek terms the 'real of capital'.

I contend in this chapter that Žižek fails to give an adequate account of capital or of political economy. This failure is directly related to his account of the act. An inadequate analysis of capital means that he cannot conceive of points of resistance and as a consequence settles for a notion of the act which is idealistic in relation to political practice. Moreover his notion of the act, which he claims to derive from Lacan's account of analysis, is an inadequate translation of analytic practice into an account of political possibility.

CAPITAL AND CLASS

Žižek's account(s) of capitalism combines an eclectic commitment to Lacan's matrix of the real, the imaginary and the symbolic, with a quasi-Marxist account of reification and class politics. Introducing a recent text he maintains that these three orders (symbolic, real and imaginary) are knotted together at the level of the social order in the relations between the real of the economy, the imaginary of democratic ideology and the symbolic political hegemony (Žižek 2004: 6). Yet this knotting has the consequence that:

> The relationship between economy and politics is ultimately that of the well-known visual paradox of 'two faces or a vase': one sees either two faces or a vase, never both – one has to make a choice. In the same way, one either focuses on the political, and the domain of economy is reduced to the 'servicing of goods', or one focuses on economy, and politics is reduced to a theatre of appearances, to a passing phenomenon which will disappear with the arrival of the developed communist economy. (Žižek 2006: 56)

It is along these lines that Žižek censures post-Marxist accounts of hegemony and politics. If the contingency of politics (which Gramsci had already linked to the Russian revolution) cannot be explained in terms of the economy, then neither can economic relations be explained in terms of the politics of contingency. He writes:

> The 'political' critique of Marxism. . .should thus be supplemented by its obverse: the field of economy is *in its very form* irreducible to politics – this level of the form of the economy (of economy as the determining form of the social) is what French

'political post-Marxists' miss when they reduce economy to one of the positive social spheres. (Žižek 2006: 56)

The implication of this is that the account of contingency defended by post-Marxists is not applicable in the realm of the real, the economy. A politics of contingency which cannot recognize the structuring of its own contingency by the form of the capitalist economy is destined, on this account, to treat the symptoms of capital rather than capitalism itself.[4] It is thus that Žižek insists, in a variety of texts, on anti-capitalist theory and politics which recognize that capitalism retroactively establishes itself as the unquestioned horizon of our time. He makes two essential points: first that the limit of capital is capital itself, not some outside to capital. Second, this limit will be reached when capitalism finally erodes the 'last resistant spheres of non-reflected substantial being' (Žižek 1999: 358).[5]

Yet the logic of this account differs from that of Marx who argues that capital generates a revolutionary class: the proletariat. For Žižek capitalism's only limit is capitalism itself. Capitalism as a system is premised on the revolutionary logic of the not-all, of a process of continual transformation, which renders everything contingent. Any critique thereof is thus likely to result in the reformation of capitalism, not its transformation, merely contributing to its own vampire-like logic of feeding on the blood of those not yet part of the system. It is no surprise that in the pages immediately following this discussion Žižek cites *Dialectic of Enlightenment*: every position of protest, every vain attempt to buck the system has already been prepared for by the system. What is innovative however is the reinvention of pessimism (there is no outside to the system) as optimism: once the system has colonized all non-reflected substantial being it will inevitably fail, because the logic of the not-all – which is what capitalism thrives on – will end. If there is any value in this argument then we need some idea of what capitalism is, and more precisely how the organization of capital has altered. We require too an account of what Marx termed surplus value. How is value generated, how is the surplus reinvested? Žižek hints at this requirement when he talks of capitalism, again following Marx, as a vampire feeding on its own blood. When the source of blood dries up, then the system collapses – no surplus can be generated, and it can longer be reproduced.

What exactly, though, does capital feed on? Žižek contends that it feeds on geographic, cultural and psychic domains of 'non-reflected substantial being'. He refers in passing to 'talents', but these are hardly 'non-reflected'. Neither, however, are the domains of geography and the psychic. Žižek's own work demands an account of how the outside that capital colonizes is itself generated by capital, an account of how the limits are internal to the system – indeed are its condition of possibility – rather than dependent upon a wholly abstract notion of non-reflected being.

Despite this odd account of implosion Žižek does indeed specify an agent of transformation, an agent that capital relies upon: the proletariat. The fantasy that capital is self-generating, that it is a system with no external reference, is in fact contradicted by its reliance on the traditional agent of revolutionary optimism, the proletariat.[6] When capitalism finally becomes independent of those who produce; when the social logic of speculative capital is released from its dependence upon substantial beings; when it becomes a purely self-referential system; only then will the collapse of capitalism occur. This is the most generous reading one can offer of this account. For, in truth Žižek does not provide an analysis of capitalism at all, other than through rather limited gestures devoid of any sustained engagement with the social logic of contemporary capital. His failure to specify its fundamental transformations means that the insistence on its implosion at some unspecified future point is mere optimism of the will, not even a calculated gamble.

Two moves that Žižek makes are problematic in this regard. I have already suggested that the notion of non-reflected substantial being makes little sense, even from Žižek's own perspective. Second, he argues that it is an error to try to keep politics and economics in view, at the same time:

> And, of course, the trap to be avoided here is precisely that of trying to formulate the totality parts of which are democratic ideology, the exercise of power, and the processes of economic (re)production: if we try to keep them all in view, we end up seeing nothing; the contours disappear. This bracketing is not only epistemological, it concerns what Marx called 'real abstraction': the abstraction from power and economic relations is inscribed in the very actuality of the democratic process, and so forth. (Žižek 2006: 56)

This is not what Marx meant when he used the term 'real abstraction', as we will see below. Moreover, this defence of the parallax view relies on the argument that economic and political logics are different. Yet Žižek should take his own account more seriously. If capitalism is viewed as an overdetermined totality, a totality which is a contingent articulation of a series of medical, economic, political, legal and other discourses, the theorist can begin to account for both the relative fixity of relations of power and economic organization, as well as their points of vulnerability. In this sense there is no object 'the economy', other than as a theoretical abstraction. Taking the abstraction seriously means precisely that other aspects of the social totality would not be seen. This blindness is then a consequence of Žižek's theoretical claims, rather than anything to do with the real abstraction: capital. However, economic relations too are criss-crossed by lines of determination which are fixed and maintained contingently. These so-called economic discourses have an integral relation to the perceptions of the actors involved in these activities, as well as to the legal and political framing of these relations. They cannot be conceptualized independently of these relations. Žižek's error is to treat contingency as if it were limited to a domain called the political, a domain which does not even exist as an independent entity. The claim that the economy determines the social in terms of its form is empty. What precisely Žižek means by form, and why he specifies form as opposed to the substantive relations that exist between relations of production and reproduction is difficult to fathom. There are at least three areas of work that Žižek should address if he wishes to add ballast to these claims.

First, reproduction has now become a means of generating capital and surplus. This overlap of production and reproduction (so that for example the sciences of life both create and privatize a new territory termed genetic life through intellectual-property law) quite literally rearticulates a new understanding of life. Life itself (so called natural life) is characterized as an overdetermined code (this is how the new functional genomics considers life: genetic function depends upon unpredictable interactions between different genes, their environment and their external environment) and this code is a key object of capitalization on global markets. Catherine Waldby terms this production of a surplus out of 'life itself' bio-value: 'Biovalue refers to the yield of vitality produced by the technical reformulation of living processes [and] biotechnology finds insertion points between living and non-living systems where new and contingent forms of vitality can be created, capitalising on life' (Waldby 2002: 310).

Second, these technologies of life which promise life extension, health into old age, greater understanding and control over the very matter that is the condition of possibility of human life are articulated with a series of other technologies which take life as their object. The key to this is a calculus of risk: life and death are articulated as forms of aggregate possibility so that gambles on individuals which do not pay off are compensated for by a majority that do. Individuals are tied into these spiderwebs of calculability which presuppose the individual as the primary unit but transcend individuality through an apparently neutral practice in which each unit is important only as a presupposition. When allied with new genetic technologies such mathematical instruments (a form of actuarial politics) generate a new territory for capital.

Third, this inclusive exclusion of life is supported by older logics of exclusion and inclusion. The various risk agencies which value life, which evaluate risk in whole societies, which are the first port of call for any form of investment – these merchants of life who operate with far more sophisticated technologies than the slavers of old who relied upon the nascent insurance industry to protect their property against natural disasters – legislate silently on which lives are worth living and which are not. The neutrality of the mechanism should not blind one to the disastrous consequences. For those whose life expectancy is low, for those whose skills are tied in to the extraction or production of primary goods, for those who live in zones of the world where there is no sovereign authority, or where war has ravaged the economy, for those struck down by HIV but who have no direct access to measurable resources the neutrality of such mechanisms is a disaster.

Marx termed the object capital a real abstraction: he recognized that no particular instance of capitalist organization would conform precisely to the general analysis, but ironed out the kinks in presenting the analysis of a totality which incorporated its own exceptions. Today what is required is just such an abstract analysis of these mechanisms whereby fine discriminations based on data analysis, the de-territorialization of capital based upon the virtual body that is the genetic code and the very health of the bodies that/who make up the body politic are co-implicated. Such an analysis would point to the agents who exercise most leverage on the system, those who may engage in the politics that Žižek wishes for. The vain hope of the implosion of capital takes us nowhere, and in its profound ignorance of the more complex mechanisms whereby contemporary forms of capitalization function, does precisely what Žižek accuses the academic Left of doing: providing mere ballast for the next consumer product.

Whilst Žižek's indicative comments about the restructuring of capitalism are never developed into what he argues is necessary (a critique of political economy), he nonetheless deems class to be the structuring principle of capitalism, that part of the hegemonic chain that sustains its horizon, the specific antagonism which overdetermines the dominant hegemony. Class structures in advance, he argues, the antagonistic struggles of contemporary societies (Žižek 2000a: 311). Žižek explains this overdetermination of society by class using Hegel's notion of concrete universality.[7] He argues that the universal will never be realized as a consequence of a necessary rather than empirical hindrance. Concrete universality indicates that moment when the universal encounters itself as particular. Any name for the universal is thus a stand in for a void, the impossibility of the universal. Žižek describes class in precisely these terms. Class is the antagonism which relates to the outside that makes the system possible, which stands in for the void, and which marks its presence as the unspoken universal. Žižek writes:

one should counter [Laclau, but also post-Marxism more generally] by the already-mentioned paradox of 'oppositional determination', of the *part* of the chain that sustains its *horizon* itself: class antagonism certainly appears as one in the series of social antagonisms, but it is simultaneously the specific antagonism which 'predominates over the rest, whose relations thus assign rank and influence to the others. . . ' I do not accept that all elements which enter into hegemonic struggle are in principle equal: in the series of struggles (economic, political, feminist, ecological, ethnic, etc.) there is always *one* which, while it is part of the chain, secretly overdetermines its very horizon. This contamination of the universal by the particular is 'stronger' than the struggle for hegemony (i.e. for which particular content will hegemonize the universality in question): it structures in advance *the very terrain* on which the multitude of particular contents fight for hegemony. . . . [T]he question is not just which particular content will hegemonize the empty place of universality – the question is, also and above all, which secret privileging and inclusions/exclusions had to occur for this empty place as such to emerge in the first place. (Žižek 2000a: 320)

Žižek like Laclau recognizes that the struggle for hegemony is not decided in advance, that a chain of equivalences is merely a system of differences unless overdetermined by a dominant antagonism. This is no different to Laclau's account of hegemony: engaged political struggle entails an understanding of contemporary forms of hegemonic politics which 'structure in advance the terrain of struggle' and establish exclusions and inclusions. The key difference lies in Žižek's assertion that one part of the chain *secretly* overdetermines the horizon of the chain, rather than the chain itself. This is reminiscent of Althusser's structural account of capital. Althusser argues that in the last instance (which he adds never comes) the economy determines which element of the structure will be dominant (Althusser 1970: 176). Žižek writes:

In the case of race we are dealing with a positive naturalised element (the presupposed organic unity of society is perturbed by the intrusion of the foreign body), while class antagonism is absolutely inherent to and constitutive of the social field. Fascism thus obfuscates antagonism, translating it into a conflict of positive opposed terms. . . The proof that class struggle is not an ontic binary opposite but a purely formal transcendental gap is the fact that, *translated into positive terms*, it always involves three not two elements – why? Because class struggle as antagonism is, at it were, its own obstacle, that which forever prevents its own direct expression, its translation into clear or symbolic terms. . . The wager of Marxism is that there is one antagonism (class struggle) which overdetermines all the others and which is, as such, the concrete universal of the entire field. The term overdetermination is used here in its precise Althusserian sense: it does not mean that class struggle is the ultimate referent and horizon of meaning of all other struggles; it means that class struggle is the structuring principle which allows us to account for the very inconsistent plurality of ways in which other antagonisms can be articulated into chains of equivalence. . . Here class struggle is the concrete universal in the strict Hegelian sense: in relating to its otherness (other antagonisms) it relates to itself, that is it (over)determines the way it relates to other struggles. (Žižek 2004: 101–102)

There are three key moments in this account of class: (1) positive elements, such as race, obfuscate class antagonism which is absolutely inherent to the social field. This argument is little different to that developed in Marxist accounts of the relationship between race and class in South Africa during the apartheid period.[8] (2) Class is a purely formal gap and this is proved (!) by the fact that it is never directly expressed, that it forever prevents its own direct expression; and yet (3) it overdetermines the whole field as the structuring principle which explains the relation between other antagonisms. This argument is extraordinary. The only evidence Žižek offers for class playing this role is that it is never directly expressed, yet despite this inherent negativity it structures the whole field. The correlate of class described in these terms is Lacan's notion of the real, but the labelling of the real as class, as the stand-in for the void performs two contradictory functions. On the one hand it allows Žižek to wear Marxist lapels; on the other he can always argue that those who fail to conceive of class in these terms make the error of presuming that class will appear in determinate form as an antagonism that can in fact be addressed. This strategy undermines two modalities of political action: Marxist claims about the imminent revolution of the working class are deemed crass; post-Marxist accounts of hegemony as dependent upon an essential contingency which reveals the performativity underlying any established power are deemed to misrecognize their own conditions of possibility. The consequence is that Žižek has to find some other account of political change compatible with his commitment to this emptied out version of Marxist political economy.

Given his conclusion that the depoliticized economy is the disavowed fundamental fantasy of postmodern politics, but that class cannot be directly expressed, his only option is to defend a radical notion of the act. A properly political act would necessarily entail the re-politicization of the economy because a gesture counts as an act only insofar at it disturbs (traverses) its fundamental fantasy (Žižek 2000a: 127). It would seem that the defence of class politics answers precisely this call: a re-politicization of economic relations (though what precisely economic as opposed to other relations happen to be is nowhere specified) that challenges the territory that capital has colonized. What type of act however would allow for this requisite re-politicization of class? I address this below.

Where does this leave us? Žižek claims that class is the structuring horizon of contemporary forms of hegemonic politics, but does not offer any sustained analysis of capital which would allow for a specification of class identity, or even the articulation of a class politics opposed to capital. Moreover, he contends that class cannot be directly expressed, that it takes on other forms. From the viewpoint of the political characterized by contingency, the determining role of class cannot even be viewed. Yet this is precisely what is required if the act is to traverse the fundamental fantasy, the disavowed of contemporary politics. In political terms Žižek's account of the act is marked by this failure.

WHAT DOES IT MEAN TO ACT?

Žižek argues that an act (as opposed to an action) 'subverts the very structuring principle of a field. . .redefining the very contours of what is possible and in so doing creating retroactively the conditions of its own possibility' (2004: 121). An act disturbs the underlying fantasy, attacking it from the point of the social symptom, addressing directly the social antagonism. An act is then related to its situation, but is issued from the standpoint of the symbolic order's inherent impossibility, that stumbling block which is its hidden disavowed principle. This is not an act in the sense in which the liberal theorist would characterize the act, as that of a self-sufficient subject in possession of its reason. Rather, one's subjectivity is transformed by the act, as none of the postulates which supported the identity of the subject lend support to the act. An act does the impossible within the existing order. Žižek describes such a challenge to the symbolic order as a 'political act of pure expenditure which changes the very coordinates of what is possible within a historical constellation' (2004: 81).

The act then is not simply outside the symbolic order. Such an act would be psychotic, and would have no bearing on the symbolic order, and could not even be considered an act. Rather, the act proper suspends the symbolic coordinates that determine the subject. In this sense an act entails self-erasure, a radical subjective destitution which installs a new master signifier. As a consequence the act has no guarantee of success: it will not be recognized, and has to establish the terms of its own recognition transforming the existing terms of recognition. It is in this precise sense that the act is a radical critique of any theory of inter-subjectivity: in acting one no longer recognizes the other as another subject, but transforms the terms on which the other is recognized, thus altering both self and other.

This notion of the act has echoes in political theory.[9] In Book II of *On the Social Contract* Rousseau outlines a notion of the general will which is not simply the will of all, but is the best possible will, of the people. He writes: 'the general will is always right and tends toward the public utility' (Rousseau 1987: 157). However the general will is constantly subverted by corruption from private and common wills even if it is apparently democratic. He concludes that the people are incapable of giving such a will to themselves, that they require a legislator to establish laws best suited to the expression of the general will:

> Discovering the rules of society best suited to nations would require a superior intelligence that beheld all the passions of men without feeling them; who had no affinity with our nature and yet knew it through and through; whose happiness was independent of us, yet who nevertheless was willing to concern itself with ours; who, in the passage of time, procures for himself a distant glory, being able to labour in one age and find enjoyment in another. Gods would be needed to give men laws. (Rousseau 1987: 163)

This extraordinary legislator transforms human nature, denies men their passions in order to give them something more than they are, denies his own passions in that he gives laws not as a ruler, but as a foreigner to the body that he constitutes through this pure act of will. In this work of legislation then two impossibilities operate simultaneously: 'an undertaking that transcends human force and an authority that is nil' (Rousseau 1987: 164).

Rousseau's legislator mirrors in essential respects Žižek's account of the act: the general will does not follow from any established coordinates; it is an act of pure expenditure in that the legislator does not benefit in any manner (there is no instrumental reason for the act); and the legislator invokes the divine in order to elect the people for themselves. There will be those who have to be forced to be free, because they refuse to recognize the validity of the general will. Rousseau insists (without using the same words as Žižek) that one can distinguish the good terror from the bad, and by implication the good terror is justified by this act of distinction which marks it as good. This Rousseauian moment is most clearly expressed in Žižek's recent text, *Iraq: The Borrowed Kettle*:

> Democratic struggle should not be fetishized; it is only one of the forms of struggle, and its choice should be determined by a global strategic assessment of circumstances, not by its ostensibly superior intrinsic value. Like the Lacanian analyst, a political agent has to engage in acts which can be authorised only by themselves, for which there is no external guarantee. (2004: 89)

He goes on to argue that there can be no guarantees for the act, no guarantee that it will be recognized, nor any guarantee that it is the correct act to take. There is a moment of radical indecision and risk which characterizes any act. Yet he also argues that the good terror, as opposed to the bad, that which is effectively a misrecognition of antagonism, might sometimes require the exercise of force, indeed of terror, especially when resisting the enemy at his best. This moment of divinity when the human actor comes into contact with the transcendental, as Žižek argues, can only be deemed an act if it traverses the fundamental fantasy. Otherwise it is mere whim. The act is derived from Lacan's account of the analyst edging the analysand toward a traversal of the fundamental fantasy. The analyst recognizes that she is not the object cause of the fundamental fantasy of the subject, and manipulates the transference but with no interest herself in the transference. The analyst avoids all danger of countertransference, and maintains within the space of the analysis an opening, a void, which the analysand must come to terms with. Yet the psychoanalytic act does not, according to Lacan, include in its agency the presence of the subject. This is the basis of what Žižek terms the act in politics:

> In short an authentic act is not simply external with regard to the hegemonic symbolic field disturbed by it; an act is an act only *with regard to* some symbolic field, as an intervention into it. That is to say: a symbolic field is always and by definition in itself 'decentred',

structured around a central void/impossibility. . ..; and an act disturbs the symbolic field into which it intervenes not out of
nowhere, but precisely *from the standpoint of this inherent impossi-*
bility, stumbling block, which is its hidden, disavowed structuring
principle. . . [T]he inauthentic act legitimises itself through reference to the point of substantial fullness of a given constellation. . ..:
it aims precisely at obliterating the last traces of the 'symptomal
torsion' which disturbs the balance of that constellation. (Žižek
2000a: 125)

Reading this one cannot but recall the distinction between race and
class mentioned above. If class is the hidden disavowed structuring
principle, the real of the economy which is the inherent impossibility, the stumbling block that renders the symbolic order contingent
then the authentic act addresses the void in addressing class. The
psychoanalytic coordinates of the authentic act allow for the identification of false acts: violence which has no bearing on the symbolic
order and is equivalent to the 'act' of the psychotic; the continual
acting out of the neurotic who avoids the act through constant delay,
the self-hindering of the obsessive who thus cannot act, and the self-
instrumentalization of the pervert who acts against himself.

There is a peculiar narcissism at play here. For the act to be
authentic the political activist has to accurately read the social
symptom, has to diagnose the fundamental fantasy, has to choose
an act which can perform the traversal of this fantasy, and in so
doing (in a moment when the distinction between performative and
constative collapses, a little like Rousseau's legislator) redefine the
co-ordinates of what can be done. This entails a subjective destitution which means that the subject cannot even evaluate whether or
not the act is in line with its basic requirements, noted above.
Contrast this with the psychoanalytic act which relies precisely upon
an analytic encounter in which the subject of knowledge does not
have its imaginary coherence verified by the analyst. Yet the presence
of the other is a crucial component of the analysis, of the passage
through the act. Such conditions simply do not apply in relation to
the notion of the act defended by Žižek in political terms. Moreover
we have already seen that Žižek, occupying the position of both
analyst and activist, has not provided an adequate analysis of capitalism and thus cannot even begin to address the fundamental
fantasy, even if it is the disavowed question of class. Even had he

provided such a persuasive account of the real abstraction, capital, which for him is the real of contemporary societies, even had he done so this notion of the act could only ever be an empty fantasy.

Let us recall the essential elements of the authentic act. The act is axiomatic and as such foundational. As in mathematics a questioning of the axioms means that one can no longer play the game. The act establishes a subject of a new knowledge, and is a moment of contact with the noumenal realm.[10] The act thus breaks with the deconstructive ethics of the limit, which posit the real as a limit, and which is positivized in various accounts of radical democracy as the impossibility of society. The assumption is that the act responds to the symptomal torsions that cut through the symbolic order, and in addressing the void establishes new rules which change possible relations to that order. Žižek seems here to suffer a melancholia less sophisticated than that of Adorno but infinitely more dangerous. For Adorno no act simply leaves the object capital behind. The idealism of the concept which presumes that this is possible without addressing its own implication in the object capital is precisely what capital allows and is already prepared for. The emptiness of the act defended by Žižek is revealed if we contrast it with Lacan's account of the psychoanalytic act which has as its condition of possibility a long and patient working through on the part of the analysand. Its idealism is revealed if we contrast it with Rousseau's account which locates the act in the realm of the divine. And its danger is obvious: if Žižek cannot even provide an adequate account of the fundamental fantasy that traverses the real of capital then the distinction between the good terror and the bad cannot be maintained.

NOTES

1 It is no mistake that Gramsci is the key reference point for writers such as Laclau and Mouffe. However, the ambiguity of Gramsci's own position vis-à-vis class determinism should be reread in light of Žižek's reading of *Capital*.

2 Žižek takes this phrase from Badiou.

3 Here Žižek's critique echoes that of Lukàcs in *History and Class Consciousness*, and Marx in the *Grundrisse*. Žižek's arguments about each of these discourses is a lot more detailed than I have the space to present here, but in effect this is his claim.

4 Žižek argues that the form of the economy has to do with the manner in which surplus value is produced and appropriated. This argument is very close to that of Althusser in *Reading Capital*, who held that the economy

determines in the last instance how the surplus is extracted and produced. It appoints, so to speak, one element of the social to effect this
exploitation.

5 This is a brutal summary of a longer quote along these lines.

6 See his discussion of this in *The Parallax View* (2006: 65).

7 For Žižek Hegel's account of concrete universality specifies, in quasi-
Kantian fashion, 'the notional network constitutive of reality itself'.
This notional network consists in a recognition of the inherent tension
within each determinate category between its necessity as a concept and
its impossibility when applied to 'reality'; second a claim that this inconsistency is the moving spirit of reality, that this spirit is not mere logic
and thus touches upon reality; and last that the only way to conceive of
the universal is as a particular which asserts itself in the guise of a particular content which claims to embody it directly and thus excludes all
other particulars as merely particular.

8 See for example an Althusserian account of the apartheid state in Wolpe
(1990).

9 I am not thinking of Badiou's account of the event, although this is the
obvious point of reference. Žižek marks his debt to and distance from
Badiou in *The Ticklish Subject* (1999).

10 We should recall here Lukàcs' account of revolution. Lukàcs argues that
the distinction between the noumenal and phenomenal that Kant develops in the first critique is in fact a consequence of the separation between
subject and object effected by the class divisions characteristic of capitalist society. The proletariat experience their objectification subjectively
and are thus the one revolutionary class capable of effecting revolutionary action, and at the same time resolving the antinomies of knowledge
developed by Kant.

ALL THE RIGHT QUESTIONS, ALL THE WRONG ANSWERS

Jeremy Gilbert

'ŽIŽEK' THE SYMPTOM

'Žižek', Ernesto Laclau was once heard to remark, 'is a force of nature'. I am generally reluctant to disagree with Laclau about Žižek or anything else, but I want to take issue with this. Like 'globalization', melting glaciers and the high price of pharmaceuticals in Africa, 'Žižek' is not a natural occurrence. Rather, the Žižek-phenomenon is a product of our times and a symptom of contemporary processes with which no one on the Left can remain comfortably complicit. It should hardly need spelling out, but I am not concerned here with Slavoj Žižek the private individual, about whom I know nothing (although some speculation as to his motives might prove interesting). Instead it is the public phenomenon – the discursive formation of writings published under the name of Slavoj Žižek and notoriously (melo)dramatic public performances of that dramatic persona with which I am interested.

Part of what I am going to argue is that Žižek – contrary to his own mythology – is not the Great Exception to the ordinary rules of academic conduct. He has published some good work and he has published a great deal of very bad work, and the good work is precisely that which is demonstrably the product of dedicated scholarship and informed engagement with specific sets of ideas. The bad work, which notoriously deals in generalizations, logical inconsistencies, groundless assertions and aimless polemics is not somehow saved or justified by Žižek's irreducible genius: it is an embarrassment, which the academic and leftist intellectual community ought to be ashamed of having tolerated for so long. The question that this assertion raises, of course, is just why it has done. I suggest that there are two broad answers to this question. On the one hand (which I will come to later), Žižek is one of very few voices in recent times to have posed a particular and particularly urgent set of questions for the post-Marxist theoretical Left, even if the answers that he proffers are very far from being useful to anyone. On the other hand, Žižek is tolerated and encouraged – even, in some quarters, feted – precisely because of the seamless fit between his practice and the ideological demands of neo-liberal culture.

Let us begin with certain indisputable truths about Žižek. In recent times an extraordinary quantity of words has been published under his name. This work has almost all been published by publishers largely known for academic publishing (although Verso, his usual publisher, is not merely an academic press). Yet this work does not even approach the standards of academic rigour that would normally be expected of an undergraduate essay. It does not include substantial references to the texts on which it offers opinions, frequently making enormous generalizations about the ideas of a particular writer or even typically of an entire field of enquiry *without a single reference to an actual page of an actual text*, and rarely cites its objects in any detail. Frequently (I am straying into the realm of the disputable here, but will justify this view shortly), Žižek actually demonstrates no greater familiarity with the work in question than that which could be acquired by any literate person standing around in a bookshop for 10 minutes, reading the blurbs on the back of books or leafing through introductory guides to the thinkers or subject in question. For the moment I make no value judgment here. We may consider it a healthy thing that books published under the name of Slavoj Žižek are not expected to demonstrate even a minimal degree of authority on the subjects they pronounce upon. We may consider it fully justified that these books are required to display a level of scholarship which would be considered pitiable in the work of an undergraduate student. We may decide that Žižek's authority is so indisputable and the quality of his analysis so extraordinary that he need not tire himself or bore his readers with such annoyances as footnotes, citations and page references. But *that* he does not do so, when other scholars and philosophers, even those of international renown, are expected to do so, is not in question.

A second truth. Žižek's main objects of attack have been on the Left. Specifically, a loosely connected set of political positions and intellectual tendencies largely associated with the legacy of the 'New

Lefts' has been the thing that Žižek has chosen to focus his critical attentions on. 'Cultural studies', 'political correctness', 'feminists', 'multiculturalism', postmodernists, post-colonial studies, historicists and deconstructionists: despite his avowed anti-capitalism, it is not capitalism and its specificities but the same litany of hate-figures that populates the fevered imagination of the American Right for which Žižek has reserved most of his ill-informed ire. We might think that this is a fully justified position. But again, my point is merely that this is indisputable. So what we are dealing with, for better or worse, is a writer whose main stock-in-trade is demonstrably ill-informed and frequently inaccurate diatribes against the legacies of the New Lefts. No one could be so crude as to suggest that this automatically puts Žižek into the same category as a William F. Buckley or a Howard Stern. But who can be entirely absolved from judgement in terms of the company they keep? It is Žižek himself, in his promotion of a 'Leninist' perspective, who reminds us today of the irreducibility of partisanship; and how would Lenin have characterized the 'objective' politics of a writer who wrote like a Right-wing demagogue, said the same things as Right-wing demagogues and attacked the same objects as Right-wing demagogues?

THE 'PROPER KNOWLEDGE' OF CULTURAL STUDIES

Before going any further, if I am going to evade charges of heinous hypocrisy on my own part, I need to offer some evidence for my charges. Let us take as one exemplary text, Žižek's *Did Somebody Say Totalitarianism?* (2001). For a start, this book opens by promising to address the 'problem' of the fact that accusations of 'totalitarianism' have become unanswerable and automatically condemnatory charges in the context of a certain post-structuralist intellectual climate. It proceeds to do *nothing of the kind*, instead offering a more or less stream of consciousness set of reflections on certain uses of psychoanalytic theory to address a disparate and frequently disconnected set of intellectual issues. At no point does the book make *any attempt* to engage with the complex intellectual history which leads to the blanket condemnation of 'totalitarianism' – the disillusion with party communism after 1968, the rigorous scholarship of Lyotard and Lefort, the influence of anarchism on the 'new social movements', etc., etc. In place of any such thing, we get remarks such as this one: 'If at a Cultural Studies colloquium in the 1970s, one was asked innocently "Is your line of argumentation not similar to that of Arendt?" this was a sure sign that one was in deep trouble' (Žižek 2001: 2).

On the one hand, this is a remark intended to illustrate a general point about the changing fashionability of Arendt's work during recent decades, to be read quickly and passed over. On the other, it sets up Žižek's entire case that there is something 'wrong' with 'cultural studies' that can be registered in terms of its changing attitude to Arendt. As such, if Žižek's initial assertion about this change is not substantiable then it raises severe questions as to the whole premise of this argument – never mind the substance of the argument itself. So wait. Read the remark again. Pause and reflect. Only one of two responses is really possible here: either silent acquiescence from someone who assumes that the remark must be reasonable (because it is made in a book by a famous authority on cultural theory published by a renowned publisher of esteem and quality), or a protesting query from anyone who knows anything at all about cultural studies and its history. Locating myself in the latter category I have to ask: what the hell is Žižek talking about? How on earth would Žižek *know* what 'would have happened' (with enough certainty to know that anything would have been a '*sure sign*' of anything else) at a 'cultural studies colloquium in the 1970s'. There was only one place in the world where one might have attended a 'cultural studies colloquium in the 1970s': at the University of Birmingham – and to the best of anyone's recollection (I have asked a number of people who were there), Slavoj Žižek never made it along to one.

Žižek may be right and he may be wrong about his substantive point. That is not the immediate issue, although we will come back to it. The important point for now is that Žižek is making an authoritative comment on something – cultural studies colloquia in the 1970s – without offering the slightest reason for the reader to put aside their justifiable scepticism as to Žižek's authority so to comment. Let us be clear about the implicit assumption here: the reader is assumed (or hoped, at least) to know even less about the subject than Žižek, and to take his word for it. Such a reader is being misled for the sake of a polemical point on Žižek's part.

This might not be so bad if what Žižek said was actually true, and in this case it cannot be well-proven that it is or is not. So let us move on to another section in the same book. In a truly extraordinary passage, Žižek writes:

In effect, the problem of Cultural Studies is often a lack of specific disciplinary skills: a literary theorist without a proper knowledge of philosophy can write disparagingly about Hegel's phallogocentrism, on film, and so on – we are dealing with a kind of false universal critical capacity to pass judgement on everything, without proper knowledge. With all their criticism of traditional philosophical universalism, Cultural Studies actually function as a kind of *ersatz* philosophy. Notions are thus transformed into ideological universals: in postcolonial studies, the notion of 'colonization' starts to function as a hegemonic notion, is elevated into a universal paradigm, so that, in relations between the sexes, the male sex colonizes the female sex, the upper classes colonize the lower classes. (Žižek 2001: 224)

The hypocrisy is breathtaking, even if we limit ourselves to this passage alone, in and of itself. First, let us ask: how do we know, or claim the authority to decide, what constitutes 'proper knowledge'? Well, at the present time such authority can be conferred by institutions and their mechanisms of legitimation (degrees, titles, etc.), or by the charisma which accrues to individuals within the circuits of celebrity. However, in the 'academic world' of which Žižek is so routinely disparaging, there is another, more democratic mechanism: the established conventions of citation and reference. As tedious as these conventions no doubt appear to a jet-setting star such as Žižek, it is essential to bear in mind that this is their primary purpose: to allow any reader whatsoever, if they want to, to go and check a writer's sources, and make their own judgments as to that writer's uses of them. The lack of such an apparatus immediately renders it impossible for such an open process of verification and potential challenge to take place. Under these circumstances, 'proper knowledge' must presumably be assumed on the basis of the author's institutional or charismatic authority, rather than on the basis of the author's capacity to *demonstrate* such knowledge by offering examples of it and evidence for it. For let us be clear, very rarely in this book or any other does Žižek offer a *single example* of 'cultural studies' or 'post-colonial studies', and he never demonstrates anything like the familiarity with the range of sources that would be expected of an undergraduate commenting on those fields. This cannot be regarded as a mere stylistic quirk. It is at once a gesture of definitive arrogance – assuming, again, that Žižek's mere celebrity is sufficient to authorize him as an agent of 'proper knowledge' – and astonishing hypocrisy given that in this very passage Žižek *himself demonstrates no 'proper knowledge' of the fields on which he himself is commentating: post-colonial studies and cultural studies.* Of course, Žižek makes no explicit claim to authority on the basis of his celebrity. It is his claim to represent 'philosophy' as such – the only 'properly dialectical' metalanguage – which is evoked here and elsewhere. But in the absence of any externally verifiable bases for his claims to speak even from this position, never mind as a commentator on cultural or post-colonial studies, the reader is implicitly invited to assent both to his claim to represent 'philosophy' and to the implicit assumption that this position authorizes commentary on other disciplines even in the absence of any apparent direct knowledge thereof, solely on the basis of Žižek's reputation and the endorsement given to it by respectable publishers. In the absence of any clearly demonstrated 'proper knowledge' of either philosophy (dialectical or otherwise) or 'cultural studies' or 'post-colonial studies', this is the only reason offered to us to take Žižek's word for it.

But still, how can we be sure that no such 'proper knowledge' – albeit legitimated by questionable means – is on display here? Simple: by noting the fact that very few examples *could* be found of anything reasonably identifiable as 'post-colonial studies' doing what Žižek says it does. Certainly none of the key figures in the formation of that area of intellectual work – Fanon, Said, Spivak, Bhabha, Gilroy, Hall – could be accused of so doing, and nor could such recent innovators in the field as Venn, Mbembe or Hallward. Žižek's remark is plausible under certain circumstances, but those circumstances depend on two possible conditions. One is the simple ignorance of the reader who knows that there is such a thing as 'post-colonial studies' but knows very little else about it. The other is a partisan predisposition to endorse Žižek's view on the basis of a wider political critique of post-colonial studies. Such a critique may well be fully justifiable, and has been made by those rigorous Marxist commentators who have called for a more specific concept of contemporary colonization (e.g. Parry 2004), but this in no way alters the fact that Žižek's remarks – which *do not*, as they could do, refer the reader to the work of such commentators – offer no grounds for the reader to accept their legitimacy and are demonstrably problematic to say the least. A parallel example is Žižek's remark on 'the shift from English to American

Cultural Studies: even if we find in both the same themes, notions, and so on, the socio-ideological functioning is completely different – we shift from an engagement with real working class culture to academic radical chic' (Žižek 2001: 226). It would not be possible to characterize such a shift, if one has taken place at all, in such simplistic terms with reference to actual published work: apart from anything, the routinely cited key figures of British cultural studies, Raymond Williams and Stuart Hall, have never been particularly interested in 'working class culture' as such (Hoggart and Thompson, the other 'fathers' of cultural studies, who were much more interested in working-class culture, have had far less lasting influence over the field) but have been much more interested in culture as a field of hegemonic and counterhegemonic struggle, as has the most prominent representative of 'cultural studies' in the USA, Lawrence Grossberg (Grossberg 1992; Hall 1988; Williams 1977).

The point here, however, is not that Žižek is strictly wrong. Of course there *is* a problem wherever 'the colonial' or 'the postcolonial' loses any specificity which might make it useful as a tool for the conceptualization of particular sets of power relations. Of course the tendency within cultural studies to substitute a set of received assumptions and intellectual caricatures (Lacan is a male chauvinist, Hegel is a fascistic 'state philosopher', class struggle is a redundant concept) for any thorough engagement with the philosophical tradition is deeply problematic. Of course the substitution of individualist liberalism for radical political positions has been endemic in cultural studies, especially where it has lost its connections to the political traditions of the British New Left, as has happened most strikingly (and unsurprisingly) in the USA (Gilbert 2003). But the solution to these problems – already manifest in the work of more rigorous thinkers from within those disciplines and adjacent to them (e.g. Osborne 2000) – is better scholarship, more diligent reading, a lesser tendency to pass judgment on whole areas of thought about which one knows nothing, and a partial return to the contingent but committed Left-partisanship of Williams and Hall. Žižek's solution is entirely opposite to this in every respect: to be even *more* causally dismissive and lazily prejudiced in his blanket characterizations of 'postmodern relativism', 'multiculturalism', 'deconstructionism', 'historicism', etc. than are the writers to whom he responds, and to argue for more – not less – Left sectarianism (an issue to which we will return).

'ŽIŽEK' THE BRAND

Žižek's ideal reader, then, would seem to be someone who knows too little about the topics on which he comments to question his authority, who does not look to other, competing sources for either corroboration (which would be difficult to find) or alternative opinions: in other words, the ideal reader implied by Žižek's texts is a 'brand-loyal' Žižek reader, assenting to the assumption that Žižek's fame is a sufficient guarantee of quality that other competing products in the intellectual marketplace need not trouble their attention. Perhaps we should not be surprised, and even less outraged, that such a phenomenon should occur at the present time. What we see here is simply the logic of celebrity culture and deep commodification extended to the field of 'intellectual' publishing, and it is virtually a truism today to acknowledge that celebrity culture is one of the most striking manifestations of the commodifying and individualizing logics of neo-liberal capitalism, logics whose widespread operation is symptomatic of the secure hegemony of neo-liberalism almost throughout the non-Islamic world (Littler 2004). The hegemony of neo-liberalism produces and is secured by a process which posits the autonomous individual in competition with others as the basic and irreducible unit of human experience and which subjects as many areas of social life as possible to the logic of commodification, constituting autonomous, unrelated monads and placing them into competition with each other in fields as diverse as cuisine and education (Harvey 2005). Just as the existence of well-defined culinary traditions and the era of culinary 'movements' is replaced by one in which individual 'star' chefs compete for public attention, the neo-liberal approach to education is to break-up coherent systems of interconnected institutions, putting individual schools into competition with each other in an open market place, struggling to outshine each other as 'centres of excellence' and even (in the UK case) explicitly seeking to attract 'star' head teachers (Whitfield 2006).

Of course, the operation of a comparable 'star' system in the field of philosophy is nothing new. At least since Socrates and Confucius, philosophy has been identified with the names of individuals and has tended to generate personality cults. In many ways, the lives of intellectuals in earlier periods seem to prefigure the fate of today's millions of mobile, insecure knowledge-workers – just think of the poor but highly mobile scholars of medieval Europe, such as Duns Scotus – and these conditions will always encourage those subjected to them to seek to secure their precarious positions (socially and financially) by promoting the idea of their individual and irreducible genius. Furthermore, the names of authors have always functioned as the marker of the unique intervention that they make in a field of thought (Derrida 1988; Foucault 1977: 113–38; Deleuze & Guattari 1994: 61–83). However, it is also true that one of the impulses behind the development of a range of institutions of intellectual life since the Middle Ages has been precisely to protect intellectual work from both the relentless logic of the market and the intrusive influence of patronage and government. While this is obviously true of traditional institutions such as academic tenure (formally abolished in the UK during the first wave of aggressive neo-liberalization and further undermined by the casualization of higher education in the 1990s), one can also argue that institutions such as the traditional apparatus of reference and citation serve a similar function, rendering all claims to knowledge publicly accountable and formally acknowledging the extent to which the production and legitimation of 'knowledge' is always a collaborative and intertextual exercise.

If academic institutions such as citation, tenure, peer-review, etc. have always in part served to protect intellectual work from the direct intrusion of both the state and market forces, then we should be particularly concerned about their erosion at a moment when the project of neo-liberalism is precisely to use the mechanisms of government to intensify the reach and ubiquity of market relations in spheres such as the university sector (Whitfield 2006a). The state and the market are no longer two definite but distinct dangers for institutions like the university today: instead the institutions of government are now collaborating towards a single common goal, doing all they can to ensure that the market meets with no inconvenient obstacles in the drive to commodify everything (Harvey 2005). In this context, a form of knowledge production which eschews these traditional protections in favour of an intellectual project legitimating itself in terms of celebrity and brand-loyalty is precisely what neoliberal strategies might have been formulated to generate, and they certainly meet with no kind of resistance in the formation of such a project. And such a project has been the career to date of Slavoj Žižek. But why then, any reader may fairly ask, does he continue to attract so much attention?

ÉPATER LE BOURGEOIS! SPECTACULAR ŽIŽEK. . .

A number of answers can be offered to this question, some of which will be more flattering to Žižek and his readers than others. It is initially difficult to resist the temptation to make a situationist analysis (Debord 1994). There can be no real question that since his earliest publications in English, Žižek has been out to shock his audience. In his first book for Verso, he notoriously berates Marxists and feminists for their excessive historicism: in other words, for failing to recognize as invariant features of the human condition upon whose variability feminism and socialism have always been predicated (Žižek 1989: 50). In some of his most recent work, Žižek declares himself committed to the rehabilitation of Lenin despite how shocking he insists this will be to the faux-revolutionaries of 'academic radicalism' (it is scarcely credible that Žižek, an international academic star, an employee of private commercial institutions such as the European Graduate School (http://www.egs.edu/), with no ties whatsoever to radical political movements outside Slovenia, regards himself as anything but a *prime example* of this category, but apparently he does).

In all such cases, however, the effect has not been to generate an outcry against Žižek's work, but merely to entrench Žižek's position as a key figure in the intellectual star-system, either a genuinely innovative figure or an 'allowed fool', irascible but harmless. There are a number of reasons for this. The most obvious is that there is simply nothing particularly shocking about these interventions of Žižek's. It had been understood by Western Marxists and feminists long before Žižek appeared on the scene that psychoanalysis posited certain features of human culture as deeply-entrenched and near-universal, and many positions had been developed which accommodated this perspective to one which retained a revolutionary commitment to the ultimate variation of those features (Mitchell 1974; Deleuze & Guattari 1977; etc.). Similarly, the idea that a 'return to Lenin' should be seen as somehow radical only demonstrates how little detailed attention Žižek has ever paid to the field in which he purports to make his 'radical' interventions. There has never been any question that Gramsci, the iconic figure of late-twentieth-century radical political theory, was heavily indebted to Lenin, even as he tried to adapt communist political methods to the new historical realities of mass democracy, mass media and Fordism. An antagonistic relationship to the neo-Gramscianism of

Laclau and Mouffe has defined Žižek's career for nearly 20 years. Yet in insisting on his own irreducible radicalism for daring even to read Lenin, Žižek does not seem to have noticed that in their classic *Hegemony and Socialist Strategy* (1985) even Laclau and Mouffe do not endorse a simple rejection of Lenin. In fact they recognize Lenin's intervention into Marxist theory as critical, posing as it did the problem of revolution and class consciousness as a political problem which could only be solved by active intervention, as opposed to that Second International orthodoxy which preached political quietism until the full evolution of capitalism made proletarian revolution inevitable (Laclau & Mouffe 1985: 64). This line of Žižek's reaches a pitch of absurdity when he writes that 'Althusser is often dismissed as a proto-Stalinist' (2001: 90), presenting his recourse to Althusser as a daring one, it not being at all clear just who is ever supposed to have made this dismissive gesture (certainly no one connected with cultural studies, where Althusser remains required reading for undergraduates to this day).

So what we seem to have here, in the case of Žižek, is a loud insistence on just how 'shocking' the work being produced is, without any evidence being available that anyone anywhere has been remotely shocked by it or was ever likely to have been. This is not a unique trope in our culture. One is reminded of the 'Young British Artists' phenomenon of the 1990s. Aping the avant-gardist impulse to '*épater le bourgeois*', conceptual artists such as Damien Hirst and Tracey Emin saw an eager public emerge for their work, happy to be flattered by the notion that in appreciating such art it was demonstrating its worldly intelligence: without a hiccup these 'shocking' artists were absorbed into the starscape of celebrity culture. Does this not sound rather like the fate of Žižek's 'revolutionary' provocations?

ŽIŽEK'S LENINISM

'Well, what of it?', Žižek's defenders might retort, 'Žižek can hardly be blamed for the fate of his interventions under conditions not of his own choosing'. Leaving aside the observation that there *are* modes of intellectual engagement which are more deliberately resilient to such appropriation (the patient scholarship of a Jacques Derrida, the deliberate anti-vanguardism of a Subcomandante Marcos), it is at this point that it is necessary to tackle in more detail the political substance of Žižek's recent interventions. Most notably,

Žižek has argued for a return to Lenin, understood as the great theorist of revolutionary practice and the advocate of an anti-capitalism which is not afraid to question the premises of liberal democracy (capitalism's tendential political form). At the other end of the scale from the anarchist-inspired tendencies which refuse any notion of political strategy as inherently totalitarian, we have Žižek calling for a return to Lenin, as the great strategist of revolutionary communism and the great advocate of the party form as the means by which political strategy should be formulated and implemented. Žižek suggests that we should return to Lenin while acknowledging that the specific content of his project in 1917 is no longer relevant to our situation today, pursuing a line of argument partly borrowed from Alain Badiou, insisting that Lenin's great contribution is to assert the irreducible value of the all-transforming revolutionary act and the necessity of disciplined, dogmatic 'intolerance' for effective revolutionary organization (Žižek 2002a).

As so often with this polemic, Žižek is once again asking exactly the right questions and getting exactly the wrong answers, and as usual this seems to be because he has not bothered to read either his opponents or his 'friends' with any care at all. Žižek is certainly right to discern a chronic and disabling lack of strategic thinking on much of the contemporary radical scene, and a similarly disabling distaste for militancy amongst so-called 'radical' intellectuals, and he is right that no attempt to get past the resulting impasse can possibly avoid an encounter with Lenin. What he seems to have conveniently over-looked, however, is that the entire political tradition from which he is most keen to distinguish himself – the Gramscian and neo-Gramscian tradition which includes, amongst others, Laclau and Mouffe, Raymond Williams and Stuart Hall – proceeds from the assumption that Lenin was right to pose the questions of political organization and strategy but that the answers which he found to those questions, arguably appropriate to the specific conditions of pre-revolutionary Czarist Russia, are not appropriate to the very different circumstances of the advanced capitalist democracies. Insofar as Žižek presents this insight *in and of itself* as distinctive to his own position, and grounds his arguments for the positions he derives from it in that claim, those arguments demonstrably lack any clear basis as anything other than bombastic assertions.

Nevertheless, it is worth thinking about exactly what Žižek thinks is specific to Lenin's thinking in the period leading up to the revolution that is so indispensable to any effective radicalism. There are two key aspects. First, Žižek is impressed by Lenin's willingness to break with Marxist orthodoxy, according to which Russia was nowhere remotely close to being ready for a proletarian communist revolution in 1917, and thereby to take advantage of a historically unprecedented situation of socio-political crisis in order to transform the historical scene in which he found himself (Žižek 2001b; Žižek 2002a: 7–12). Secondly, he is impressed by Lenin's willingness to abjure the niceties of consensual liberalism in order to defend a militant position of revolutionary anti-capitalism (Žižek 2001b; Žižek 2002a: 167–78). Let us deal with these one at a time.

First: it is clearly true that Lenin's break with Marxist orthodoxy was in some senses exemplary, both theoretically and pragmatically. However, Žižek's characterization of the nature of this break is both reductive and counter-productive in its implications. Žižek almost invariably presents Lenin's break as an example of pure volition, unmediated will, a fundamental act in the most metaphysical and individualistic sense. Although he does write that 'Lenin is not a voluntarist "subjectivist" ' (Žižek 2002a: 10), Žižek nonetheless writes as if Lenin simply decided, in the face of a historically unprecedented set of circumstances which no established theoretical framework could comprehend, to remake the world in some wholly inventive manner, as if Lenin's decisions were not the outcome of years of Bolshevik theorizing and practical politics, as if Russia in 1917 was simply in a condition of absolute social dislocation into which any imaginable intervention could have been made, as if the complex specificities of the situation were not the irreducible context within which Lenin had to act. For example:

> It is rather as if, in a unique suspension of temporality, in the short-circuit between the present and the future, we are – as if by Grace – for a brief time allowed to act AS IF the utopian future is (not yet fully here, but) already at hand, just there to be grabbed. (Žižek 2001b: 26)

To the contrary, I would argue that Lenin's decision to push the revolution to its logical conclusion was *not* some miraculous accession to grace, but the product of a careful strategic calculation and a willingness to recalibrate the terms of that calculation in the face of emergent events. Far from being the singular intervention which changed everything, Lenin's decision was the product of a willingness to accept that he could not control events and that no theoretical dogma could predict them. Lenin had to accept the fact that the revolution was not unfolding according to the classical Marxist scheme and hence to take political opportunities as they arose.

It was therefore an openness to the incalculability of the future which characterized Lenin's perspective and distinguished it from later Stalinist dogmatism. It was a willingness to accept the fact that his actions were always already caught up in a destabilizing network of causes and effects which forced Lenin to act as he did, not some pure moment of revelation. Žižek does seem to acknowledge this much when he describes Lenin's attitude as one of 'authentic historical openness' (Žižek 2001b). But let us be clear: this undermines his entire position. As Žižek himself might put it, does not this final resort, in the very last phrase of a substantial essay on Lenin, to a rhetoric which is clearly Derridean and Levinasian in inspiration, reveal the ultimate instability and unsustainability of Žižek's own position? More importantly, it entirely undermines Žižek's own defence of Lenin's 'revolutionary intolerance'.

Žižek carries out this defence according to his classic mode of caricaturing the positions of a vast range of people with whom he wishes to disagree as being fundamentally identical to each other and then, having failed to offer any justification for this classificatory gesture, proceeding to press home his case merely by taking issue with the most crude and idiotic position to be found amongst the horde which he has lumped together. So, Žižek identifies all those thinkers who try to defend some ideal of democratic engagement and all postmodern critics of totalitarian thinking (including, amongst others, Jean-François Lyotard and Chantal Mouffe) with those who regard liberal democracy as the untranscendable horizon of all legitimate or even possible politics. This is simply a demonstrable mistake. One of the key reasons as to why thinkers informed by currents of thought such as postmodernism and deconstruction resist any attempt fully to shut down debate, dialogue and dissensus is precisely so that we never again repeat the mistakes of the pre-Leninist Marxists of the Second International, in holding on to a theoretical paradigm which is no longer useful and no longer capable of generating effective political intervention in the face of contingent and unpredictable circumstances (Gilbert 2001).

What is most extraordinary about all of Žižek's polemic against critics of Leninism, is that he writes now as if the entire history of Leninism and its consequences were not deeply problematic. One need make no reference to the Soviet experience to understand the problems here. The British Left has its own traumatic memory of Leninism, to which Žižek seems entirely oblivious. There can be little argument that the period 1983–84 marked the moment when socialism in the UK was killed as a political force, utterly defeated by Thatcherism and undone by its own internal divisions. This was the moment when the Labour Party, standing in the 1983 general election on the most radical manifesto in its history, was almost wiped out as an electoral force. Perhaps even more significantly, 1984 is burned into the memory of the British Left as the year of the miners' strike: this was the longest industrial dispute in our history, when the most politicized and widely supported strike since 1926, by a group (coal miners) who had at several points (most recently in 1974) succeeded in winning major victories for the labour movement, was roundly defeated, never to recover.

Importantly, one of the reasons for the political defeat of the strike was the refusal of the miners' leader, Arthur Scargill, to ballot the union's membership on support for the strike. This was and still is seen by many of Scargill's supporters as an almost baffling gesture. There is little question that the strike had majority support amongst members of the National Union of Mineworkers (NUM) as well as amongst a broad cross-section of the public, yet Scargill refused to hold a formal ballot to demonstrate the fact, provoking a major split within the union which made it far easier for the Thatcher government to break the strike. Why? The answer is still a matter of historical conjecture, but one of the most persuasive explanations is that as a committed Leninist, Scargill regarded demands for a formal ballot as degenerate concessions to bourgeois liberal democracy, believing that in a situation of immediate struggle, revolutionary discipline demanded that the union membership submit to the decisions of the leadership. The refusal of one section of the union to concede to this view, instead seceding from the union, was decisive in breaking the strike.

Of course, there were many other factors in play. The East Midlands NUM branches who broke away to form the Democratic Union of Mineworkers were notoriously Right-wing, were defending specific privileges not enjoyed by other British miners, and were justifiably suspected of looking for any excuse to break the strike. Nonetheless, no one who remembers that time can read Žižek's blasé appreciations of 'Leninist intolerance', especially of 'liberal democracy', without being reminded of the political consequences of Scargill's bloody-minded intransigence, which ended in the farce of his ill-fated 'Socialist Labour Party' failing to make any electoral impact while succeeding in splitting the left of the labour movement just when it faced the challenge of nascent Blairism. On a personal note, no one who witnessed the appalling destruction of mining communities in the wake of the strike's defeat can happily accede to Žižek's views. This does not mean that Žižek is wrong, but it does suggest that something is amiss in his failure even to acknowledge this history when writing for an anglophone readership, and when attacking intellectual projects (post-Marxism, cultural studies) with *direct* roots in the specific experiences of the British Left during the period of its great defeat (1974–84).

WHY ŽIŽEK IS RIGHT

Of course, this raises once again the question of why Žižek is so popular. The explanation offered above, that his audience simply enjoy or are flattered by the harmlessly commodified spectacle of the 'militant' intellectual 'shocking the bourgeoisie' could well still stand here (how many young Western Leninists over the years have been merely trying to shock their parents, actual or symbolic?). And yet, like most situationist explanations, this offers us only a general and condemnatory critique of the Žižek-phenomenon. It still touches little on the substantial reasons why a large public may be attracted to some of these ideas other than because of their hopeless complicity with bourgeois ideology. Now at last then, I want to propose two more substantive reasons as to why Žižek's work is so popular: it is often right, and it is occasionally perceptive and persuasive.

To say that Žižek is right is not to say that I agree with his proposed solutions to the problems of contemporary radical theory. However, even from the point of view of disagreeing with those solutions, it is perhaps more fundamental to acknowledge that Žižek is quite right to identify the problems that he does. In particular, Žižek's general perspective is clearly a response to a certain political impasse within much of contemporary cultural radicalism. Let us be fair to Žižek: for all of the anecdotal nature of his evidence, we know what he is talking about with his condemnations of 'cultural studies' (especially in the USA). No one who has tried to work in cultural studies from a perspective which is even conscious of the global hegemony of neo-liberalism and its social consequences can fail to be dismayed by the atmosphere of complete disengagement which seems to infuse so much 'cultural studies' and related areas of thought: the sheer absence of any sustained attempt to analyse the current political conjuncture within those fields is enough to drive many people into the arms of Lenin and Badiou.

In all this, Žižek's intuition that most of post-1960s intellectual radicalism has become largely complicit with the hegemonic liberal culture of advanced capitalism and shies away with making any effective challenge to neo-liberalism (not that he ever uses a concept as specific as 'neo-liberalism') is undoubtedly correct. The problem with Žižek's responses to this situation is not that they are 'too militant' but that they are *not political enough*. For example, Žižek observes that sexual libertarianism has become part of the common sense of capitalist culture (Žižek 2001: 116–17) but he writes as if it were enough merely to observe this fact, without thinking at all about the political history whereby neo-liberal culture has successfully articulated social and cultural liberalism to the ideological norms of competitive individualism, while the leftist sexual utopianism of the past has been marginalized. Indeed, if anything, Žižek's analysis of this situation simply reproduces the norms of extreme Right-wing critique, blaming 'political correctness', 'multiculturalism' and an undifferentiated 'capitalism' for this situation, instead of seeing it as the outcome of a specific political defeat for the Left. At a moment of political crisis for the Western Left, this is hardly the perspective we need.

Similarly, Žižek is quite right to observe that the distaste for any kind of partisanship which pervades the 'postmodern' Left is crippling, but his solution is ridiculous. Rather than observing that there already *is* an emerging coherent movement against neo-liberal capitalism to which the Western intellectual Left could ally itself in a new spirit of anti-capitalist partisanship, he calls for a deliberate cultivation of 'Leninist intolerance', while disparaging the activists of the anti-capitalist movement in wholly misinformed terms. Is this position not just a little too comfortable? The academies of the developed world are clearly full of apolitical elitist scholars just dying to be told that their anti-populist distaste for cultural studies is justified, their inability to come to terms with feminism is not their fault, and their disengagement from any real political struggle is precisely what characterizes them as true revolutionaries. Should the ease with which Žižek tells such an audience exactly what it wants to hear not make us just a little uncomfortable?

Finally, however, one must acknowledge that there are moments when Žižek's interventions are of great value. Two of his more recent works spring to mind here: *The Ticklish Subject* (1999) and *Revolution at the Gates* (2002a). In the former work, whether one agrees with the conclusions or not, one must acknowledge that Žižek presents a reasoned and well-researched set of arguments carefully differentiating his position from those of recent key thinkers. At the same time, he offers some substantial evidence that his brand of Lacanian analysis can be of use in analysing contemporary cultural and political phenomena from a recognizably leftist perspective. In particular the chapter 'Whither Oedipus?' takes an approach which is entirely at odds with the psychoanalytic dogmatism with which he is often charged (Butler 1993), acknowledging that contemporary social developments, driven by changes in the nature of capitalism, might undermine the very psycho–social structures which Freud and Lacan identify, and reflecting on the political consequences and offering a persuasive account of 'Third Way' politics as one response to this situation. In the chapters on Badiou and Butler, Žižek makes a detailed engagement with specific writings by those authors (not as detailed as would be expected from anyone else, but never mind). Here, at least, Žižek demonstrates that he can make a rigorous direct engagement with the ideas of others and their political implications.

In *Revolution at the Gates*, Žižek goes even further, taking the brave step of simply presenting the whole set of writings by Lenin that he bases his argument on in the second half of the book. This is a courageous move, especially given that any reader can see how little Lenin offers with which to support Žižek's arguments. For example, Žižek mobilizes Lenin in support of his belief in the singular, all-transforming revolutionary act which is entirely self-authorizing in nature (Žižek 2002a: 243). One of the ideal examples of such an act cited by Žižek and Badiou is the conversion of St Paul (more precisely, this conversion is understood by Badiou as an ideal-typical 'Truth Event' (Badiou 2003), fidelity to which in the act of founding the Christian community Žižek seems to regard as a true

Lacanian 'act' (Žižek 2000: 92–97). Yet on only the second page of the writings from Lenin included in that volume, Lenin writes:

> There are no miracles in nature or history, but every abrupt turn in history, and this applies to every revolution, presents such a wealth of content, unfolds such unexpected and specific combinations of forms of struggle and alignment of forces of the contestants, that to the lay mind there is much that must appear miraculous.
>
> The combination of a number of factors of world-historic importance was required for the tsarist monarchy to have collapsed in a few days. (Žižek 2002a:16)

There are no self-authorizing acts in this perspective: only overdetermined conjunctures of a thoroughly Gramscian character. Surely Žižek must realize how radically this problematizes his whole argument, and could easily have left the obscure letter from which it derives out of the collection without many people noticing. Let me be clear: I am not drawing attention to this inconsistency as evidence of the idiocy of Slavoj Žižek, but as evidence that he is capable of considerable openness and courage when he decides to make his sources explicit. What is more, the long essay included in this volume is full of considerable insights. Its reading of the cinema of Lars Von Trier, for example, unexpectedly concludes a perceptive analysis of the role of fetish in *Dancer in the Dark* with a more conventional (but *none the less correct*) critique of the sadistic misogyny which informs the 'gaze' of these films. The essay's anecdote about the problems of 'political correctness' points to the problems inherent in its tendency towards abject individualism (a tendency which risks full complicity with neo-liberal ideology) and therefore has a clear political purchase for a leftist perspective (Žižek 2002a: 214), rather than merely reproducing reactionary clichés. One could go on.

What these books have in common is quite simple. They appear to be written with the aim of developing a leftist critical perspective rather than simply attacking the legacies of the New Lefts, and they appear to be written on topics about which Žižek knows something, as is demonstrated by their adequate presentations of source material (containing either the actual texts under discussion or a comprehensive set of references). In particular, they read so differently from the other works mentioned here simply because one comes away with the sense that Žižek has actually been reading before sitting down to his keyboard. What might one conclude from this observation? Well, the simplest explanation is that Žižek is, after all, a talented scholar and a valuable thinker of the Left, but that he too often (far too often, most of the time, almost always) gives in to the temptation to write a polemical and wholly ill-informed treatise on a topic he clearly knows little about in the secure knowledge that the publishers will take it, the public will buy it and profit will thereby ensue.

This is not the place to condemn Žižek or anyone else in moralistic terms. How many of us could honestly resist the temptation to believe it if Verso told us, in effect, that anything we happened to jot down on paper was of immense value and would be treated as such? How many of us would truly fail to comply with the demands of celebrity culture if all we had to do in return for its rewards was to knock out a few books which were not quite as well researched as they should have been? It is not Žižek who should be condemned for such complicity, nor even the struggling progressive publishers who desperately need to sell anything they can: it is we, Žižek's willing public who are to blame. All evidence suggests that when Žižek is not trying to comment on a topic merely because it is fashionable or supposedly shocking to comment on it, when he is left quietly alone actually to do his research and write accordingly, when he spends some time on a work and chooses his targets with an eye to their political status rather than to the ease with which attacking them will provoke controversy amongst his audience, he produces work of great value to the radical intellectual Left. Who can doubt that it is only if he continues in the latter vein that posterity will judge him kindly? Who can doubt that if he remains trapped in the permanent gaze of an intellectual culture too lazy and too complacent to point out his failings, then he will only become more and more ridiculous? It is our complicity with this situation which is the real problem here.

More to the point, however, is the very precise disjuncture between the appropriateness of Žižek's questions and the absurdity of his solutions. Žižek rightly raises the question of what political commitment means in a postmodern context, and what it means for the legatees of a political tradition whose highest aim – the substitution of capitalist social relations for forms of society based on cooperation and mutuality – has been so comprehensively marginalized by the success of neo-liberalism. But his proposed solution – to practice deliberate 'intolerance', to spend most of his time *attacking the*

Left – is nothing but a recipe for that petty and self-regarding sectarianism which has always plagued this tradition. If an ethic of anti-capitalist partisanship is what is required in the current situation, then this is no way to encourage it, just as under-researched and casually dismissive engagements with cultural studies are not an effective response to under-researched and casually dismissive engagements with philosophy. As ever, Žižek seems to be offering all the wrong answers to all the right questions.

CODA

Immediately I had completed the final draft of this chapter, Žižek published an article in the *London Review of Books*, arguing that the apparent philanthropy of socially conscious liberal entrepreneurs such as Bill Gates – 'liberal communists' as Žižek calls them – should be treated with circumspection by anyone concerned about the implication of neo-liberal capitalism in contemporary social problems. Žižek casually remarks that 'it may be necessary to enter into tactical alliances with liberal communists in order to fight racism, sexism, and religious obscurantism' 2006b: 10. This is extraordinary. For if it is allowed that in the course of fighting a Gramscian 'war of position', it may be legitimate to enter into such tactical alliances, then every single one of Žižek's attacks on 'the academic Left' or 'radical chic' since the late 1980s is without foundation, and concepts such as 'revolutionary intolerance' and the philosophy of the 'act', are clearly illegitimate. So one really has to wonder if the whole business of reading and commenting on Zizek since 1989 has not been an enormous waste of time. . .[1]

NOTE

1 Thanks to Paul Bowman, Stuart Hall, Neil Lazarus, Mica Nava, Richard Stamp and Bill Schwarz.

THE INSUFFICIENCY OF GROUND: ON ŽIŽEK'S SCHELLINGIANISM

Iain Hamilton Grant

> The fascination issuing from Schelling's metaphysics is due to its intel-
> lectual excavations reaching strata where the roots of beings no longer
> lie, but where all roots decompose; they attain an unground of reason
> that is equally its presupposition. . . In this conception there are
> glimpses of a modernity we have not yet attained.
>
> (Hogrebe 1989: 127)[1]

Amongst all the forms occurring in contemporary philosophy,
amidst the clamour of being, Žižek is not alone in proclaiming the
truth of the overcoming of metaphysics. Unlike most, however, he is
explicit as to how this overcoming is to be achieved, drawing its
resources from the eruption of metaphysics following Kant, as
against the completed form in which Hegel sought to resolve it. Of
this 'German Idealism', Žižek writes that it ' "returns", within psychoanalysis. . . what was repressed in post-Hegelian thought: the
subject's prehistory' (1991a: 49).

Žižek's repeated forays into Idealist territories, from *Le plus
sublime des hystériques* (1988) to *Tarrying with the Negative* (1993),
follow Heidegger (1985: 165) in taking Schelling's so-called 'philosophy of freedom' as the 'acme of German Idealism', which Žižek
explores in *The Indivisible Remainder* (1996), 'Selfhood as Such is
Spirit' (1996a), and in the 'Abyss of Freedom' (1997b), with the aim
of producing a 'materialist reading of Schelling' (1996a: 11).

When we hear of 'materialisms', we imagine a sober philosophy
that acknowledges the ground of reality as lying in physical *nature*.
Yet since Marx, a radical political realism conversely places 'materialism' on the side of *freedom*. Philosophically, these two orientations
are classically antithetical. By calling his a 'critical materialism',

82

Žižek aligns his *materializing* with *freedom* against the 'crude materialism' of *nature*. Accordingly, he dismisses Schelling's 'philosophy of nature' as merely 'preparatory' and 'anthropocentric' (1996: 65), setting out instead to recover that author's *Ages of the World* (henceforth *Weltalter*) as 'the founding text of dialectical materialism' (1996: 37). Importantly, this division of materialisms follows the extraction of Schelling's 'proto-ontological domain of the drives' from 'simpl[e] nature' (2004b: 32) and its reinsertion into the 'materialist notion of the subject' (1996: 65). As a preliminary characterization of Žižek's 'materialism', then, we may say that it extends from the 'drives' (that, as 'proto-ontological', *are* not yet) to the subject. Crucially, it is 'critical' insofar as it rejects primordial being and eliminates 'simpl[e] nature'. Critically, it opposes 'Idealism' insofar as it is premised not on the completed odyssey of consciousness Hegel proposed in the *Phenomenology of Spirit*, but on 'incompleteness', remaining within the subjective and the partial.

This chapter accordingly demonstrates that Žižek's 'return' to Schelling's philosophy resituates 'critical materialism' not as a materialism at all, but only as an incomplete *idealism*. In this respect, Žižek is not simply erroneous, but *exemplarily* so. Incompleteness, that is, is not self-evidently the index of 'materialism' Žižek takes it to be.[2] In other words, 'incompleteness' is no guarantee that the *Idealist* philosophy of consciousness is not rather *completed* than 'eliminated' by the 'materialist notion of the subject'. Thus, just as 'Lacan is fundamentally Hegelian, but without knowing it' (1988: 7), so Žižek's odyssey from Hegel to Lacan reveals a self-misrecognizing Idealism at the heart of contemporary philosophy, characterized by the self-evidently limited or 'parochial' ontology that, in the name of 'materialist subjectivity', 'critically' eliminates *Nature* and the *Idea*. Since this is the very issue that separated Schelling's from Fichte's philosophy, Žižek's 'Schellingianism' is really, as we shall see, an unacknowledged *Fichteanism*.

There are therefore three principal reasons why this 'exhibition' of Žižek's encounter with Idealism may be taken as indexical for contemporary philosophy. *First, morphology*: the insistence on the 'incomplete', on the figures of failure, applied to metaphysics and its systems, are practically universal in contemporary philosophy. *Secondly*, Žižek's insistence on accounting for *freedom* nevertheless stipulates a metaphysics, one that sums up the history of modern dualism, from Sartre to Lacan, that Kojève reinvented through

Hegel,[3] although it is sourced in Fichte. *Thirdly*, that Žižek's return to Schelling, rather than to his Idealist counterparts Hegel or Fichte, is explicitly directed at the problem of *ground* (like Badiou, our other great Lacanian), and marks out, despite itself, both the historical and contemporary antithesis to predominant Fichteanism. As we shall see, it is *nature* – which Žižek, with Fichte, rules out from the first – that provides the ground through which this alternative can be developed. With Žižek, we therefore take the problem of ground as the root of our inquiries.

THE NATURE OF GROUND

Otherwise known as the 'principle of sufficient reason', the problem of ground has exercised modern philosophy since Leibniz. The principle makes two interrelated stipulations: first, that, simply put, *there is a reason for everything that is*, thus answering the metaphysical problem of 'why there are beings rather than nothing?' The second stipulation, as efficiently stated by Isabelle Stengers (1997: 25), acquires particular force in physics: 'the full cause is *equivalent* to the entire effect'. The particular issue here revolves around *equivalence*: the efficacy of the cause is given as and by the extent of the effect. For example, this is the 'best of all possible worlds', argues Leibniz, because the actual (and *therefore* the best) world is the extent of the effect, so that its cause must have sufficient 'fullness' or perfection to actualize it. Since, as Leibniz states in the *Theodicy*, only God could be the cause of such perfection, then by the principle of sufficient reason, God is *equivalent* to the actual world. We will see below that the 'reversibility' of cause and effect derived from the *physical* stipulation of the principle of sufficient reason is crucial to Žižek's account of Schelling's '*Ungrund*' as 'the abyss of freedom', although Žižek takes the *cause* of freedom to be 'the sudden suspension of the principle of sufficient reason' (1997b: 3).

It is Kant who turns these relations into the contemporary philosophical problem to which Žižek reacts. On the one hand, the physical-causal function of ground forms 'an abyss [*Ungrund*] for human reason' insofar as the pursuit of 'the ultimate bearer of all things' (Kant 1958: 513 [A613/B641]) can reach no conclusion that is self-sufficient: for any given cause, that is, a reason for it may in turn be sought, *ad infinitum*. The only option, Kant concludes, is to establish a *transcendental* ground *over* this abyss, a 'supreme reality [which] must condition the possibility of all things' (1958: 492–93 [A579/B607]). It is from this problem that the *Critique of Judgment* sets out: 'there must be a ground uniting nature and freedom' (Kant 1987: 15), which, because it must *ground* both, cannot *be* either. The Idealist philosophers succeeding Kant – Schelling, Fichte and Hegel, each propose different solutions to this inherited problem: Hegel's absolute Mind, Fichte's generative antithesis of I and not-I, or subject and nature, and Schelling's 'unground'. For present purposes, these divide into two: Schelling pursues ungrounding rather than ground, but does so not transcendentally, like Kant, but 'descendentally', through *nature* (XIII, 151n).[4] By contrast, Fichte attempts to deploy freedom to unground 'first' nature and then to redeposit a *second nature* as the *product* of freedom. The issue, then, is this: finding room in nature for freedom *extends* an ontology grounded on the former; having nature produced through freedom, by contrast, restricts ontology to the one being supposed capable of acting independently of nature – the conscious subject.

It has always been the tendency of materialist critiques of Idealism to assume it incapable of nature, just as 'crude materialism' is supposed incapable of freedom. Yet Schelling's 'descendental rather than transcendental' (Hogrebe 1989: 124) investigation of grounds upsets this common assumption. Thus the *Philosophical Inquiries* declare freedom 'inexplicable' unless its 'roots. . .are acknowledged in the independent grounds of nature' (Schelling VII, 371; 1986: 47), clearly stipulating nature as the ground of freedom. However, because these grounds are 'independent', they cannot be derived by driving phenomena back to their preceding causes, reasons or principles, since this leads, as Kant warned, only to regress (on what does Atlas stand to support the world?) Instead, the pursuit of phenomena leads only to *ungrounding*, to the chaos from which 'grounds' first emerge:[5] 'the essence of ground', writes Schelling, 'can only be what *precedes* all grounds, that is, the Absolute as such, the Unground' (VII, 407–408; 1986: 88–89). This same irreversible priority of unground over ground forms the basis of Wolfram Hogrebe's (1989) 'reconstruction' of Schelling's metaphysics, which Žižek (1997b) takes as his guide, in terms of the irreversible priority of 'being' (onto-) that any 'ontology' *only then* determines. It follows from this real priority that no ontology can exhaust being, of which it is just one expression, since grounded on 'something positive', it necessarily leaves an 'irreducible remainder that cannot be resolved into reason' (Schelling VII, 360; 1986: 34).

While it is clear that Schelling's interrogation of the essence of ground as Unground *universally* breaks the symmetry by which the principle of sufficient reason operates, Žižek claims that, according to Schelling, 'the enigma of freedom, of the sudden suspension of the principle of sufficient reason' (1997b: 3) consists in the 'inversion of the "proper" relationship' (1997b: 12) between 'symmetrical polarities' (1997b: 7). Yet, as its causal–physical application makes clear, the principle of sufficient reason grounds precisely the *reversibility* of symmetrical or polar opposites. Žižek's 'enigma' is not the *suspension* of ground, but its *fulfilment*: ground is the reverse of freedom, and vice-versa. Thus Žižek cites Lacan's hypothesis concerning an Ideal or 'cured' subject emerging when it 'becomes its own cause':

> Lacan conceives the conclusion of the cure as the moment when the subject, by way of its own destitution, changes into a 'being of drive' and becomes its own cause. (1997b: 87)

The manner in which Žižek holds this Lacanian 'cure' to be key to his account of a 'Schellingian reconciliation' of past and present in the (unwritten) third of the 'ages of the world', or the divine future, is instructive in two ways. First, that such a wholesale recovery of the past in a future is possible violates Schelling's 'irreducible remainder', and is expressly rejected by Schelling: the future, he writes, is not the unity of the system of times, but rather 'eternity in three times' (1994: 134). Secondly, that this recovery *can be*, even if as an 'Idealist fantasy', effected through the 'overcom[ing] of the egotism of the contraction-into-self', presents all possible solutions as lying within the domain of the subjective. Thus Žižek prepares the *Weltalter* to become the metaphysics of subjectivity once it has been 'rid of. . . material inertia' (1997b: 77), so that its schema can be reconciled with that of the Lacanian cure. While Žižek understands himself simply to be paraphrasing Schelling, this getting rid of the 'material inertia [of] bodily reality' is in strict conformity with his later edict that what is 'preontological' in Schelling is 'not simply nature' but 'drives' (Žižek 2004b: 32). Once rid of material nature (of the 'not-I'), the subject is free when it recovers the drives (actions) prior to being as its *own* (as 'I'). The *morphology* of the thought that is key: that the symmetrical polarity of nature and subjectivity – of a *nicht-Ich* and an *Ich* – is no paraphrase of a Schellingian, but rather of a Fichtean '*Grundoperation* of Idealism', is evident as soon as it is stated;[6] but the importance of this is not simply that it indicates a flaw in Žižek's promiscuous hermeneutics, but rather that it demonstrates *a persistent*, if largely unacknowledged,[7] *commitment of contemporary philosophy to Fichtean Idealism.*

The morphology of Fichtean Idealism consists in the repeated iterations of a single imperative. Declaring himself Kant's heir in the critical philosophy, Fichte set about reducing theoretical to a branch of practical reason on the grounds that:

It is not in fact the theoretical power which makes possible the practical, but on the contrary, the practical which first makes possible the theoretical. . .reason itself is purely practical. (1982: 123)

The consequences of this collapse of Kant's transcendental faculties are not simply to reduce theoretical reason – which has nature and experience as its domain – to morality, but to make the transformation of nature, the 'modification of matter' (Fichte 1982: 269), into a *practically ontologizing* imperative. Fichte understands this as a transformation of the dogmatic 'the world *is*. . .', to the critical 'the whole universe *ought to be*. . .' (Fichte 1962 [II-3]: 247). That nature *must be* determined by freedom gives this metaphysics its morphology, which Fichte characterizes as the striving of the *Ich* to reduce the *nicht-Ich* to zero: the goal of freedom is the systematic expansion of the sphere of freedom by means of the reduction of that of nature. Here, then, a symmetrical polarity between freedom and nature is evident, but gains a 'dynamic' element through the 'striving' of the *Ich*. The symmetry is confirmed in a certain 'wavering', however: while the ontological imperative leads Fichte to insist that the proposition 'that intelligence. . .is a higher power (expression) of nature. . .is obviously false' (Fichte 1971 [IX]: 362), he will in turn postulate that 'nature has destined the human being. . .for freedom, i.e., for activity' (Fichte 2000: 184). There is, in Fichte, a permanent *crisis* of grounding, a striving to revert to grounds to demonstrate the *necessity* or *causation* of freedom as lying in nature, and a counter-striving to unground necessity through what Kant called the 'sublime quality of freedom to be itself an *original cause*' (Kant 1993: 226).

Again, Fichte more properly corresponds to the inverting incompletion, or the insufficiency of Being, that Žižek holds to be the distinguishing feature of 'materialist thought' (1996: 7).

Hence the polar ideal represented by Fichte's 'law of inverse pro-
portion': freedom rises as nature falls, and vice versa. Again, this is
no 'sudden suspension', but simply the 'inversion' or reversal guaranteed by sufficient reason: its premise is precisely the symmetrical
reversibility of full causes and entire effects. Rather than thinking
freedom, however, this approach eliminates it: it cannot think
freedom because it requires freedom to be equally necessary as nature
(there *must be* freedom) and not necessary (the free act is by definition not a necessary act). Nor, although it wants a 'ground' of autonomy, can it think *autonomous*, or 'self-operating ground' (Schelling
VII, 381; 1986: 58): by the symmetrical reversibility between freedom
and nature, the becoming-causal of freedom *is* the 'practical' elimination of nature as cause of freedom. The necessity at the core of the
Fichtean approach to the problem, echoed by 'critical materialism',
is conceived according to the parochial ontology that, in order to
have the kind of freedom it desires, restricts it to a single class of
beings – 'human and all other finite natures', as Fichte stipulates
(1982: 249) – by its symmetrical elimination from all others. Žižek
puts the point in terms sympathetic to 'modern' sensibilities:

> Modern subjectivity emerges when the subject perceives himself
> as 'out-of-joint', as excluded from the order of things, from the
> positive order of beings. (1999: 157)

This is why Schelling's 'self-operation of the ground' (VII, 381; 1986:
34) exceeds Fichteanism's subjectivist metaphysics: the ground of
freedom is extended to the operations of nature, rather than
restricted to a single class of beings.

These, then, form the two axes for the interrogation of
Schellingianism today: either ungrounding in nature *will* be symmetrically completed by the emergence of isolated freedom (the
'cure', as Žižek says; or 'critical materialism': the fulfilment of an
exclusively practical ontology), or *all* grounds emerge in asymmetrical consequence of a universal unground. Either, that is, the 'principle of sufficient reason' is sufficient insofar as it is practically
reversible, or ground must be rethought through the irreversibility of
ground as nature.

Having witnessed the first through our initial consideration of Žižek's approach to Schellingian ground through the problem of freedom, we will follow the second through Hogrebe's route through Schellingianism below, while noting Schelling's own accounts of the problems. At stake, as Hogrebe notes, is a metaphysics as yet unexplored due to the overarching and insensible dominance of another.

It is important to repeat that our aim is not simply to criticize Žižek for a false or Fichtean Schellingianism, but to illuminate the precise variety of Idealism as practised in contemporary philosophy. The striving to eliminate nature, disregarding for the moment whether the implied incompleteness of the 'striving' is indeed a hallmark of 'critical materialism', extends the morphology of Fichtean Idealism beyond philosophy into every theoretical architecture premised on incomplete constructivism, in those, that is, in which grounds for appeal are short-circuited by the assertion of a discursive, semiotic, or economic dependency of 'the real', and where 'nature' therefore emerges as the *product of freedom* (a social/historical/political construct). The illusion of absent grounds is sustained only by a covert insistence on freedom as the ultimate ground of all Being, from which standpoint may be issued outright rejections of its converse. These are not ungroundings at all, but rather small-town critiques of the wider world. Accordingly, we call this approach *ontologically parochial.*

'NATURE IS APPARENTLY MISSING. . .' GROUNDS WITHOUT NATURE

How could such an ontology acquire credibility? It is at this juncture in the history of the problem of ground that Heidegger's interrogation of ground and sufficiency intervenes, pincering the options for contemporary philosophy. Between *Vom Wesen des Grundes* (1931) and *Der Satz vom Grund* (1957) – between essence (*Wesen*) and proposition (*Satz*) – Heidegger undertakes to exhaust the possibilities of ground, or to explicate the question 'why there are beings, rather than nothing'. In the later work, Heidegger unsurprisingly critiques naturalistic and materialistic conceptions of ground, in the course of which his project betrays a powerful procedural affinity with Hegel's phenomenology: 'materialism is simply not something material [but] itself a frame [*Gestalt*] of mind' (1957: 199). Regardless of Heidegger's own form of phenomenological Idealism, the applicability of this to the *critical* materialism Žižek advances cries out for expression: whatever the purchase of the critique of 'crude' materialism, critical materialism articulates precisely an ideality concerning matter, premised in turn on the Fichtean imperative that matter itself be 'modified'. Heidegger's earlier essay, by contrast, while betraying a more Kantian complexion, undertakes to reinvent Kant's transcendental as ground *within*, rather than distinct from, nature. Heidegger writes:

> Although nature is apparently missing. . .in the analytic of *Dasein* – not only nature as the object of natural science, but also nature in the more originary sense – there are reasons for this. It is decisive in this regard that it [nature] can neither be encountered within an environment or circumference, nor above all as primarily something *towards which we comport* ourselves. Nature originally reveals itself in *Dasein* because the latter exists as found and attuned *in the midst* of beings. Yet because foundness (thrownness) belongs to the essence of *Dasein* and comes to expression only in the unity of the full concept of *care*, it is here alone that the *basis* for the *problem* of nature may be reached. (1931: 36 n.)

Nature as ground is therefore supplanted by *Dasein* as the ground of nature. Although once again we find the same inversion as in Žižek's Fichteanism, Heidegger does not make ground dependent on (the elimination of) nature, but instead seeks the possibility of ground in the transcendental. Transcendence is *Dasein*'s 'climbing above itself' to world, or its self-projection into its own worldly possibilities. This self-transcendence to *transitive* willing is, Heidegger writes, precisely 'freedom itself' insofar as *Dasein* 'projects itself' in the world (1931: 43). Reciprocally, world thus finitizes *Dasein* so that 'grounding emerges. . .from the finite freedom of *Dasein*' (1931: 49), a reciprocity Heidegger designates by the explicitly Schellingian concept of the *Seinkönnen* (capable-of-being):

> Freedom stands in its essence as the transcendence of *Dasein* as *Seinkönnen* in the possibilities that are spread before its finite choice, i.e., in its destiny. (1931: 54)

The Leibnizian roots of Heidegger's solution to the problem of ground are striking: just as the world owes its actuality to God's free choice amongst possible worlds, divine selection, far from being constrained as to which one *is* 'best', necessarily confers actuality upon the selected world which *becomes* best *because* it is *actualized*. Moreover, since the principle of sufficient reason states that the perfection of the cause is equivalent to the entire effect, divine freedom is equivalent to actual necessity (the actual world). Although therefore Heidegger is telling the familiar story of the emergence of freedom as spontaneity, *Dasein* achieves it not by eliminating the world, but by climbing over itself towards a world that spreads its destiny before it as its only possibilities. If 'primary ground is nothing other than a *projection* of transitive willing' (1931: 45), this ground *itself* has no ground. Answering the question, 'What is the reason of ground?', in other words, 'reiterates' the problem of the ground of grounding, just as Kant warned. Heideggerian transcendence or 'projection' raises the dimension of height, opening chasms in ground in exactly the opposite direction to Schelling's *'philosophia descendens'* (XIII, 151 n.). Heidegger's ontology-as-project enables us to entitle it a *projective ontology*. While its incompleteness ought to recommend it for inclusion in the Milner–Žižek line of critical materialism – all the more so due to Heidegger's overtly Idealist criticism of materialism as, in effect, a 'frame of mind' (1957: 199), or a figure in Hegel's great odyssey of consciousness – Žižek's qualification of this incomplete ontology as 'the *subject's* prehistory' (1992: 49) enables us to entitle Žižek's an *Idealism of subjective projection*. Perhaps this is why Žižek *has himself inserted*, as the explication of the implicit observer, into scenes of 'perverse' cinematic voyeurism.[8] While sharing with Heidegger a projective ontology, Žižek's subjectivism makes its essential Fichteanism clear.

Although we have seen the varieties into which contemporary Idealisms may be arranged, and noted the divergence between Schellingianism and Žižek's projective ontology, there is a further element of Heidegger's account of ground that will serve to reintroduce Schelling into our discussion. Heidegger's positive evaluation of Schellingianism is well known through his lectures on the *Philosophical Inquiries into the Essence of Human Freedom* (see Heidegger 1985); but it is already evident not only in the *Seinkönnen* we previously noted in *On the Essence of Ground*, but also in the 'zone of eruption' that is the *Ungrund*, and in the 'formal, endless iteration' by which Heidegger here characterizes the recurrent problem of 'the ground of grounds' (1931: 52–53). The problem for our purposes arises, however, when Heidegger invokes a resolution of depth in height through an '*Umwillen*' that, rather than a transitive willing-in-world, simply inverts willing into the ground of grounds. Where Schelling memorably defined the problem in terms of 'the Unruly that lies ever in the ground as though it might again erupt', he adds that this 'incomprehensible basis of reality in things, the irreducible remainder which cannot be resolved into reason. . . remains always in grounds' (VII, 359–60; 1986: 34). Heidegger accepts the constancy of the 'eruptive potency' of the ground of grounds but, in place of Schelling's irreducible remainder, sets freedom: 'The eruption of the *Ungrund* in grounding transcendence is rather the original motion that freedom completes with us and gives us thereby to understand, i.e., as original world-content' (Heidegger 1931: 54). Freedom 'pulls itself together' from the erupting *Ungrund*, grounding us and our relating to the world and its grounds, while the world makes 'man. . .resonant with possibilities [as] *a being of distance*' (Heidegger 1931: 55), distances filled by projections. While Heidegger's conception of freedom is radically impersonal – freedom *itself* completes ungrounding, throwing *Dasein* into the world, rather than 'our' freedom having as its aim the recovery of its own prehistory – it is all the more suspect, on Schellingian lines, for that very reason. To pursue this, along with the implications of the 'irreducible remainder' for Schellingian ground, we will now contrast Žižek's Schellingianism to Hogrebe's: what precisely is the modern metaphysics Schellingianism has yet to realize?

DESCENDENTAL PHILOSOPHY AND TRANSCENDENTAL GEOLOGY

The real basis of the theory of the *Weltalter* is modern geology.
(Sandkühler 1984: 21)

Žižek's central claim regarding the 'system' of the *Weltalter* remaining 'incomplete', is broadly speaking accurate: Schelling never progressed beyond reworking book one of three: *The Past.*[9] What, however, if the descent into the past were *necessarily* incomplete? Precisely this follows from Hogrebe's account of the irreversible priority of being over its expressions as ontology; every ontology is accordingly 'incomplete', and entails an 'asystasy' of many systems, each an expression of being. Hence Schelling's tasking 'The Nature of Philosophy as Science' in 1821, with 'discover[ing] a system of knowing or, otherwise and better put, to glimpse human knowing *in a system*' (IX, 209). The pointed rephrasing makes the objective of philosophy as science quite clear: 'human knowing' is no *self-enclosed* system, but is knowing at all, and human knowing in particular, only insofar as it is grounded in the systems from which it emerges. If the ground of human knowing cannot therefore, as Fichte thought, be sought in knowing itself, the question is, in *what* systems is it grounded?

Hogrebe begins his reconstruction of the *Weltalter* with Schelling's characterization of the same problem a decade later, in *The Foundations of Positive Philosophy* of 1832–33: 'The entire world lies caught, as it were, in reason, but the question is: how has it gotten into this net?' (Schelling 1972: 222). The statement only superficially suggests the sufficiency of *reason* as the ground of the 'entire world'. By confronting this sufficiency with the priority of 'world' to 'reason', Schelling opens a chasm at the core of world-reason that descends into the chaos before the world, denying the sufficiency of reason as ground of world, just as human knowing was earlier 'ungrounded'. Thus, where transcendental philosophy starts from the premise that knowledge can be systematic only by grounding itself not in the world, but on the *a priori* conditions of human cognition, 'descendental' philosophy pursues the '*a priori* route' by seeking the '*prius* and *posterius*', the primary and the derived, 'in nature' (Schelling 1994: 146). Distinguishing between '*being prius*' and 'being known *a priori*', Schelling writes of 'the absolutely positive *prius* of which I may say *that it is* and is cognizable because it is and, to that extent, is known *a posteriori*' (1998: 85). Nature, accordingly, is the *prius* of all cognition.

Where Schelling overtly pursues the *prius* and *posterius* in nature, Hogrebe exploits the same asymmetry in reason. Hogrebe asks – with Schelling, but as though reducing the problem of sufficient reason to semantics – 'why is there sense rather than nonsense?', which he draws into two arguments based on reconstructing the *Weltalter* as a metaphysics of predication or judgment (Hogrebe 1989: 39, 114), as exemplified in the following passage: 'The beginning may not know itself as a beginning. In the very beginning, nothing is or discerns itself as merely ground or beginning' (Schelling VIII, 314; 2000: 86). The first of Hogrebe's arguments is that the structure of predication (X is *p*), is grounded in Being, or in a 'non-predicative, pre-rational reference to something that exists'

(1989: 126); without, that is, there being something (= X) to which predicates may be ascribed, predication could not take place. The second, that the transition from pre-predicative indeterminacy or 'unground of reason' (1989: 127) to predication is a *becoming* of being, that is, it is *ontogenetic*, and not merely cognitive (1989: 92–93). Being, that is, is the *prius* of judgment, and judgment the *posterius* of being; yet judgment is itself a modification of primary being, which is therefore the beginning of judgment while not yet having become it. This is also the sole ground for Schelling's frequently cited claim that 'created from the source of things and the same as it, the human mind has a co-science [*Mit-wissenschaft*] with creation' (VIII, 200; 2000: xxxvi, trans. modified). Rather than asserting the sufficiency of human knowing as the ground of creation, thus fulfilling the principle of sufficient reason, Schelling's *Mit-wissenschaft* consists in the identity of the asymmetrical beginnings of both nature and Idea. Nor does it assert that these beginnings are the *same*, and that therefore the human mind accesses the past of creation *directly*. There are two reasons for this. First, far from disdaining naturalistic and empirical investigation, Schelling scolds those 'precipitate beings' who race directly to 'inspired concepts and expressions rather than descending to the natural beginnings' (VIII, 286; 2000: 63), that is, to the *prius* that produces it. Since, however, 'even the smallest grain of sand' is the product of an inexhaustible 'course of productive nature' (1946: 120–21; 1997: 121–22), let alone the ascent from silicates to organics, and the subsequent development of mind, 'nature is an unground of the past [which] is what is oldest in nature and remains at the remotest depths' (VIII, 243; 2000: 31). Nature therefore entails the *necessity* of an inexhaustible past for every cognitive event, the 'irreducible remainder that can never be resolved into reason' (VII, 360; 1986: 34), and denies reason's sufficiency to the nature that irrecoverably precedes it.

Secondly, the 'system of times' at the core of the *Weltalter* consists not of 'passages' between the beginning or past, the present, and the future – 'the one does not come to an end in the other' (Schelling 1994: 150) – but of a 'succession of eternities' (VIII, 302; 2000: 120–21), which *qua* eternities, *remain* rather than succeed one another. Schelling thus constructs a *stratified* rather than a *sequential* theory of 'times', for each of which, what is past – the systematic entirety of their conditions or *prius* – *remains necessarily unrecoverable* for reason. For any becoming, therefore, its 'first beginning = eternal beginning' (1994: 167), to which descendental philosophy 'returns' as its 'past' (1946: 112; 1997: 113). Even when 'the work of thousands of years' is 'stripped away, to come at last to the ground' (1946: 120; 1997: 121), 'the essence of ground', as what 'can only *precede* all grounds', turns out to be 'unground' (VII, 407–408; 1986: 88–9).

Thus Schelling fleshes out the 'irreducible remainder that cannot be resolved into reason' (VII, 359–60; 1986: 34): the irreducibility of past to present, or – *pace* Žižek (1997b: 77) – the resolution of the two into a future, introduces a radical asymmetry into the problem of ground which prevents the symmetrical resolution of ungrounding as the ground of freedom. Although Žižek celebrates the 'breach of symmetry' (1997b: 16) that undoes 'any dualism of cosmological principles' (1997b: 5) as well as the reversible polarities that, he holds, characterize the principal failing of Idealist 'systems' (see 1997b: 11) – and that characterize, he adds falsely, Schelling's 'early. . .symmetrical polarity' between the real and the ideal (1997b: 6–7) – he nevertheless asserts precisely the symmetrical and reversible relation between *Grund* and *Ungrund*: 'prior to *Grund*, there can only be an abyss (*Ungrund*)' that, of course, turns out to be 'the abyss of pure Freedom' (1997b: 15). Reversible symmetrical relations, as we have seen, persist in the notion of 'passage', which is, however, written into the entire scheme whereby Žižek engages Idealist philosophy: 'German Idealism returns what was repressed in post-Hegelian thought: the process of constitution *qua* the subject's prehistory' (1991a: 49). The medium presupposed by such passages is nothing more than the odyssey of tortured consciousness, a consciousness that has as its parallel and reciprocal condition a nature or a real so fragile it can easily be broken: 'Freedom. . .designates the abyss of an act of decision that breaks up the causal chain, since it is grounded only in itself' (1997b: 32). *At last we have it*: the self-grounding of freedom common to all the Idealist philosophies, Schelling's included, says Žižek (1997b: 12), provides the *necessary* 'subject's prehistory'; to what else *could* it lead? How capable is Being (*Seinkönnen*) of anything other than subjectivity, and moreover, of a subjectivity narrowly conceived within the rubric of a freely acting self-consciousness, whatever its constitutive lacunae? As regards ground, the holes in things provide Žižek's speleological tunnels, leading ever and again from these cavernous 'ungrounds' to the freedom spied in the cinematic light where they cross. While

Heidegger notes that, ontologically, much can be accomplished by 'projection', he has at least the good grace to admit that such projection acquires its particular morphology from the world, as the insuperable destiny of all freedom.

By contrast, writes Schelling, 'the root of freedom' must lie 'in the independent grounds of nature' (VII, 371; 1986: 47): nature shatters the convenient symmetry by which, Žižek argues, the ground of freedom is the non-existence of nature. The *Inquiries*' titular 'human' therefore refers not to the one, restricted, supra-natural domain wherein freedom arises, but rather extends natural freedom to the 'self-operating ground' (VII, 381; 1986: 58). From this 'geology of morals', we arrive at the following conclusion: that freedom is everywhere in nature precisely because there is no reversibility between the ungrounding that is the eruption of beings and their futural determination: in terms of the principle of sufficient reason, there is no equivalence between any effect and its causes. Hence the naturalism of the *Weltalter*, which Žižek's 'critical materialism' misses not accidentally, but programmatically: the 'proto-ontological domain of drives', he writes (Žižek 2004b: 32), 'is not simply "nature"'. If the *Ages of the World* remain 'stuck in the past', we might say, this is not because of Schelling's failure, but due to the imperatives of descendental philosophy. The problem with any critical philosophy – whether or not it bears a materialist stamp (or has one projected onto it) – is that it is condemned to the Parmenidean problem of granting actuality to 'what is not': denying the 'materiality' of Idea and nature, in other words, leads necessarily to a philosophy that rejoices in incapacity: the grounds of the necessity of the incomplete are therefore equally those of an Idealism of the *Nicht-seinkönnen*.

If, finally, we return to the question of system, the following problem arises: insofar as Schelling notes an 'asystasy', a lack-of-system or 'incompleteness', reigning throughout philosophy-as-science, this might be taken precisely as the preparation for the total system commonly associated with Idealist philosophies. However, it is the 'nature of philosophy as science', Schelling states, not somehow to bend asystasy *into* a system that recovers itself from its past, or will do so in the future, but rather to 'glimpse' the system of asystasy. What does this 'glimpse' mean? That the irreducible multiplicity of expressions of being – eruptions of the *Ungrund* – is not a barrier to the systematic pursuit of asystasy, just as univocity (everything is an expression of being) does not entail the eventual satisfaction of the principle of sufficient reason, as Hogrebe shows. Thus Hogrebe's call for a renewal of Schellingian metaphysics is key not because it presages precisely that futural completeness Žižek envisages would be consequent on Schelling's 'failure to fail', an eternal resolution, or absolution, of time or the reduction of the remainder; it is important because it demonstrates that undertaking to complete the *Weltalter* could not *reduce* asystasy to system, because the past is non-eliminable in every system.

If it is the task of physics, as Hogrebe accounts it, to establish the grounds of beings, that is, to ascend from conditions to conditioned, it is the unavoidable task of metaphysics not only to descend to the first origin of things, to the ground of all grounds, but to *unground* grounds, to press towards the unconditioned, 'the Absolute, the Unground' (Schelling VII, 408; 1986: 89). Yet descendental philosophy does not begin from nowhere, but rather from amidst the asystasy that is the expression of being; in other words, philosophy systematically ungrounds the totality of systems that compose the asystasy of real – physical and ideal – systems, grounded only because they are first and eternally, ungrounded. Incompleteness, it turns out, is indexical not of the 'frame of mind' called *materialism*, but of nature.

NOTES

1 Such excavations as Hogrebe here invokes have equally characterized the two years of intensive reading of Deleuze's metaphysics in *Difference and Repetition*, the roots of which may be evident here, undertaken by Jeremy Dunham, Peter Jowers, Sean Watson and myself. Since these collective labours form an indispensable substratum to this essay, the cited passage equally provides a 'mantic', as Hogrebe would say, for their fuller and more public expression.

2 'Incompleteness' is chief among Jean-Claude Milner's enumeration, which Žižek cites favourably, of 'the features which distinguish great works of *materialist* thought, from Lucretius' *De rerum natura* through Marx's *Capital* to the work of Lacan' (Žižek 1996: 7).

3 That a fundamentally dualist ontology should emerge from a materialist reading of Idealism echoes precisely the project Kojève incited his audience – Lacan amongst them – to pursue in his *Introduction to the Reading of Hegel* (1969: 215n).

4 All further references to Schelling, *Sämmtliche Werke* (1856–61), will be given as a roman numeral (indicating volume) and page.

5 Schelling's account of ungrounding is repeated by Deleuze in *Difference and Repetition*, where he writes 'grounds can only be assigned in a world

already precipitated into universal ungrounding' (1994: 202). The tradition of what Deleuze calls 'transcendental volcanism' (1994: 241) extends from Plato's *Statesman* through Schelling and the geologist Heinrik Steffens, to Heidegger and Deleuze.

6 Žižek is overt in his claim that, as regards the problematic of freedom, the solutions of Schelling, Fichte, Hegel and even Kant, are structurally the same, consisting in a 'perversion or inversion' of the 'proper' relationship (1997b: 10–12) between the *'symmetrical* polarity' of the potencies' (1997b: 7). It is this that Žižek calls 'ungrounding', or the *'Grundoperation* of German Idealism' (1996: 76).

7 Not universally so, however: Eric Alliez has recently suggested the utility of a re-evaluation of Fichteanism as a strategy for exploring the Deleuzian legacy in contemporary philosophy. See Alliez, *The Signature of the World* (2004: 30n).

8 See the recently aired *A Pervert's Guide to Cinema* (Žižek 2006a), wherein he accomplishes this feat.

9 There are three principal *Weltalter* drafts: 1815 (VIII), 1811 and 1813 (in Manfred Schröter's *SW Nachlassband*, cited as Schelling 1946). Žižek 1997 prefaces Judith Norman's translation of the 1813 draft (Schelling 1997), while Jason Wirth has retranslated Frederick de Wolfe Bolman's version of the 1815 draft (Schelling 2000). Additionally, Siegbert Peetz has published a transcript of Schelling's 1827–28 lectures entitled *System der Weltalter* (Schelling 1998), while Klaus Grotsch's *Weltalter-Fragmente* (Stuttgart-Bad Canstatt: Frommann-Holzboog, 2002) contains drafts from the period 1810–21.

ACTING AND THE ACT: ON SLAVOJ ŽIŽEK'S POLITICAL ONTOLOGY

Oliver Marchart

One of the most surreal characters in movie history is the deplorable guy in Woody Allen's *Deconstructing Harry*, played by Robin Williams, who is 'out of focus'. His contours remain blurred even where, at a party, he stands among people whose contours are absolutely clear. This character has a precursor in Jacques Lacan himself. On one of the photographs taken by Brassaï of the party crowd who in March 1944 gathered at Michel Leiris' apartment in order to witness or act in Picasso's play *Le Désir attrapé par la queue*, one sees the whole group, among them Picasso, Sartre, Camus and Simone de Beauvoir, in perfectly clear shape. The only one in the group who remains 'out of focus' is Jacques Lacan. Without the distinctive feature of his ears sticking out, it would be difficult to recognize the blurred face at the upper left-hand corner of the photograph as Lacan's. Whether Lacan deliberately moved his head in order to produce a photographic effect of estrangement, or whether he simply could not stand still, is an unresolved question. But how could we not think, as a contemporary analogy, of Slavoj Žižek's public appearance as somebody who simply 'moves too fast', who seems to be simultaneously presenting papers at the four corners of the universe, and to write more books, and faster, than any audience can read? The resulting effect of estrangement is not due to the fact that Žižek's work is not clear – his arguments and provocations are perfectly clear. On the contrary, every argument and provocation, considered by itself, stands out against the background of professional academia around Žižek, which in turn appears 'blurred' and, more often than not, evasive in comparison. The blurring-effect sets in when everything – all jokes, theoretical claims and political provocations – are considered in their ensemble (if it is possible at all to keep track of this ensemble). As his own editors remark, one can find Žižek throughout his texts 'reversing his position many times', as he writes 'prolifically and seemingly with little concern for consistency' (Butler & Stephens 2005: 2). Let us restrict this observation to two levels of his thought: if we consider the purely theoretical level, then it is possible to find, next to the dogmatic Lacanian, a – most often openly disavowed – *deconstructive* Žižek. As Ernesto Laclau once remarked: 'Žižek is a staunch monogamist (Lacanian) in theory, who, however, makes all kinds of practical concessions – this is his obverse, obscene side – to his never publicly recognized mistress (deconstruction)' (Laclau 2000: 76). On the *programmatic* level of political theory, the later Leninist Žižek stands in blatant opposition to the earlier radical-democratic Žižek, even as, when they fit the argument, earlier positions easily re-surface.

Apparently, in order to discuss the work of somebody who says one thing and the opposite, one necessarily has to make the decision of carving out *a* Žižek rather than discussing '*the* Žižek' – an object as evasive as Lacan's head on Brassaï's photograph. This will engulf the attempt to re-focus Žižek by pinning down some slices of his thought while leaving aside others and perhaps contradictory slices. What I will seek to pin down in the following chapter is Žižek's notion of *the act* which I take to be the cornerstone of his political ontology. It will be argued that the implicit relation between *acting* and *the act* – or, what amounts to the same, between *politics* and *the political* – is premised upon the ontological difference in the Heideggerian sense which makes it impossible to play out one term against the other – as many variants of political theory do (favouring *acting*) and Žižek does (privileging *the act*).

Instead, it will be claimed that it is absolutely imperative to *retain both terms* in all their radicality if we do not want to give in to either pure empiricism or pure decisionism. Understood in the correct sense, this re-framing of the ontico-ontological difference as political difference will show us the only way out of the *cul-de-sac* of either a merely ontic or a purely ontological approach to politics. Two productive conclusions will flow from it. First, by taking into account the hidden Heideggerian roots of both deconstruction and Lacanianism (did not Lacan start from the Kojèvian position of a *Heideggerized* Hegel?), it will be possible to avoid Žižek's over-stressed *incompatibility* argument and to focus more clearly on the overall *compatibility* of these approaches, without however neglecting the differences. And second, if we retain the difference between acting and the act *as a difference*, rather than abandoning it, then it follows that some ('Leninist') *revolutionism* can no longer be played out against 'radical-democratic' approaches for every radical politics will be, paradoxically, revolutionary *and* reformist at the same time, or rather, it will escape this historically overcome and entirely unproductive way of framing radical politics.

ŽIŽEK'S ACT

For Žižek, an act in the most radical sense is an 'impossible' intervention that changes the 'reality principle' of a given situation, that is, the parameters of the possible. An act is not 'the mere endeavour to "solve a variety of partial problems" within a given field', but should rather be understood as 'the more radical gesture of subverting the very structuring principle of this field' (Žižek 2000a: 121). For the same reason, the act does not find support in the symbolic order that precedes it. An act touches at the real, and is entirely of a groundless nature. Notwithstanding this unfounded character of 'the act', acts do occur in reality. Žižek gives all kinds of comparatively mundane and modest examples from the political field, including the case of Pinochet's arrest in the United Kingdom which dramatically changed his perception back at home in Chile. Suddenly, Pinochet did not appear any longer as an all-powerful *éminence grise* but as a humiliated old man (Žižek 2001: 169). Along similar lines, Žižek claims that 'an authentic political *act*' would be achieved 'if, when Kissinger was on a world tour promoting a new book, some (preferably West European) country arrested him just as they arrested Pinochet' (2002a: 265). The implementation of Clinton's healthcare reform, under today's conditions, also would have amounted to a radical act – had it ever occurred.

I call these examples 'modest' because they do not involve the fantasy of a radical break with the past on a world-revolutionary scale. What they involve is an alteration, to put it in Gramscian terms, of the thinkable and sayable within a given hegemonic constellation. This leaves open, as we will see later, the possibility of a more deconstructive re-configuration of Žižek's political ontology. Most often, however, Žižek is not satisfied with the mundane political reality of today's politics. He then resorts to an all-or-nothing argument which does not follow from the premises. Žižek's arch-example here is

Lenin's lonely decision – without any guarantee in the big Other – to pursue a 'second', Bolshevist revolution and seize state power:

> With Lenin, as with Lacan, the point is that the revolution *ne s'autorise que d'elle-même*: we should venture the revolutionary *act* not covered by the big Other – the fear of taking power 'prematurely', the search for the guarantee, is the fear of the abyss of the act. That is the ultimate dimension of what Lenin incessantly denounces as 'opportunism', and his premiss is that 'opportunism' is a position which is in itself, inherently, false, masking a fear of accomplishing the act with the protective screen of 'objective' facts, laws or norms. (2002: 8)

As Žižek writes on another occasion, to perform an act is 'not a matter of strategic deliberation' (2001: 162), it is the leap into a strategic vacuum:

> The Leninist stance was to take a leap, throwing oneself into the paradox of the situation, seizing the opportunity and *intervening*, even if the situation was 'premature', with a wager that *this very 'premature' intervention would radically change the 'objective' relationship of forces itself, within which the initial situation appeared 'premature'*. (2001: 114)

There are a couple of obvious problems with this account of the act. First of all, one cannot avoid the impression that, while mobilizing all his energies for his attack on 'opportunism' as the ideology that renders impossible any act in the radical sense, Žižek falls into the obverse trap. For what he comes to defend as an alternative – a purely abyssal and decisionist act that is to be achieved without any strategic considerations of circumstances – Lenin himself would have considered a clear case of 'adventurism' or 'Blanquism'. There will be, without doubt, *an aspect* of adventurism in all acting, otherwise we would stay at home paralysed, but from the premise that in our acts we cannot rely on 'objective laws' that would guarantee success it does not follow that acts occur in a vacuum where all strategic considerations are suspended. Tightly connected to this anti-political assumption – anti-political if politics necessarily involves some form of *strategic* acting – is the all-or-nothing logic of Žižek's argument. At times, Žižek argues, particularly when attacking liberal democratic 'reformists' and 'opportunists', that only a redemptive revolutionary act by which the world is turned on its head will achieve the impossible. However, since world revolution seems to be on nobody's political agenda at the moment, Žižek in the meantime resorts to the idea of installing a radical break by way of separatism and escapism, recommending 'radical attempts to "step outside", to risk a radical break, to pursue the trend of self-organized collectives in zones outside the law' (2004a: 81–82). As an example he refers to the nineteenth-century Canudos community in Brazil, a sort of forerunner of twentieth-century sects like the Davidians. The fact that the existing space of the state is completely negated by such communities is enough for Žižek to affirm: 'Everything is to be endorsed here, up to and including religious "fanaticism"' (2004a: 82). What seems to count for Žižek is not the content of an emancipatory project, but the purely formal fact that a radical break is established vis-à-vis the existing order. But to sustain the idea of a clear-cut and total break, it is necessary for this order to be conceived as a homogeneous and self-sufficient block in the first place. Once again, the all-or-nothing logic of the argument leaves no room for any strategic and thus political negotiation between a counter-hegemonic project and the established order. Either the break is total, or no act has occurred.

MACHIAVELLI'S LESSON

Before eventually addressing the phantasmatic aspects of Žižek's political recommendations, let us evaluate the theoretical merits of his political ontology. Everything hinges on the differentiation between the ontic level of politics and the ontological level of the political, or between *la politique* and *le politique*, a difference immensely prominent in post-foundational political thought.[1] Most theorizations of the political difference would assume that if the most radical features of the act – ungroundedness, contingency, etc. – can only be ascribed to the ontological level of the political, the ontic level of politics designates the realm of *acting* rather than *the act*. While Žižek is well aware of the difference between politics and the political, his theory of the act tends to ignore the ontic level of politics and acting altogether. When insisting that 'there *are* (also) political acts', he does not refer to *political* and thus *strategic acting*, but on the contrary explains that there *are* political acts 'for politics cannot be reduced to the level of strategic-pragmatic interventions' (2004a: 80), since 'an act is neither a strategic intervention *in* the existing order, nor its "crazy" destructive *negation*; an act is an "excessive", trans-strategic intervention which redefines the roles and contours of the existing order' (2004a: 81.)[2] If Žižek simply claimed that every 'ontic' form of acting, including strategic acting, participates to *some* extent in the ontological structure of the act – the 'madness' of decision, etc. – there would certainly be no problem with this assumption. But he promotes his argument through a general denigration of strategic acting which, as a consequence, leads right into a new form of quasi-existentialist adventurism and decisionism. By cutting the link between politics and the political, and retaining the side of the political or ontological only, Žižek develops a 'political ontology' of the act which is not a *political* ontology because every relation to actual politics, in the Machiavellian sense of strategic action, has been lost. Concomitantly, the result is a hypostasization of the act at the expense of acting.

To be sure, the problem with this move is not to be found in Žižek's *ontological* account of the act, which makes perfect sense. The problem lies in the evacuation of the ontological of all politics. In order to exemplify this point, let us consider the specific temporality of the act (and the event), as presented by Žižek. The Lenin of 1917, according to Žižek, is the prime example of somebody achieving an act because he 'discerned the *Augenblick*, the unique chance for a revolution' (2002a: 5). This *Augenblick* is the moment in which the usual flow of time is halted, in which temporality as such is suspended. It is as if, 'in a unique suspension of temporality, in the short circuit between the present and the future, we are – as if by Grace – briefly allowed to act *as if* the utopian future is (not yet fully here, but) already at hand, there to be seized' (2002: 259). For this reason, 'the question of timing, of "seizing the moment"' is crucial, as Žižek explains elsewhere with reference to Lukàcs:

> The art of what Lukàcs called *Augenblick* (the *moment* when, briefly, there is an opening for an *act* to intervene in a situation) is the art of seizing the right moment, of aggravating the conflict *before* the System can accommodate to our demand. (2001: 117)

And, designating such stance as 'Gramscian', he goes on to explain that: 'the lukàcsian *Augenblick* is unexpectedly close to what, today, Alain Badiou endeavours to formulate as the Event: an intervention that cannot be accounted for in terms of its pre-existing "objective conditions"' (Žižek 2001: 117).

This concept of the *Augenblick* is not only present in Lukàcs. Much more prominently it figures in Heidegger and, as a Messianic conception of *political* temporality, in Benjamin and in Arendt.[3] And since Arendt is Žižek's as well as Badiou's *bête noir* of lukewarm 'liberal' thinking, it should be noted, if only in passing, that for her the suspension of temporality in a 'short-circuit between the present and the future' is precisely the defining ontological characteristic of ontic political action. Acting, as men's capacity to begin something new, takes place in the very non-temporal *gap* between past and future, in the 'hiatus between the end of the old order and the beginning of the new' which in history is precisely the moment of revolution (Arendt 1990: 205). Yet Žižek is not willing to see, let alone to concede these parallels, as he takes at face value the de-radicalized picture of Arendt currently painted by mainstream political thought and the Habermasians. Instead, he refers to Badiou, which is all the more revealing since Badiou rules out strategic action just as Žižek denigrates it. For this reason, the accompanying reference to Gramsci is entirely misleading, insofar as Badiou's model is *anti-Gramscian* (next to being anti-Arendtian) to the extreme. 'Acting', for Badiou is only another form of 'thinking' anyway, is a matter of retaining the umbilical cord of *faith* towards an ontological event, without paying attention to the changing ontic circumstances of the 'mundane' world of politics. The act consists in a decision to invest faith into a contingent event (by which the subject is only touched in a moment of grace). Politics is thus replaced by an ethical relation towards the event, a relation that subjugates all questions of strategy and tactics to a form of quasi-religious adherence to what we have 'encountered'.

The Gramscian approach to acting and the event (as a figure of contingency) is significantly different and can best be explained with regard to the most important – and historically primary – political theorization of the category of *Augenblick*: namely, Machiavelli's notion of *fortuna*. With Machiavelli, the classical idea of *kairos* – the fleeting but decisive moment allegorically portrayed as a young man on wheels whose proverbial forelock has to be grasped when he passes by – is given a thoroughly modern and political turn. In the sense of good or bad luck, *fortuna* confronts us as an unforeseeable event, as in Machiavelli's famous example of dangerous rivers that 'when they become enraged, flood the plains, destroy trees and buildings, move earth from one place and deposit it in another' (1988: 85). Today we see in *fortuna* an allegorical figure of contingency: it is not in our hands to pre-determine and calculate the emergence of 'fortunate' events, nor can we wilfully forge an event into existence. Yet Machiavelli draws neither fatalist nor voluntarist conclusions from his notion of *fortuna*. Even though we cannot foresee the coming of an event, such as the arrival and immediate departure of *kairos*, it is a matter of political wisdom to be prepared for the moment of, following Machiavelli's example, the river's flooding: 'to take precautions, by means of dykes and dams, so that when it rises next time, it will either not overflow its banks or, if it does, its force will not be so uncontrolled or damaging' (1988: 85). Modern inheritors of the Machiavellian legacy, among them Gramsci and Arendt, were very well aware of this. Gramsci's whole idea of organizing a 'collective will' through organic intellectuals (including the party as a collective organic intellectual) should in no way be mistaken for voluntarism, since to be organized forms a necessary precondition for the 'fortunate moments' to be seized in the protracted process of building up a counter-hegemonic formation. Otherwise, these moments will be passing by or, what is worse, seized by the enemy.

For her part, Arendt was very determined in pointing out that revolutions cannot be made, that power in a revolutionary situation lies on the streets and has to be picked up by the revolutionaries, for otherwise, again, the fortunate moment vanishes. If such a situation is not at hand, 'what could pave the way for a revolution, in the sense of preparing the revolutionaries, is a real analysis of the existing situation such as used to be made in earlier times' (Arendt 1972: 206). What Arendt recommended to the revolting students of 1968 in this interview was another *mode* of 'revolutionary action', as she was sure that no revolutionary situation was at hand.[4] This mode of 'paving the way' would consist in something similar to the preparatory practice of Marx, Lenin, Trotsky and other revolutionaries, when they were studying at libraries as a way of preparing for the *kairos* of revolution. The aim of their preparation, of course, was not to kill time in libraries and coffee-houses until the moment was right, but to analyse the strategic situation better to determine the moment when power would be lying on the streets. So, when Lenin in 1917 came to a different conclusion to that of his fellow-revolutionaries, this was not because he was prepared, existentially, to 'take a leap', but because he arrived at a different strategic assessment of the situation.

This leads to a further Machiavellian category: *occasione*. At first sight, *occasione* may seem to be just a slightly different version of *fortuna*, but in actual fact it designates the very situation in which a fortunate (or unfortunate) event occurs. As a term for opportunity, *occasione* can provide favourable (or unfavourable) conditions for acting and, conversely, it is a matter of *virtù*, defined as the capacity to think and act politically, to recognize those conditions and make strategic use of them. The difference is decisive: if *fortuna*, in its purest form as a figure of contingency, is located on the 'ontological' level, then *occasione* is a category of the 'ontic' level, describing the ever-changing conditions with which all political action is confronted. It is *fortuna* – in other words, contingency as a condition of possibility of all political action – which provides for *occasione* as the favourable historical or political conditions within which we act. As a result, *fortuna*, strictly speaking, cannot be analysed, whereas *occasione* can. When Trotsky was reading newspapers in a coffee-house he was studying *occasione*, in order to be able to realize the moment when *fortuna* would be passing by – even if this moment could never be determined with objective certainty. Similarly, *fortuna*, because of its essentially evasive character, cannot be made an object of political calculation nor can *fortuna* be made the objective of an 'authentic act' on the ontological level. Being the ontological condition of all acting, *fortuna* can never be 'enacted' directly, she can only be approached *obversely*. Put differently, it is only possible to engage in a strategic game with *fortuna* by way of *occasione*.[5] Contingency is never encountered in a vacuum, but only within determined 'ontic' conditions. The quasi-transcendental, that is, ontological conditions of *contingency* and the ontic conditions of opportunity are therefore intrinsically related, and it is precisely because of this necessary intertwining between the ontic and the ontological, between *occasione* and *fortuna*, between acting and the act, that a pure act – an act *out of context* – is unachievable, or achievable only phantasmatically in an ideological, not in a political way. But if this is the case, then to 'play' with contingency necessarily involves to strategically account for, to borrow a term from social movement theory, the 'opportunity structure' of a given hegemonic force field.

The crucial point here is that only by way of this tensional relation between the ontic and the ontological, between the politico-historical situation in which we act and the quasi-transcendental conditions of all acting, action is made possible in the first place. Otherwise we would indeed find ourselves in either the ontic universe of rational-choice theory, which is a place of total calculability; or in Žižek's (or Badiou's) ontological universe of ethico-political purity, of 'faith' and 'the act'. In both cases the possibility of *acting*, the strategic game with the unforeseeable under hegemonically determined conditions, would be ruled out. It is in this latter Machiavellian sense of acting, understood precisely as the virtuous play with *fortuna* through the strategic assessment of *occasione*, that the Lenin of 1917 acted as a Machiavellian (and Gramscian), not as a sectarian of truth à la Badiou (whose 'Political Organization' basically consists of three people), nor as the political adventurist as which he is portrayed by Žižek.

DIS-EMBRACING THE ACT

What has to be elaborated today are tools for a theory of acting on the ontic plane which, nevertheless, takes into account the ontological plane of the act – yet as something which can never be achieved in its purity. It is exactly at this point where we discover the line of separation between a Gramscian, or deconstructive, and a Žižekian approach. In Žižek's numerous conjurations of an 'authentic act' one seems to witness a romantic longing for such purity. Without doubt, Žižek is entirely right when claiming that the '*obliteration of the dimension of the Act proper*' (by New Age discourses, for instance) in fact implies a form of ontological closure where 'nothing New can emerge, no Event proper can occur; everything can be explained away as the outcome of already-present circumstances, all the gaps in the edifice of the universe can be filled' (2001: 176). But the idea of an 'authentic act', achievable in its ontological purity, is as phantasmatic as the opposite idea of a total ontic obliteration of the act. It is certainly true that today's dominant discourse rules out any ontological dimension, thus producing an effective implosion of the ontico-ontological difference by which the act is reduced to the level of ontic calculation. But does not Žižek, on his part, reduce acting to the ontological, thus again eradicating the ontico-ontological difference *as difference*? Žižek is not only aware of his denigration of the ontic at the expense of strategic acting, he even proudly proclaims that:

In a truly radical political act, the opposition between a 'crazy' destructive gesture and a strategic political decision momentarily breaks down. This is why it is theoretically and politically wrong to oppose strategic political acts, as risky as they might be, to radical 'suicidal' gestures à la Antigone, gestures of pure self-destructive ethical insistence with, apparently, no political goal. (2004a: 204–205)

Well, it might indeed be wrong 'to oppose' acting and the act (which would be inadmissible even from a Heideggerian perspective, as the ontological difference is not at all an 'opposition'), but why should it be wrong to retain this minimal yet chiasmatic difference between the ontic and the ontological? If one prefers a Lacanian to a Heideggerian framing of the same point: where the symbolic is sacrificed at the expense of the imaginary (of, for instance, the New Age discourse) or the real (as in Žižek's advice to 'take a leap'), what is lost is not only the symbolic register of differences but the *very differentiation between the three registers.*

Put differently yet again, what Žižek in fact proposes is a politics of the real at the expense of the symbolic, which thus runs the danger of being carried out, exactly, within the imaginary. For in all its 'authenticity', such a politics of the real, as Žižek well knows, could only be 'enacted' through a *passage à l'acte*: 'a true Leninist is not afraid of the *passage à l'acte*, of accepting all the consequences, unpleasant as they may be, of realizing his political project' (1999: 236). However, it is well known that for Lacan there is only one case of a successful *passage à l'acte*, and this is the case of suicide (Miller 1989). For this reason there is a certain consistency in Žižek's tendency to revert – in some of his examples which oscillate, as mentioned before, between the ordinary and the hilarious – to models of a suicidal or self-destructive act, since 'in a situation of the forced choice, the subject makes the 'crazy', impossible choice of, in a way, *striking at himself*, at what is most precious to himself' (2000a: 122). Although Žižek would like to separate self-destructiveness from the achievement of the act through a fine displacement – the act for Žižek aims at the destruction not of the subject but of what is 'most precious' to him or her – an act will be 'successful' in the full sense of a *passage à l'acte* only if the subject disappears. Only from her disappearance can we infer that a 'true act' has been successfully accomplished. But what sort of politics would such a strategy entail other than the very end of politics? If a politics of the real (of the act) cannot be enacted without leaving the realm of politics altogether, it can only be envisaged in an entirely phantasmatic fashion. The following example given by Žižek for an 'authentic act' may testify to the phantasmatic aspects of an ontological act supposed to be fully 'realized' within the ontic:

> There is a will to accomplish the 'leap of faith' and *step outside* the global circuit at work here [in the Canudos community], a will which was expressed in an extreme and terrifying manner in a well-known incident from the Vietnam War: after the US Army occupied a local village, their doctors vaccinated the children on the left arm in order to demonstrate their humanitarian care; when, the day after, the village was retaken by the Vietcong, they cut off the left arms of all the vaccinated children. . . Although it is difficult to sustain as a literal model to follow, this complete rejection of the enemy precisely in its caring 'humanitarian' aspect, no matter what the cost, has to be endorsed in its basic intention. (Žižek 2004: 83)

This example is difficult to sustain for an emancipatory project of the Left, not because of the gory details with which Žižek loves to shock and entertain his audience, but because of the phantasmatic aspects of the endeavour. The possibility of a 'complete rejection of the enemy' is premised, as in the Canudos example, on the idea of a clear-cut break, of the possibility to get rid of the last traces of everything which may prove to be heterogeneous to one's own project. Consequently, the cutting-off of the children's arms must be understood as a sanitary effort at purification (a form of 'counter-purification' directed against the vaccination programme), and in this sense participates in the ideological fantasy that it is always the 'enemy within' – the spy or collaborator, those who were *infected* by the enemy – which constitutes the greatest danger to the pure homogeneity of one's own project. If 'to strike at oneself', the hallmark of a 'pure' act, is supposed to serve as a generalizable recommendation for actual politics, it runs the danger of turning into a recommendation for political purification, and, in the last instance, extermination.

Žižek is prepared to run this risk because he believes himself to be in possession of clear criteria to distinguish between the 'good' leftist act from the 'bad' fascist act (or act-simulacrum). His criteria are clearly unconvincing, though. First, an empty formalism is introduced into the argument, when Žižek defines fascism as 'nothing but a certain formal principle of distortion of social antagonism, a certain logic of its displacement by a combination and condensation of inconsistent attitudes' (1999: 186). (Elsewhere he claims that 'the difference between Fascism and Communism is also "formal-ontological", not simply ontic' [2004: 99].) This definition is insufficient because, on a formal level, *every* politics is based on the articulatory logics of 'a combination and condensation of inconsistent attitudes', not only the politics of fascism. As a result, the fundamental social antagonism will always be displaced to some degree since, as we have noted earlier, the ontological level – in this case, antagonism – can never be approached directly and without political mediation. It follows that distortion is constitutive for every politics: politics as such, not only fascist politics, proceeds through 'distortion' and, what is more, occurs on a terrain which is always already distorted by the absence of ground, the play between the ontic and the ontological and, if one wishes, the fundamental antagonism.

So, a purely formal description does not provide sufficient criteria to distinguish fascist politics from any other politics. In order to do this, Žižek has to smuggle in an additional feature on the level of content. He, secondly, submits that:

> [Fascism] emphatically does *not* pass the criterion of the act. Fascist 'Revolution' is, on the contrary, the paradigmatic case of a pseudo-Event, of a spectacular turmoil destined to conceal the fact that, on the most fundamental level (the relations of production), *nothing really changes.* (1999: 200)

The criterion here is not change or non-change (which would again be an empty formalism as the political action of any ideological camp may lead to change), the positive criterion is change in a particular ontic realm which then serves Žižek as a ground of the social, as 'the most fundamental level': the relations of production. The purely 'formal' logic of fascist politics is first given 'content' as an ontic field, and then assumes the ontological role of foundation. This might convince only the most orthodox Marxists, whilst for everybody else the claim that *ontological privilege* be granted to the economy (rather than recognizing its immensely important function in society, which on an ontic plane is undisputed) has to be theoretically substantiated. But Žižek sees no need to provide any further arguments. The economy is simply posited as a new – or not so new – ground. In the end, it becomes a question of simply *believing* in Žižek's economism. We know however, that fascism, apart from 'leaving the relations of production unchanged' (a claim that is partly debatable anyway), did change a lot for many people, and for some it changed *everything*. To reduce our criteria for fascism (in comparison to any supposed 'revolutionary' ideology) to the mono-thematic yardstick of whether or not the relations of production were affected, leaves us with a thoroughly reductivist and economist picture of fascism which for good reasons has been overcome by students of fascism and Nazism since the 1960s. The same insufficient argument unfolds with relation to the analogous question of 'class struggle'. Žižek claims that fascism phantasmatically fills up society's fundamental antagonism with 'race' as a 'positive', substantial content. So far so good, yet Žižek himself smuggles a positive content into the 'real' of antagonism: in his account, the fundamental antagonism is 'class struggle', and 'class struggle' only. Thereby the purely negative ground of antagonism is given a new (or simply orthodox) grounding positive content: class.

REVOLUTION RECONSIDERED

The problem with Žižek's revolutionary account of the act is not that we do not have political (ontic) tools in order to discern between Left and Right; the point is, rather, that we are simply not in possession of a formal criterion and, thus, an *ontological guarantee* to discern the 'good', emancipatory act from the act in all its 'ugly' versions. For this reason it does not make much sense to denounce as reformist, 'opportunist' and liberal 'radical democrat' everyone who does not subscribe to Žižek's own economic foundationalism. Where the notion of the act is concerned, we will also have to abandon the terrain of Žižek's all-or-nothing model: either the 'rules of the game' change drastically as a result of an 'authentic act'; or everything stays the same (which then is considered to be the proof, in this circular argument, that an 'authentic act' did not occur). But the truth of the matter is that nothing ever stays the same, that the 'rules of the game' are altered every time they are enacted, simply by virtue of their enactment under changing conditions (they always have to be enacted against 'rival' attempts at re-defining the rules).

Much more than this being the Derridean point of *iterability*, it is in actual fact the basic lesson of Gramsci. From a Gramscian point of view, Žižek appears as a nostalgian of the war of manoeuvre, as somebody who recommends storming the Winter Palace as the only possible strategy. As Gramsci underlined, under certain conditions it may be a good idea to storm the Winter Palace, yet in the countries of the West with their extended trench-works of civil society, it is impossible to condense political acting into the single sweeping act of conquering the power centre. If there was a *single* rule of the game, then Žižek would be right, and through an 'authentic act' the rule could be altered. But if the social – Gramsci's 'civil society' – is an embattled terrain where conflicting forces struggle over hegemony – that is, over the very definition of rules – then Žižek is wrong: no single act would ever be effective enough to change the hegemonic formation *in toto*. What is required is a multiplicity of acts organized into a 'common will' or hegemonic project.

'Revolution', in a modified sense, is not ruled out by such an approach and certainly 'reformism' is far from being the only imaginable consequence. Nor is a deconstructive take on politics necessarily incompatible with a Lacanian approach. It is enlightening to see how one of Žižek's main adversaries (and, following Laclau, 'unrecognized mistress'), Jacques Derrida, defined revolution – in what might be, for some, a surprisingly Žižekian way – as a rupture with the established order:

> I believe in the Revolution, that is, in an interruption, a radical caesura in the ordinary course of History. In any case, there is no ethical responsibility, no decision worthy of that name, that is not, in its essence, revolutionary, that is not in relation of rupture with a system of dominant norms, or even with the very idea of norm, and therefore of a knowledge of the norm that would dictate or program the decision. All responsibility is revolutionary, since it seeks to do the impossible, to interrupt the order of things on the basis of non-programmable events. A revolution cannot be programmed. In a certain way, as the only event worthy of the name, it exceeds every possible horizon, every *horizon of the possible* – and therefore of potency and power. (Derrida and Roudinesco 2004: 83)

If we put aside the ethical notion of unconditioned responsibility (yet the Lacanian ethics of the real is less remote from it than Žižek wants us to think), this could very well be a quote from one of Žižek's books. Yet there *is* a difference, which becomes clear if one continues reading:

> But if we want to save the Revolution, it is necessary to transform the very idea of revolution. What is outdated, old, worn out, impracticable, for many reasons, is a certain theater of revolution, a certain process of seizing power with which the revolutions of 1789, 1848, and 1917 are generally associated. (Derrida and Roudinesco 2004: 83)

To 'save the Revolution' one has to liberate it from the very revolutionary fantasy of a war of manoeuvre, not in order to contain it but to widen its effects on a strategically complex terrain. Rather than to a containment, such a deconstructive move amounts to the radicalization and expansion of the revolutionary moment – a moment which necessarily escapes the outmoded dichotomy of 'revolution' and 'reformism'. Such a move runs counter to what I call the *rarification argument* which can be found in many theorists, Žižek included. For rarification theorists, of which Badiou, once again, is the most outspoken exponent, an authentic act or event is rare by nature. Žižek himself seems to subscribe to the rarification argument when he claims that 'from time to time, something genuinely New can emerge *ex nihilo*' (2001: 176). However, if the act is to serve as an *ontological condition* of all ontic politics and of all acting, it cannot be rare by definition. It cannot simply occur 'from time to time', but will always be present as a dimension within every political *acting* (which of course does not provide us any guarantees that such acting will be emancipatory).

In the Machiavellian tradition, one has always been conscious of the fact that we will wait in vain for the single redemptive event – which is precisely the reason that we will have to act in the *now* of constantly changing conditions. As Hannah Arendt put it: 'no single act, and no single event, can ever, once and for all, deliver and save a man, or a nation, or mankind' (1968: 168). Yet Arendt, in a proto-deconstructive insight, also perceived the implication of this fact. Since if what Žižek calls the 'authentic act' is impossible, this does not preclude the possibility of acting, it rather serves as the very condition of the latter. As a result, the field of contingency, of *fortuna*, is significantly expanded, and together with it our ability to act strategically or *virtuously*. In the end we have to come to realize that, apart from mere revolutionary rhetorics, the idea of the potential dispersion of acts and of events throughout the whole register of the social is much more radical and politically enabling than the romantic longing for a single redemptive Act. Hannah Arendt, unjustly taken by Žižek for a liberal, has expressed this idea in her notion of the event as a 'miracle':

> History, in contradistinction to nature, is full of events; here the miracle of accident and infinite improbability occurs so frequently that it seems strange to speak of miracles at all. But the reason for this frequency is merely that historical processes are created and constantly interrupted by human initiative, by the *initium* man is insofar as he is an acting being. Hence it is not in the least superstitious, it is even a counsel of realism, to look for the unforeseeable and unpredictable, to be prepared for and to expect 'miracles' in the political realm. (Arendt 1968: 169)

Here is a thinking of 'miracle' not as the grandiose moment of the end of times, but as the interruptive *Augenblick* of the political which can occur – and does occur – in every single moment in which people start *acting*.

NOTES

1   For the genealogy and contemporary use of this difference, see Marchart 2006a.
2   Whereby he contradicts his own Canudos example on the following page, which certainly counts as a case of 'crazy' destructive negation of the existing order. Žižek explains this in a passage where he counters a critique by Stavrakakis (2003), based on the defence of a radical democratic ethics of the real. Žižek's counter-attack borders at the comical, since Stavrakakis does little more than defend Žižek's own arguments of a couple of years earlier. Yet Žižek reacts to these arguments as if they were the most absurd and hilarious things anybody could imagine, without with one word mentioning that it was he (Žižek) who played a large part in imagining them in the first place.
3   See Marchart 2006a.
4   Far from speaking out against a revolution, Arendt in actual fact criticized the impotent pseudo-revolutionary rhetorics of the students, thus reminding them that a revolution needs more than that (including, as Žižek also seems to forget, an organized group of revolutionaries): 'At the moment, one prerequisite for a coming revolution is lacking: a group of real revolutionaries. Just what the students on the left would most like

to be – revolutionaries – that is just what they are not. Nor are they organized as revolutionaries: they have no inkling of what power means, and
if power were lying in the street and they knew it was lying there, they
are certainly the last to be ready to stoop down and pick it up. This is
precisely what revolutionaries do' (1972: 206).

5   It is true that Machiavelli in his infamous 'fortune is a woman' line
assumes that 'she is more inclined to yield to men who are impetuous
than to those who are calculating', which is why one has to 'treat her
boldly' (1988: 87). Of course this implies that, as a rule, in a moment of
doubt it is better to act than not to act. Yet this must be understood as
strategic advice for 'virtuous' *acting*, not as a quasi-ethical injunction to
take an existential leap into *the act*.

TRAUMA ENVY

John Mowitt

HAVING ONE'S *TIZZY* AND EATING IT TOO

The initial incarnation of this chapter assumed the form of a response. The details are presented below. This, its second incarnation, is also a response, but to a rather different call. In fact, the second call might fairly be characterized as 'invaginating', that is, a call that in soliciting the Truth In Žižek (TIZ) reaches into the pocket of my chapter and turns it inside out. Once thus inverted, a discussion of trauma studies that made reference to the work of Žižek, is now recast as a discussion of Žižek that makes reference, perhaps even central reference, to trauma studies. As Derrida forewarned, the pocket may always be larger than the garment into which it is tucked.

Noting this might well suggest that in this incarnation my essay invites a rather serious overhaul. At the risk of defanging invagination entirely, reducing it to the banal cataclysm of turning a glove inside out, let me suggest why no such overhaul is warranted. At the heart of the earlier discussion of Žižek's work stood the concept of trauma. Indeed his work allowed me to sketch with a limited rigour the theoretical anaclisis that allowed trauma studies and psychoanalysis to hold each other up. As a result his work, notably the early *The Sublime Object of Ideology* (1989), could be read as a rhizomatic line constituting, obviously in part, the genealogy of trauma studies. What precisely is to be read there – the subordination of the political to the ethical – may matter to the TIZ, even as trauma studies necessarily takes on a more minor role. By this I do not mean to suggest that Žižek and trauma studies are two names for the same thing, although those caught up in the high drama of the former's recent wedding may disagree, but that what they share survives the contextual reorientation effected here.

This said, it is important to observe that for Žižek, much has happened since *The Sublime Object*. I am thinking not only of his many books (some I know better than others), but also his regular contributions to publications like *In These Times* where his has been a singular and bold voice in a journalistic context dominated by, as Lacan famously put it in *The Ethics of Psychoanalysis* (1992), fools and knaves. Given that my criticism of Žižek's early work challenges his theoretical commitment to politics (we all know about his political practice, his campaign for office, etc.), it is important to honour an intervention when honour is due. One is, just the same, entitled to pressure such interventions when they stake out convictions that do not live up to the standards set by the interventions themselves. I am thinking here of the sustained recourse in Žižek's corpus to the concept of trauma. It appears, essentially as an alias for capitalism itself, in the much more recent debate with Butler and Laclau, and insofar as it glosses the Ur-concept of the real – whether framed in the context of his counterintuitive reinvigoration of Pauline Christianity or not – trauma endures in a way that allows the genealogy sketched below to retain its pertinence. To be sure, what emerges sharpened is the important question regarding the becoming-ethical of politics. Can this take place even in the practical sphere of political behaviour? If, as Žižek argued in *The Sublime Object*, ideology takes place in what we do, then this becoming-ethical need not be a stranger to the global field of what we once called *Realpolitik*. It all depends on how the alignments formed through the discourses conditioning our thought operate in our practice whether theoretical or not.

TIZ brings to mind, no doubt more readily to some, Alain Badiou's 'subject of truth', and if it makes sense to forge this link here it is because the first incarnation of this chapter has been criticized by none other than Dominick LaCapra – on the pages of his recent, *History in Transit: Experience, Identity, Critical Theory* (2004) – who detects a certain political alignment between Badiou's approach to ethics and mine. He calls it 'old Left'. There is, of course, much to say here, and someone of LaCapra's stature deserves a more systematic treatment than can be offered here, but if the gist of his challenge comes down to reminding me that 'trauma envy' is reductive (it presumably fails to recognize not only that many different lines make up trauma studies, but that some trauma studies partisans resist the becoming-ethical of the political), then one is entitled to wonder whether the same error has not been committed in calling up the plainly reductive and dismissive category of 'old Left' and throwing me and Badiou (needless to say I am flattered, even intimidated, by the distinguished company) into it. Frankly, and here I will simply wear my reductivism on my sleeve, the 'subject of truth', indeed the whole fascination with the evangelism of the event (let us not forget that Žižek too is interested in Paul), might be construed as a certain neo-existentialist revival (let us not forget that one of LaCapra's important early studies was of Sartre), that is, a concerned resuscitation of the human agent who can again speak truth to power. The conflicted subject, responsible even for its bungled action, emerges as the ethical subject par excellence. Whether it is also political – and here the more urgent question appears on the horizon, namely, how are we to think and act the political from within the Western/ Northern university now that truth can no longer simply be counterposed to power – is what calls for discussion. I make no pretence here of 'doing justice' to Badiou's discussion of ethics, but as a rejoinder, however oblique, to LaCapra it is important to suggest how the genealogy sketched below might let some light shine between my position and that of Badiou's. Beyond the reductivism of reductivism lies the problem of getting some fix on, to bastardize Freud, where ethics came from. Doubtless this will help in the urgent struggle to figure out whether the ethical belongs fundamentally to the negativity contained in 'never again'.

SHAKEN, BUT ALSO STIRRED

The call which this chapter answers characterized its prospective topic via the antemetabole: 'Theorizing Trauma/Traumatizing Theory'. At the pivot of this rhetorical figure, literally around the virgule, spins trauma. Seizing the opportunity presented by the play conditioning all such pivots, this essay seeks, while acknowledging the attendant methodological risks, to traumatize trauma. Because theory too is caught up in this antemetabolic spin, and in that sense can no longer be all that it can be, trauma will be approached through its study. Specifically, my aim is to present trauma studies with a sketch of its genealogy. To the extent that trauma has, through its study, come to designate an expressive limit – the unspeakable event – confronting the tendency within trauma studies to speak of history and/or memory, while exhibiting a certain reticence about its own history, subjects trauma studies to trauma. At first glance, of course, there is a profound difference between 'the unspeakable' and the 'as yet unspoken', but it will be the argument of this chapter that this glance, in the very obviousness of its immediacy, misses something crucial. To spell this out, it will be necessary to reflect upon the institutional context of the emergence of trauma studies and the importance there of psychoanalysis as a theoretical practice, indeed a practice claiming specialist knowledge of both the limits of speech and traumatic injury. Ultimately, the gesture of traumatizing trauma, by charting the envy at work in the analytic debate over castration, will help to illuminate what I regard as the troubling contemporary tendency to displace the political with the ethical; a tendency – though hardly unique to trauma studies – that, to my mind, speaks volumes about the failure of its institutional success.

The issues at the core of this chapter first attracted my attention as I was writing about drumming and the 'new' men's movement during the fall of 1995. In that study – now the concluding chapter of *Percussion: Drumming, Beating, Striking* (Mowitt 2002) – I found 'trauma envy' analytically productive as a way to frame the affective dimension of the relation between an emergent (or merely alternative, as Williams might have insisted) politics of masculinity and 'second wave' feminism. Adorno's bold gloss on Nietzsche's aphorism, *'Du gehst zu Frauen? Vergiß die Peitsche nicht!'* provides the gist of the matter.

> Whatever is in the context of bourgeois society called nature, is merely the scar of social mutilation. If the psychoanalytical theory is correct that women experience their physical constitution as a consequence of castration, their neurosis gives them an inkling of the truth. . . Without a single exception feminine natures are conformist. The fact that Nietzsche's scrutiny stopped short of them, that he took over a second-hand and unverified image of feminine nature from the Christian civilization that he otherwise so thoroughly mistrusted, finally brought his thought under the sway, after all, of bourgeois society. He fell for the fraud of saying 'the feminine' when talking of women. Hence the perfidious advice not to forget the whip: femininity itself is already the effect of the whip. (Adorno 1974: 96)

Though unnamed, the 'neurosis' invoked here would appear to be, given the reiterated thematization of castration, *Penisneid*, that is, penis envy. In his critique of Nietzsche what Adorno seizes upon is the now familiar feminist insight that 'femininity', as a designation for the essential nature of women, represents little more than the gesture of consolation offered to the victims of male supremacy by its beneficiaries. In confusing femininity with women, Nietzsche reputedly misses the social character of the violation enacted through such a gesture. I take Adorno's point, though I think the matter is complicated by a detail that he overlooks. Specifically, Adorno misses that it is a woman who is represented as articulating the aphorism in question. This detail suggests that, in fact, Nietzsche wanted everyone and no one to read that Zarathustra's demand had produced a deeply ironic, if not openly contemptuous retort. This, however, is a diversion. It is more important that Adorno discerned the logic of *ressentiment* in the repudiation of femininity missed by Nietzsche, and did so in a way that enabled me to understand something important about the men's movement, namely, the fact that its adherents felt wounded by a feminism that had deprived them of what Lacan would no doubt call the phallus, that is, the mark of meaning or, to put the point more provocatively, the capacity to naturalize male supremacy by rendering it synonymous with the logic of signification. This led to my characterization of the men's movement as mobilized by castration envy, that is, the desire – perhaps even the drive – to take possession of the wound fantasized as that which allowed women to make men answerable for the wound of castration.

The 'new' men do not, however, want what psychoanalysis took from women. Instead, they seek the specifically moral authority that is now invested in this injury. To acquire it, another prior and preferably greater injury must be made to belong to men. Odd though it may seem, a blatantly masochistic drive, indeed a certain desire for suffering, appears now to have acquired a pronounced political value. Those familiar with Wendy Brown's provocative *States of Injury* (1995) will recognize its discussion of 'wounded attachments' in such formulations, and needless to say this is not entirely by chance. Indeed, the framing of my subsequent remarks relies, in significant ways, on her account of the socio-political and historical moment in which wounds come to be invested with moral authority, thus justifying a brief elaboration of her project, particularly as it comes to thematize the Nietzschean problematic of *ressentiment*.[1] For the sake of expediency let us say that Brown is attempting, among other things, to situate identity politics within the discursive antinomies of liberalism. She nowhere pretends either to account fully for, or judge, such politics, but her study moves inexorably toward the conclusion that identity politics is hopelessly compromised by its 'wounded attachments' to liberalism, that is, the very socio-political discourse through which the reprehensible violence of contemporary social relations is legitimated. In this her argument shares much with the Judith Butler of *Excitable Speech* (1997), and with Slavoj Žižek's various attacks on 'multiculturalism' (I will revisit this matter at length, below). Lest I be misunderstood, this kind of pushing of the Left's political envelope represents a terribly important political initiative, and while Brown and I apparently disagree over the legacy and viability of contemporary Marxism, her account of the enabling conditions of identity politics bears repeating.

In Brown's contribution to Gordon and Newfield's *Mapping Multiculturalism* (1996) this account appears in summary form. It is elaborated under two headings: capitalism and disciplinarity. Both are deployed to establish how in the era of late modernity (conspicuously not postmodernity) identity is at once disinterred and dispersed. Disinterred because capitalism has unmasked the aggressively particularist character of the state while at the same time uprooting its relation to national territory; dispersed because, through concomitant proliferations of disciplinary investments – at once bureaucratic, commercial and cultural – recognition (both personal and political) has been indexed to a logic of hyper-differentiation where, alas, size again matters. To wit, the smallest differences have assumed enormous importance. Although, as I have argued elsewhere (Mowitt 1992), disciplinarity bears immediately upon the institutional organization of academic knowledge production, Brown prefers not to take advantage of this aspect of the concept, keeping the broadly political character of liberalism in the foreground instead. This allows her to argue that all political discourse that is recognized as such and which appeals to the labour of specifying identity's minute particulars, invariably repeats the conditions of its own elaboration, thus aligning itself – in the name of satisfaction – with the very cause of discomfort. Identity politics is, for Brown, the consummate embodiment of such a discourse, and despite its persistent donning of the mantle of radicality, this politics folds neatly back into the impasses of classic liberalism which, for Brown, is a perspective that engulfs the distinction between democrats and republicans.

Perhaps with the now forgotten passing of Lucien Goldmann, who, it will be remembered, was given to situating theoretical projects (especially those of his opponents) within their often unspoken socio-historical contexts, we feel compelled to separate political discourses from theories (whether critical or traditional) about them. To be sure, we have come a long way from Part I of *The German Ideology* (1970), where Marx and Engels 'situated' Feuerbach's secular humanism within the 'ruling ideas' of nineteenth-century Germany. We recognize the bedevilling complications that arise when drawing material links between ideas and institutions. However, if it makes sense to situate liberalism in relation to capitalism and the micro-politics of everyday disciplinarity, then surely it makes similar sense to situate *States of Injury* (Brown 1995) which, after all, at no point presents its analysis as emanating from any 'other scene'. Aware that projects in cultural studies are often dismissed as fatuously ensconced in performative contradictions, Brown manoeuvres to theorize, to become response-able to/for, such charges. Whether she succeeds or not is best left to her readers, but her dialogic anticipation of this sort of dismissal sets a standard worth preserving. In particular, such a standard invites us to think similarly about the concept of trauma itself, not in order to determine whether its various elaborations are free of performative contradictions, but to reflect upon the relation between trauma – especially our comparatively recent theoretical preoccupations with it – and the logic of *ressentiment*. Indeed, the remainder of this chapter will strike out toward this end.

What are the stakes involved here? First, of course, there are the genealogical issues that arise as one seeks to situate a particular movement within contemporary academic (though not exclusively so) theoretical practices and the mode of production conditioning them. To borrow Foucault's diction: what inscription and destruction of the body is articulated in the 'moment of arising' of trauma studies? Which lines of force converged to condition this moment and what capacity for cultural critique finds its limits there? Second, given that for Nietzsche (as well as for Brown) *ressentiment* belongs to a genealogy of morals, what symptomatic status does trauma studies have with regard to what I earlier called the displacement of the political by the ethical? Precisely to the extent that it embodies a

certain disavowed politics, does this displacement itself not represent a privileged moment in the contemporary struggle over the critical character of cultural critique?

THE GAIN OF PAIN

When Cathy Caruth spoke last year at the University of Minnesota
she addressed herself to, among other things, loss. The loss of life
among troubled teens, the loss of death in *Beyond the Pleasure
Principle* (Freud 1964), the loss of her mother. To this sombre list
one might also have added the loss of trauma, for it was clear that
Caruth was keenly aware of the academic (but not merely academic)
'trauma industry' that had risen up around her work, depriving it, in
a certain sense, of its ontological dignity. With the precise sense of
timing that renders existence itself perverse, the loss of her own
mother was made to coincide with the loss of her disciplinary object,
that is, the literary work ravaged and adorned by trauma. I say this
not out of any disrespect for Caruth (whose *Unclaimed Experience*
I admire enormously), nor in order to exaggerate her importance,
but simply to draw attention to the genealogical fact that the prob-
lematization that had made trauma studies possible appears, of late,
to have suffered a structural transformation. But this is putting the
proverbial cart before the no less proverbial horse. What, after all,
made trauma studies possible in the first place? My colleague Tom
Pepper has proposed, in his essay 'A Night on Earth' (an unpublished manuscript), that we include the following enabling events in
a description of the field's emergence: the publications of Caruth,
Felman and Laub, La Capra et al.; the de Man scandal and its
impact on the cultural politics of literary criticism; the return of historicism and the pruning back of theory; the advent of Holocaust
studies; but perhaps most importantly the perception shared by
many academic intellectuals that a certain *ek-stasis* buckled us to the
moment, now lost, when, to use Heidegger's zinger, we had actually
begun to think. All of this makes a great deal of sense to me, and yet
if we are to avoid the vaguely theological narrative wherein trauma,
at a certain moment, falls into its industry, then it is necessary to
grasp the possibility, indeed the likelihood, of this development in
the very emergence of trauma studies. Of course, in the loneliness of
the last instance this possibility derives from the increasingly corporate character of the university within contemporary capitalism. But

ultimately, in thereby saying everything, one ends up saying very little. Here, Brown's analysis of liberal political discourse, strikes me as invaluable, for I see no point in treating academic thought as somehow above or beyond the ideological fray, since, as Kant reminds us, its very autonomy was bestowed upon it by an imperial state. This does not imply that thought is somehow *merely* ideological, only that its concerns – even when utterly inaccessible to taxpayers – are forged in conflict. Trauma studies, precisely to the extent that it articulates the unspeakable, crafts itself on a discursive field it does not, and cannot control. While this suggests, rather obviously, that trauma theory can be read as a wounded attachment, its 'fall' into industry, or more particularly the pathos associated with that fall might actually constitute something else. About this there is, of course, more to say, but the dependence of trauma upon its study, that is, the source of 'both its ontology and its and "voice"', produces a structure that necessitates, nay invites, capitalization. To be continued.

Thankfully, the matter I now wish to broach has been beaten to death. This no doubt peculiar expression of gratitude reflects the fact that I can be spared a certain rehashing of the all too familiar, while at the same time exploiting it, knowing full well that a certain danger has passed. I am thinking, of course, of the so-called Culture Wars and in particular of those skirmishes that, in the works of Allan Bloom, William Bennett, Dinesh D'Souza and Roger Kimball, centred around the reputed decline of the university, a decline indexed directly to the supposed incursion there of 'tenured radicals'. For me, and for many others, this is all part of a protracted national struggle over the political and cultural legacy of the 1960s, a legacy that, in being emblematized in the resignation of Nixon in 1974, has been resuscitated in the failed *coup d'état* or revenge farce called 'Monicagate'. Why is it important to frame these issues in this way? There are essentially two reasons. First, when attempting to situate an event like the emergence of trauma studies it is vital that one engages the discourses contending for legitimacy in the very site of this field's emergence. They help us conceive what is at stake in the struggle over new intellectual initiatives within the university, even when such initiatives do not immediately pose the question of the university. This is because nine times out of ten legitimacy is purchased through the cultivation of studied silences. Second, beneath the forensic cliché – that in charging tenured radicals with having politicized knowledge neo-conservatives were themselves engaging in political work – lies an important 'affective' element in the emergence of trauma studies, one worth lingering over as an element of the liberalism challenged by Brown. If embarrassment were actually capable of halting the forward march of Christian soldiers, then perhaps it would be enough to establish the hypocritical character of the neo-conservative stance on post-secondary education. Unfortunately, it is not. Moreover, what such an emphasis potentially misses is the *ressentiment* at work in the neo-conservative attack on the academic Left. Just as there is some truth in the claim that what the Left was blocked from gaining at the national political level during the 1960s, it later sought to gain academically, it is likewise true that neo-conservatives in the 1980s (the decade of trauma studies' emergence) resented the cultural influence enjoyed by Left academics whose teachings sought to engage the cultural political map redrawn during the 1960s. For neo-conservatives, the political crises of the 1960s – crises emblematized in Nixon's resignation – retained their menace as long as their cultural supports maintained their legitimacy. Confronted with this sort of challenge it is indeed worth denouncing the hypocritical character of a position that decries the political character of culture while elaborating a cultural politics that draws its energy from this very power source. But, as I said, hypocrisy is not the issue.[2]

Instead, if one concentrates on the dynamics of *ressentiment*, what comes into focus is the way in which the particular resentments agitating the neo-conservative meditation on the university belong to a national discourse persistently involved in the moralization of 'wounded attachments'. To elaborate this it will be necessary to engage the theme of trauma envy directly, drawing upon it to recontextualize the preceding discussion of the legacy of the 1960s. As anyone who was involved in the Left during the 1960s knows (and I am speaking here, obviously, of the so-called New Left, thereby acknowledging that there is a much more complicated story to tell here), it did not make its gains as a result of effective organization. Indeed, one might even say that it made its political gains almost in spite of itself. If gains were indeed made (and they were), it was because the movements the Left sought to engage and organize (especially the Civil Rights Movement and the Women's Liberation Movement) were out ahead of it, even if today, these movements are struggling, as it were, to stay in the streets. These movements won ground because their members were able to demonstrate that the paradox of democracy (its formal abstraction from all the particulars it is understood to protect) could be made to register their differences and the demands that gave voice to them. If neo-conservatives regard these gains as having definitively 'levelled the playing field', it is not because race relations have indeed been fully democratized, but because they are promulgating a discourse driven by a self-sustaining logic of, yes, *ressentiment*. Which means what? With regard to racism, it means that neo-conservatives want to equate it with a painful past that has now been lived through. For them, only racists or perverts would want to relive this pain by, as we say, playing the race card. More generally, neo-conservatives wish desperately to foster a link between traumatic injury and moral authority; a link that can be forged out of the conflicted legacy of the 1960s.

What one recognizes in the neo-conservative stance on the Culture Wars is something like an envy for what neo-conservatives construe as the moral authority ceded to the Left during the 1960s. Note that especially today, as Michael Eric Dyson would no doubt insist, the national memory of Dr King pivots around his 'promised land' speech in Washington DC instead of those speeches in which he elaborated the political analysis that made him an ally of striking sanitation workers. As we shall see, envy shares a volatile border with guilt and it is this sharing that invites us to consider whether the Right in general and contemporary neo-conservatives in particular remain wounded by the guilt their partisans were made to feel as a result of the gains won during the 1960s by the 'new social movements'. A certain white, middle-class and predominantly heterosexual male perception and experience of the USA was effectively exposed and shaken during the 1960s. As a result, the struggle over this legacy on the part of neo-conservatives has driven itself on the energy generated by envying the efficacy of guilt, by, in effect, seeking the opportunity to visit upon the Left the guilt, perhaps even the shame, 'inflicted' upon the Right during the 1960s. Two points: first, it is vital here that one recognizes the distinctly moral character of the feeling of guilt that arises when it is articulated within a discourse inflected by what Nietzsche would call the Judaeo-Christian tradition. In other words, guilt is the mask worn by neo-conservative partisans seeking to snatch victory from the jaws of defeat while at the same time denying the existence of hostilities. Second, it is equally vital to recognize the stakes of any move to reduce trauma to a moral problem. In short, inscribed in such a reduction is the recipe for generating a desire to experience that which authorizes the specifically moral condemnation of others, or what I am calling, the envy of trauma.

Lest I be misunderstood, I am not suggesting that the 'new social movements' of the 1960s moralized the traumas of racism, sexism, class and sexual privilege. On the contrary, my proposal is that Benjamin was right. History, now as before, remains in the hands of the victors and regardless of how shaken it was by the crises of the 1960s the Right has retained its right to write history. The work of Noam Chomsky among many others – all devoted to exposing the illusion of a 'liberal' media bias – has made this point well, and though this work might be usefully supplemented by that being done on the ideological narrowcasting of contemporary television (take, for example, Avital Ronell's essay 'Trauma TV' (1994)), nothing I might say here could render it any more compelling. To put the basic point very reductively: the issue is not whether, for example, sexual promiscuity is condoned on television, but whether hetero-norma-tivity is. The very fact that the debate over alleged bias is cast in such narrow terms (is adultery punished? are fathers 'bashed?'), is evi-dence of a certain cultural hegemony of the Right. Under such cir-cumstances, our collectively mediated memory of the 1960s becomes subject to an agenda that profits from the moralization of trauma, from, that is, a reconstruction of the 1960s as a nationally traumatic decade lacking the 'moral compass' neo-conservatives now carry. Thus, it is precisely in the representation of trauma that the work of moralization begins. To grasp what is at stake here it is important that one recognizes the neo-conservative desire to deny that its partisans bear any properly political responsibility for the traumas inflicted upon blacks and women (in strictly juridical terms this introduces the spectre of 'compensation'). Surely I am not alone in my continual astonishment over the aplomb with which fervent believers in 'origi-nal sin' insist that they are innocent of the crimes of their fathers, that only those 'directly responsible' for hate crimes and the like are answerable to the charge of racism. Privilege, as it were, has its priv-ileges. At work here is an interest, perhaps even a desire, to deprive the guilt produced by, say, the charge of racism, of any socio-politi-cal cause, any basis either in the political behaviour of neo-conserv-atives, or the survival of capitalism now confused both here and abroad with democracy itself. As is well known, these relations are often reconciled with a certain evangelical Christianity through the exertions of management gurus like Mack Hammond, whose televized *Winner's Minute* daily exhorted CEOs to teach their employees how, in effect, to wriggle through the eye of a needle.[3]

Once deprived of any social provenance or dimension, all traumas become grist for moral discourse, not just in the sense that they are treated as resulting from the moral failings of their perpetrators (when human), but more decisively, in that they authorize a mode of criticism that necessarily calls for moral redress. Trauma serves in such a context to name the stunning wound that produces moral authority. As such, it facilitates the constitution of a plane upon which 'reverse discrimination' becomes not only commensurable with racial discrimination, but the very conceptual means by which one might reduce protest about the latter to the morally suspect logic of 'tit for tat'. In relation to such a plane, one can argue that a far more serious trauma is inflicted when privilege and competence are subordinated to the morally 'primitive' desire for compensation than when privilege was first secured. The second state of affairs is deemed innocent, perhaps even naïve, whereas the first is regarded as deliberately vindictive. The refusal to offer the other cheek, in its repudiation of sublime alterity, is made to verge on immorality. By teasing out the logic of *ressentiment* at the heart of contemporary liberalism, Brown's *States of Injury* (1995) argues precisely that the current avatar of the 'new social movements' of the 1960s, namely, identity politics, is caught up in this political nightmare, a nightmare in which the struggle for radical democracy authorizes itself through 'wounded attachments', or, in my terms, trauma envy. In this sense the circle has now been closed: envy for an authority defensively construed as moral on the part of neo-conservatives, now expresses itself in an envy for the end of 'mere' politics, that is, for an ethics of difference that, in recasting the political as mere might, steers us away from the task of rethinking it. The circle must be broken.

A more thorough genealogy of the phenomenon I am tracing would have to take up Isaac Ray's *The Medical Jurisprudence of Insanity* (2000) and the still controversial McNaughtan Rules. These last are the procedural guidelines developed in Britain for pursuing the now much used and much maligned 'insanity defense' first deployed by Daniel McNaughtan when he was arraigned, in 1843, on the charge of attempted assassination. And this is not because insanity is the standard to which all so-called extenuating circumstances aspire, but because by admitting the prior history of the perpetrator, the British courts made it possible for defence attorneys throughout the Anglophone world to deploy the forensic strategy of comparative trauma calculation. Thus, when more than a century later Leslie Abramson sought to confront the jury of the Menendez brothers with the abusive history of their childhood, she was explicitly asking its members to weigh the two traumas of parricide and child abuse. What is of interest here is not the legal reasoning at stake (Abramson's was proven wrong), but rather the symptom that it represents. When the law itself is traumatized, that is, when it is confronted with an unspeakably infinite regress of violations, each one madder than the next, trauma acquires transcendental status. Everything is potentially traumatic. Under these circumstances, trauma has come to be invested with such authority and legitimacy that it elicits a concomitant desire to have suffered it, or if not the unspeakable event itself, then the testimonial agency it is understood to produce. The fact that Nicole Simpson did not survive the trauma of domestic abuse did not stop Clark and Darden from attempting – in advocating in her (and, let us not forget, Ron Goldman's) absence – to weigh the traumatic character of her experience off against the trauma of institutional racism proffered continually by her husband's defence team. In the end, one might even argue that the reassuring reiteration of mixed couples (Nicole and O.J./Marcia and Chris) ultimately worked to intensify the specific gravity of institutional racism as a traumatic element. Certainly few would be shocked to learn that parties sympathetic to O.J. were keen on having the rumours of a relationship between Clark and Darden circulate as widely as possible.

But what specifically does this have to do with trauma studies? Some might argue that, to the extent that coming to terms with the Holocaust was a crucial aspect of its emergence, trauma studies is very much aligned with a distinctly academic incarnation of identity politics. My point is somewhat different however. In accordance with a strictly dialectical dynamic, the very banalization of trauma that renders it unspeakable in daily life and the euphemisms of medical jargon ('repetitive trauma syndrome'), finds its antinomy in academic obsession. To no historical materialist's surprise, this dialectic, indeed its very sublation, is to be found in the concept of trauma. In this sense, trauma was always inclined toward capitalization. In a social context where its centrality to political debate has rendered it subject to the verbal equivalent of a *Bildverbot*, it was necessary, perhaps even inevitable, that this strategic reticence be counteracted by a certain explicitness. That this explicitness has been tinged with a certain desperation might well reflect the fact that the preoccupation with it emanated from an institution that seemed destined for ruin throughout the decades of the 1980s and 1990s, indeed an institution where the relation between speech and freedom has become variously politicized. That scholars in danger of losing their careers would turn to the task of thinking through and inventorying the traumatic character of their lives is hardly surprising. Nor is it particularly problematic. What is unsettling is the way that the academic study of trauma, perhaps in an act of sublime defiance, has rarely if ever sought to reflect upon the turf it shared with what Brown calls liberalism. In saying this I am, of course, aware of how politically charged the legacy of liberalism itself has become. However, if we are ever to find 'the real killers', it will be because a movement has emerged that refuses to argue with the Right on its own terms. There is no danger in letting liberalism go, once we recognize that democracy and capitalism are not synonyms.

TRAUMATIC COLONEL

There is, obviously, a great deal more to say here about the unsettling character of the academic study of trauma. I will not be able here, if indeed anywhere, to say it all. However to say some of what needs to be said, and, in the process, to further illuminate my association of trauma with envy, it is essential that the centrality of psychoanalysis to trauma studies be addressed squarely. Rather than assume the burden of engaging the entirety of the often brilliant work being done on this front I will instead concentrate on the justly influential re-reading of psychoanalysis (especially Lacanian psychoanalysis) still underway by Slavoj Žižek. Although his work is not typically included within the trauma studies canon, what makes it especially pertinent here is Žižek's persistent recourse to the concept of trauma. Indeed, whereas Freud was more inclined to invoke trauma (for example, 'war trauma') as a repercussive event (however complex), Žižek has moved to render trauma as something of an ontological category. In the brilliantly provocative rearticulation of Marx and Freud that organizes *The Sublime Object of Ideology* (1989), this move occurs as the motor of ideological identification comes to be lodged, not in the realm of the imaginary, but in the subject's structural relation to the limits of symbolization. Additionally, Žižek's work has the virtue of being involved in a historical reading of Lacan which, on the one hand, facilitates the 'plotting' of the concept of trauma, while on the other, it prompts us to think about the moment, the situation, of Žižek's reading.

Conditioned by the serendipitous fusion between a word processor and *schtick*, Žižek's writing invites a reading attentive to the rhythms of serial variation. Even a casual glance over 'The Object as a Limit of Discourse: Approaches to the Lacanian Real' (1988a) and 'Which Subject of the Real?' from *The Sublime Object of Ideology* (1989) reveals that whole sections have been lifted from the earlier essay to the later one, a fact duly noted in the acknowledgements. No doubt because a later preoccupation with the subject replaces that with the object, the sequencing of sub-sections is changed, but – as if to supplement the statement of his point with its enunciation – the real returns repeatedly, and the question that his analysis prompts us to pose is: which instance of the Lacanian real is this? Is it the McGuffin/MacGuffin or, perhaps, the mute embodiment of an impossible *jouissance*? Though interesting in their own way such questions are not mine. Instead, let us try to make sense of two things: (a) the link between trauma and the real and (b) the political value of such a link in the context of what I have called the trauma industry.

As concerns the link between trauma and the real, consider the following formulations:

> The real is then at the same time the hard, impenetrable kernel resisting symbolization *and* a purely chimerical entity which has in itself no ontological consistency. . . As we have already seen, this is precisely what defines the notion of a traumatic event: a point of failure of symbolization, but at the same time never given in its positivity. It can only be constructed backwards, from its structural effects. All its efficacy lies in these effects, in the distortions it produces in the symbolic universe of the subject. The traumatic event is ultimately just a fantasy-construct filling out a certain void in a symbolic structure and as such the retroactive effect of this structure. (Žižek 1988a: 107)

The *déjà vu* to which this citation refers is triggered in a prior section where the aim was, through a discussion of 'traumatism' (Žižek

1988a: 103), to persuade us that during the 1960s and 1970s Lacan's approach to the real resembled more his approach to the imaginary as elaborated in the 1950s. This invites two comments. First, not only is the real 'actually' linked to traumatic events, but, as these remarks make clear, it is conceptually linked to them as well. In other words, the real is like trauma in that the latter's cause – like the real itself – is subject to the work of metalepsis, or retroactive construction. Moreover, this 'likeness' is rendered intelligible through an apparently necessary appeal to Lacan's account of traumatism, as though without such an appeal the real would lack definition. To be sure, other appeals could have been made, but one of the risks consistently taken by Žižek requires that the gesture of exemplification be transferable. Here, this implies that traumatism can serve as a metonym for a series of which it may also be nothing more than a member. Žižek's appeal to traumatism warrants scrutiny under the broad heading of what might be called the 'politicization of theory', about which more will have to be said.

The second of my two comments bears on the historical register of Žižek's reading. Throughout Žižek's work one finds him engaged in a low-intensity but nevertheless steady conflict with post-structuralism. When this conflict rises above the quick and dirty thrills of caricature, it seems clear that it is driven by Žižek's desire to cast post-structuralism as the thief of his (or perhaps psychoanalysis') enjoyment. In accord with a logic specified by Žižek himself, what the former enjoys is an obscene relation to the real that it refuses to psychoanalysis. To wit, instead of the specific impossibility of the real constituting its reality, post-structuralism posits the impossibility of any real intelligible to us. To expose this theft or defect, Žižek outmanoeuvres most extant Lacanian criticism – criticism which has long centred around the conceptual bric-a-brac of the imaginary and the symbolic – by setting out to unearth the Lacanian real. Almost immediately he discovers that this real has a history, indeed the very decade-graduated timeline charted in the discussion of traumatism. Here too, an enabling disjunction between the statement and its enunciation is exploited if not exactly pronounced: just as the real is theorized as that which arises, as it were, after the fact, it is shown to be returning to where it always was in every decade prior to the 1980s, that is, prior to the publication of the text in which its inevitable return is cast as an expression of its ontology. Its dialectical status as both kernel and chimera, predicting as it does the very procedures of

Žižek's reading, is difficult to regard as anything other than an effect of that very reading, and no accumulation of 'illustrations' (whether from film, opera or contemporary geopolitics) can erase this bond with post-structuralism, which must then be cast as what deprives Lacanian psychoanalysis of its full enjoyment of the real thing. What interests me here is not, however, the question of Žižek's critique of post-structuralism. Instead, what is crucial is the appeal to trauma as the concept (and, presumably, the experience, since lately we have been treated to more and more of Žižek's 'army stories') through which one gains access to the real, or, to cleave closer to the terms of the citation, through which the dialectical character of the real is made manifest through a failure of symbolization that is, properly speaking, traumatic, if not trauma itself.

When all is said and done, Žižek's appeal to trauma is not really driven by a theoretical need to clarify the concept of the real, but instead by a political need to forge a link between the real and trauma that allows psychoanalysis to have, as it were, the last word about trauma. That word is 'void'. To the extent that 'void' also designates the inessential essence of the subject, thereby grounding the agency of the subject in trauma, its theorization is an expression of trauma envy. Given the link forged within liberalism between trauma and moral authority, the current preoccupation in and around psychoanalytical theory with things ethical should come as no surprise.[4] Thus, one might say, the quarrel with post-structuralism is a feint. The 'real' enemies, as becomes clear in 'Multiculturalism, Or, the Logic of Multinational Capitalism' (1997a), and 'A Leftist Plea for "Eurocentrism"' (1998a) are those partisans of identity politics who, by insisting upon the traumatic character of racism, colonialism and the countless quotidian violations that maintain the cultural and political hegemony of the West, have called into question both the analytical integrity and the political efficacy of psychoanalysis. Their point is not the familiar rant against the 'bourgeois' character of psychoanalysis, but rather such partisans seek to 'smear' psychoanalysis with the charge of complicity, as if to say: 'what adjustment must be made to the analysis of how to "go on" *dans la merde*, when one indeed lives in shit?' Lest I be misunderstood, I am quite sympathetic to Žižek's attack, particularly on multiculturalism (indeed his position shares much with Brown's), especially as he seeks to confront it with the task of reflecting upon its own relation to multinational, or as we now say, global capitalism. But when these critiques invoke 'traumatic *jouissance*' to clinch their arguments (as, for example, occurs in 'Multiculturalism' [Žižek 1997a: 34]), one cannot help but recognize a certain envy at work within them. It is as if psycho-analysis must be released from its guilt over the matter of its com-plicity in 'real traumas', and to do so it is bent to the task of discovering within its own conceptual resources the 'mother of all traumas', the trauma that trumps the moral authority of all comers, the trauma that is the subject's relation to the real itself. Armed with this strictly fetishistic concept, Žižek is in a position to undermine the credibility of all witnessing, arguing that Eurocentrism is not racist, it is the multiculturalists – precisely in their implied repudiation of the irreducible antagonism structuring the social order – that are the real racists. As stunning and intellectually provocative as such rever-sals are, they appear to be driven by a politics of theory that, even as it insists upon the need to reflect upon the nature of 'true politics', never quite manages to follow through.

When at the commemorative conference that produced the volume, *Michel Foucault: Philosopher* (Armstrong 1992), Jacques-Alain Miller identified the need for an 'archaeology of psycho-analysis' (1992: 64) he blazed a path that few others have taken. Žižek, who has discovered Lacan's teachings in every nook and cranny of the West's cultural storehouse, would appear to number among the few who have, and yet this is precisely what seems lacking in his approach to the Lacanian real. The point is not that this real must be subordinated to a realer real, for example, the one Sokal and Bricmont think that they are defending from post-structuralists and other science-phobes.[5] The point is rather to situate a concept so that its emergence can be projected across a complex graph that registers the intricate and uneven antagonisms that structure cultural politics. Doing so would render more conspicuous the appeal of trauma as a concept on which to prop up an account of the real. To be sure, one would have to foreground here Žižek's desire, as a Slovenian public intellectual writing in the aftermath of 1989, to find the 'common ground' on which to open a dialogue with potential interlocutors, but even so a certain vigilance remains necessary. Without it, the proximity between what Brown calls 'wounded attachments' and the mantra, 'the wound is healed only by the spear that smote you', passes un-remarked.

Some concluding thoughts, then, about envy. In my opening, envy was attached to the trauma of castration. I want now also to link it to the displacement of politics in the domain of theory. Within the corpus of psychoanalysis envy is one of the more under-theorized concepts, and this despite the fact that it plays a decisive role in Freud's account of sexual difference. Freud himself had little more to say about it. Even in the 1920s when he returned to the problematic of the *Three Essays* (1953) and the concept of *Penisneid*, he tended to foreground the latter's relation to *Eifersucht*, or jealousy. And, while Ernst Jones was among the very earliest to probe and ultimately contest the symmetry organizing Freud's account of sexual differentiation, it is Melanie Klein in the pages of *Envy and Gratitude* (1957) who squarely confronts the task of thinking through the concept of envy. However, before turning to the details of her discussion and discerning there the 'recipe' for a displacement of the political, a prior, albeit contextual, observation is called for. One of the features of Freud's return to the *Three Essays*, for example, in 'Some Psychological Consequences of the Anatomical Distinction Between the Sexes' from 1925, is the prominence there of a distinctly anti-feminist rhetoric. Nowadays this hardly bears repeating. However, what I am concerned to stress is that woven tightly into the very theoretical articulation of envy is a struggle between psychoanalysis and an earlier avatar of what we would now characterize as one of the leading columns in the march of contemporary identity politics, namely, Western feminism. Thus, in addition to tracking how envy serves to frame the 'trauma' of sexual differentiation, it will be important to consider how this intellectual and ultimately political struggle remains indissociable from the frame. Part of why envy emerges here as the pivotal concept has to do with this very situation.

Klein, of course, inherits a vital legacy within the international emergence of psychoanalysis; a legacy that certainly reaches back to Jones and Karl Abraham (one of her own analysts) but even more immediately to Helene Deutsch and Karen Horney. Horney in particular is crucial, not only because Klein credits her with being the first to examine the link between Oedipus and the castration complex, but because in essays like 'On the Genesis of the Castration Complex in Women' (1924) and 'The Flight from Womanhood' (1926), Horney lays the groundwork for the displacement of castration that Klein's own discussion of envy presupposes. Specifically, in 'Womanhood', where Horney is concerned to reinstate the analytical centrality of maternity, she makes inspired use of Georg Simmel's *Philosophische*

Kultur (1983), to argue that if Simmel is right – that 'our whole civilization is a masculine civilization' – then would this not apply to psychoanalysis in general, and to Freud's account of female sexuality in particular? After thematizing the methodological problem mythically resolved through the figure of Tiresias, she then proposes a critique of the masculinist character of Freud's account of castration; an account that centres on a clearly retroactive over-investment in the penis. Ultimately, this leads Horney to split envy (between primary and secondary envy) thereby discovering in the greater guilt experienced by women the motor for Simmel's 'masculine civilization' and the devaluation of maternity. This discovery is important for Klein's work because, although her 'feminism' is less conspicuous, the notion that psychoanalysis might be caught up in the dynamic of cultural reproduction and as such a partisan enterprise is fundamental to her treatment of envy. Because Simmel was part of the intellectual circle that informed Adorno's consciousness, surely it would be fair to say that this orientation might well be what is expressing itself in the latter's reading of Nietzsche. As I have argued, this reading recognizes without yet thematizing the dynamics of trauma envy.

The work that was to culminate in *Envy and Gratitude* began in 1955 with the presentation before the 19th Congress of the International Psychoanalytic Association of a paper later titled 'A Study of Envy and Gratitude'. The key proposition of the later study was formulated here, namely, that envy is not first directed toward the penis, but toward the breast. Long regarded as psychoanalysis's quintessential 'breast woman', Klein's position in this comparatively late text is far from surprising. However, certain of its details invite elaboration. First, of course, is the fact that in this construction Klein is carrying forward Horney's insight about 'masculine civilization'. By subordinating the penis to the breast she, in effect, recasts the trauma of castration as an echo of the more primordial trauma of nursing and ultimately weaning. Here not only is the logic of sexual difference indexed to one's relation to the female and ultimately maternal body, but clearly the defining trauma of castration has been displaced by another trauma. Secondly, this displacement is lodged at the heart of a full-blown psychoanalytical account of envy. Though reluctant to characterize this in terms of necessity, a brief elaboration of Klein's account of envy will show why the displacement of the penis by the breast is not linked simply by accident to the theme of envy.

As though she had consulted either a dictionary or a commentary on the seven deadly sins, Klein opens her discussion by attempting to isolate envy from jealousy and greed. She writes: 'Envy is the angry feeling that another person possesses and enjoys something desirable – the envious impulse being to take it away or to spoil it' (Klein 1986: 212). This feeling arises in nursing because the breast, though a vital potential source of gratification, is also, for structural as well as physical reasons, fallible. Consequently, the 'good feed' as Klein dubs it, is elusive. For this reason the child (male or female) comes to divide the breasts along moral lines, that is, between the good and the bad, treating the breasts themselves as both the source of the child's enjoyment and the bane of its existence. The breast appears to withhold, almost sadistically, that which the child most enjoys thereby stirring the envious impulse. It is crucial here that Klein characterizes one of the aims of this impulse in terms of a desire 'to spoil' the breast, and by extension, the creativity of the maternal body. I stress this not simply because such a characterization underscores the extent to which the theory of castration fits within the movement of a certain analytical misogyny, but because it decisively complicates the concept of envy. How so?

When Klein writes: 'the envious impulse being to take it away or spoil it', she invites us to consider that the object of envy is susceptible to two sorts of action, one conspicuously more 'virtual' than the other. 'Spoiling' the breast, involves (at least in English) the doting that parents often complain about in the parenting of others; yet it can also involve a strategy that, in reframing the breast's meaning, recasts the relation between the child and its mother so as to ruin the breast for her, and in effect, to deprive the mother of the breast symbolically. It is no longer what the mother values the breast as, but rather what the child's behaviour implies that s/he values it as. If the breast thereby becomes a 'gift that takes', then the child is positioned so as to proclaim, with all the ruthless precision of belatedness, its victimage. Envy, then, is not simply organized around an object. Instead, it takes as its object a condition of relating, indeed, the very condition where the guilt that might arise from an envious impulse can be causally attributed to, and thus in effect, be made the responsibility of, another. Gratitude, of course, is the counterweight here. It is clear, however, that the gratification from which gratitude derives has been all but pre-empted by the constraints operating on the 'good feed', obliging Klein to concede that its relevance arises primarily in the struggle to give shape, typically within analysis, to the psychic contents at play in belatedness. With regard to this last, Klein is no innovator. For her, as for Freud, belatedness designates the structural delay that organizes the link between meaning and experience. However, though both envy and gratitude are rooted in the vicissitudes of nursing, the significance of gratitude exhibits what might be called a belated belatedness. It comes later, and is thus more accessible, in a certain sense, to the work of analysis. Precisely why this is so remains unclear in Klein, but her discussion prompts one to conclude that giving thanks is predicated on the perceived receipt of a 'unique gift' which would thus appear to be as quixotic as grace itself. The step from the gift of gratitude to forgiveness is a short one, and once taken it is possible to discern Moses (the law-giver) and Christ (the saviour) in Klein's two breasts.

One provocative consequence of this treatment of envy is that in it envy is made to share something essential with trauma. In Klein's formulations this sharing expresses itself in the cause of envy, a cause that in depending for its legibility on its own effects remains indissociable from envy itself. When we recognize that this trauma is expressly designed to displace another (what Deutsch herself had called the 'trauma of castration'), not only are we invited to regard Klein's account as envious, but we are positioned to recognize what constrains or otherwise limits cultural critique in the stealth pleonasm of trauma envy. What is at stake here is the political itself.[6]

One need not turn to those passages in Klein where envy and resentment are aligned to discern the presence of *ressentiment* in her text. That it is there has less to do with her than with the psychoanalytical field itself at mid-century. The significance of its presence, as Brown acknowledges, has been forcefully articulated by Nietzsche who spun out the concept of *ressentiment* as perhaps the red thread in the genealogy of morals. As precursor to psychoanalysis, he was unlikely to have discerned the unconscious in what he called 'willing against the will', but it is difficult to imagine that he would have failed to recognize the significance of the proximity between the past, present and future illusions of Christianity and those of the hetero-normative family. Of course, in *On the Genealogy of Morals* (1996), Nietzsche makes only passing reference to envy, but it is clear that his entire account of breeding 'promise keepers' and the necessary link between memory and pain presupposes the importance, nay the centrality, of trauma. This is vital because it underscores the link between trauma and morality, not just in the sense that trauma might be construed as essential to the emergence of morality, but in the sense that morality is thus cast as the essential remedy for trauma, thereby vanishing into the chimera (or is that the kernel?) of the absent cause. Max Scheler, in his own study of *ressentiment* (Scheler 1972), has drawn attention to the distinctive ways in which this construction of morality belongs to the political and cultural triumph of the bourgeoisie. While I remain unconvinced by his effort to separate Christian love from the genealogy of morals, the indisputable merit of his project lies in its clarification of the link between morality and capital, a link thematized in Nietzsche's discussion of *Schuld* (both guilt and debt) and remarked in Brown. The redemption of Christian love in Scheler is clearly motivated by Nietzsche's bad press, that is, the oft-repeated contention that any wholesale repudiation of morality leads implacably to fascism. This is, beyond question, a crucial problem. Indeed, I hope it is clear that my quarrel with the ethical is not about its necessity, but its sufficiency. However, if the rich and conflicted scholarship on the Holocaust of the last half century has taught us anything, it is that what remains most difficult and urgent to discern about this catastrophe is not its moral significance or character, but how the conditions for it arose within a world that *remains* ours. True, these conditions include the status of the ethical, but it is nevertheless a remarkable feature of liberal discourse in the West that the Holocaust, as the event that cleaves the moral universe from top to bottom, is regarded as providing humanity's moral compass with its poles. In relation to it 'we' know with a certain certainty where we stand. Indeed.

What troubles me here is not, however, this certainty, which is, of course, another matter altogether. Rather what troubles me is the way this casts the political in relation to the ethical. For me the issue is not about priority, but about efficacy. When the political is conceived as a matter of taking sides, and specifically sides separated along the fault between good and evil (whether banal or not), its link to the labour of 'making' sides, of producing and advancing positions, is obscured. What is risked in this obscurity is not just the elaboration of the ethical as such (its production as 'that which matters most'), but the importance of the political as the field within which groups struggle in and for power. Here, I would submit, the vital question is not 'whose trauma provides one with greater moral capital' (as though the matter of efficacy could be exhausted in the 'capture of speech'), but 'what kinds of institutions, relations, practices need to be forged so that the trauma of capital accumulation can be abated?' Here I share Guttierez-Jones' impatience with the objective of inclusivity to the extent that the value of this principle is based on the presumption that it offers a moral remedy for a political problem. Obviously, the conditions analysed in this chapter require – given its deliberate aim of traumatizing trauma – that this characterization of capital accumulation be deemed, in turn, envious. I appreciate that, but insist all the same that the question of the political value of trauma and its theory still needs to be posed explicitly. What follows is up to those who hold themselves response-able to and for such an act. For my part, I suspect that regardless of the fate of trauma studies, my partiality for red over green will persist.

NOTES

1   It should be said, of course, that Brown's study was preceded by William Connolly's *Identity/Difference: Democratic Negotiations of Political Paradox* from 1991. Indeed, in focusing on the vicissitudes of identity politics, Brown can be read as an elaboration and response to Connolly. In this vein, it is appropriate to acknowledge the impact on this chapter of Carl Guttierez-Jones' 'Injury by Design'. Guttierez-Jones and I share an interest in disciplinary objects, though his study is focused on American studies. And since, in his words, trauma 'is more singularly oriented toward addressing the victim's experience of loss' (Guttierez-Jones 1998: 77) he leaves it to the side of his discussion of injury. I would argue that he remains more confident, as a consequence, about psychoanalysis and concentrates his political analysis on the remedy of 'inclusion' even as he acknowledges its ethical, and therefore politically ambiguous cast.

2   Here it is again appropriate to acknowledge that Guttierez-Jones, in examining the significance of the conflation of race and racism in D'Souza's *The End of Racism* (1996), has pin-pointed a key later articulation of what I am calling hypocrisy. In linking this articulation to the resentful liberal account of race relations, he underscores the urgency of displacing the critique of hypocrisy by exposing its often unacknowledged investment in normativity. This is a start, but the relation between this investment and the general accumulation of something we might call moral capital needs to be elaborated.

3   A recurrent segment of the morning news and weather programme broadcast by the local ABC affiliate in Minneapolis, the *Winner's Minute*, is now off the air. For nearly 24 months, however, it buttonholed sleepy middle-class commuters, beseeching them to bring biblical principles to bear on

their careers. Addressing specifically managers, the host/sponsor, Mack Hammond used his 60 seconds to propose, in a tone utterly devoid of irony, that a strict analogy obtained between Christ's relation with his disciples and a manager's relation with 'his' employees, thereby distancing himself from those who simply insist that the *Bible* does not oppose the accumulation of wealth. Some of his juxtapositions were quite chilling, so chilling in fact that his 'ministry' has now morphed into the more typical format of the business seminar, having lost his television audience. Real TV indeed.

4 I realize, of course, that here I appear to be treating ethics and morality as interchangeable. No less a figure than Lacan, in the opening of Seminar VII (1992), might be invoked as my warrant, but since it is clear that I have a quarrel with the ethical turn, this is a gesture that would not ring true. In lexicographic practice a certain professional and secular orientation is used to separate out the properly ethical from the moral, and since Lacan was persistently contesting the grounds of his school's exclusion from the international psychoanalytical community, such a focus makes considerable sense. However, Habermas, in chapter 4 of *The Structural Transformation of the Public Sphere* (1991 [1961] – thus roughly contemporaneous with Seminar VII) provides one with the historical and perhaps even political means to distinguish the two. His discussion is far too rich to summarize in a note, but one of its conclusions is that ethics come to serve as the means by which – through the medium of the bourgeois public sphere – politics is brought under the sway of morality. Kant's discussion of pure practical reason figures prominently here, as it does in Lacan. And while I realize that my concern about the displacement of politics would thus appear predicted in the very concept of ethics, what Habermas alerts us to is the more consequential matter of thinking about the university as an institution caught up in the structural transformation of the public sphere. Is an ethical stance sufficient to forestall the ruin of an institution whose ordinary routines and procedures are predicated on the maintenance of an ethical articulation of the relation between morality and politics? I have my doubts.

5 In *Fashionable Nonsense* (1999) Alan Sokal (best known for the hoax he perpetrated against the Left academic periodical, *Social Text*) and Jean Bricmont launch a full scale attack on French post-structuralist philosophy, arguing that it is largely based on widespread and wanton misuse of scientific concepts. Motivating this misuse is, they allege, a repudiation of scientific realism, which has its roots – and here the nationalistic character of their rhetoric is unmistakable – in Cartesian rationalism. I have waded in on this debate elsewhere (see Mowitt 1997).

6 Throughout *A Critique of Postcolonial Reason* (1999) Gayatri Spivak draws on Klein's treatment of envy as a way to problematize the status of the political within post-colonial discourse. Squaring off against her redoubtable sparring partner, Benita Parry, Spivak uses Klein to legitimate the concept of a constitutive violence that founds the political whether at the institutional or geopolitical level. Her expressed aim is to

repudiate the claim – typically, in her mind, advanced by feminist scholars – that if approached with sufficient theoretical and practical care, all geopolitical grievances can be redressed. While I share with Spivak a commitment to re-treat and reiterate the political, especially once we have attempted to reckon with the concept of a constitutive violence, the preceding discussion of trauma implies that Klein's concept of envy may be, well, spoiled.

THE TRUTH ABOUT OVER-IDENTIFICATION

Ian Parker

The concept of 'over-identification' is drawn from the armoury of psychoanalysis and forged by cultural activists in the *Neue Slowenische Kunst* (NSK) into a weapon against Tito–Stalinism and contemporary neo-liberalism. Over-identification works because it draws attention to the way the overt message in art, ideology and day-dreaming is supplemented by an obscene element, the hidden reverse of the message that contains the illicit charge of enjoyment. When over-identification brings that double-sided ambivalent aspect of the message to the light it can be a more subversive strategy than simple avoidance. However, Žižek's particular path from psychoanalysis to politics entails some more dubious over-identification tactics that entangle him all the more closely in the ideological apparatus he claims to dismantle. We will come to that.

Let us begin with two ways of approaching the concept and practice of over-identification. To put the distinction between the two rather schematically: one way proceeds from what is imagined to be a powerful fixed reasonable locus of thought, which views entanglement with the chaotic and irrational as profoundly problematic; while the other way mobilizes anarchic and unreasonable symbolic forces to discomfit and disturb hierarchical social systems organized around fixed points of authority. It is worth being clear about how each of these takes on over-identification operates, and then whether we try to work with it or against it.

OVER-IDENTIFICATION: THE DOMINANT CLINICAL PROBLEMATIC

The first way of approaching over-identification attempts to conceptualize it in such a way as to avoid it. This is what we can term the dominant clinical problematic, and it manifests itself in a number of different forms.

Over-identification, when it is named as such, is often treated as an institutional problem, and it revolves around the process of recruitment of different categories of subject. The institutional apparatus concerned is usually that of so-called 'special education', and the word 'special' here is something that should alert us to the production and regulation of excess, a surplus that is at once necessary and disruptive to a symbolic system. Žižek has often commented on how symbolic authority requires such an excess and then needs to keep it in check, and here the obscene superegoic injunction to 'enjoy' has been a useful elaboration of Lacan's comments on the role of the superego (Žižek 1991: 25). In 'special education' in the United States the 'over-representation' of African-American students is viewed as just such a problem. Certain 'discrepancy formulas' are used to determine that when, for instance, these students make up 12 per cent of the student population and have a 30 per cent presence in special education, this is way above the margins of chance, and it is then termed an 'over-identification problem' (Education Commission of the States 2005). It should be noted that while 'over-identification' is assumed to be synonymous with 'over-representation' in this context, it is not: since these terms are signifiers they operate in chains of equivalence and difference that are symbolically structured – from a Lacanian point of view there is no such thing as a synonym, a point we will return to presently.

This kind of institutional problem betrays a lack of balance in the management of the educational apparatus, and perhaps of the wider system of which it is a part. The correct weighting of different categories of identity, handled by careful and judicious rule-governed choices about rates of inclusion and exclusion, should in this view be one that is reasonable. This is why when things seem to slip out of kilter, the normative functioning is often viewed as being beset by irrational prejudice that may have seeped in and upset rational appraisal. Žižek has drawn attention to how ostensibly balanced economic systems only function by virtue of what escapes the judgement of reasonable agents, how the object cause of desire is produced and lost and so operates as the obstacle that is simultaneously the condition of possibility and impossibility of the system (Žižek 1993: 142). When the Connecticut State Department of Education noticed that 'black and hispanic students are more than twice as likely to be identified with intellectual and emotional disabilities than their white peers', these were seen as 'issues of overidentification and disproportion' (LRE News 2003). The signifier 'disproportion' here is equated with 'over-identification' in such a way as to evoke underlying assumptions about how the system should and could function, proportionately.

We should also note how over-identification figures within a dominant problematic in clinical practice, for this is where the historical roots of the term lie in relation to identification. Here it is typically configured as a seductive and harmful part of what is termed, in the dominant psychoanalytic tradition in the English-speaking world, 'countertransference'; this 'countertransference' indexes the 'resistance', 'inner conflicts' and 'blind spots' that afflict the psychoanalyst. These may be treated as interferences that mislead the analyst and throw them off track, or as their 'appropriate emotional responses' that cue them into what the analysand is feeling and attempting to communicate to them (see Sandler, Dare & Holder 1979). The desirable aspect of countertransference in this tradition is seen as what has been called an 'echo of empathy', which calls upon a conception of the analytic relationship that Lacanians will have difficulties engaging with because it is something too close to the line of the imaginary – an illusion of direct communication between analysand and analyst. This reference to empathy also serves to draw attention to what the 'countertransference' is understood as 'counter' to, to transference conceived as feelings and thoughts that may not be easily conveyed from one individual to another. Lacan, in contrast, saw transference as operating through and in relation to signifiers, a field of symbolic material in which analysand and analyst are both, if asymmetrically, a part (see Lacan 2002c).

Work carried out within what I have referred to as the dominant clinical problematic – in the Center for Torture Victims in Sarajevo, for example – exemplifies how over-identification is then seen as brought into play as part of an 'inadequate countertransference'. Here it is seen as the opposite of and complement to 'avoidance' (avoidance which may include paternalism, rejection, a conspiracy of silence and unwarranted resort to medicalization); this over-identification may be driven by 'shame and helplessness', a 'non-declared ethnocentric alliance' or by the 'pitfall of solidarity' (Dizdarević 2001). There will be undesirable consequences for the analysand, of course, but this form of over-identification is primarily a problem for the analyst who is drawn into material that should be consciously attended to and sifted through.[1] Particular kinds of profoundly traumatized patient may evoke such reactions; other examples in the literature include students in psychiatric residency training referred to as 'special patients' who may be inclined to idealization of their therapists and may elicit over-identification (Kay 1981). It should be noted here that in a psychoanalytic tradition that places some value on identification – including seeing the end of analysis as entailing identification between the ego of the analysand and that of their analyst – there is an impetus to conceptualize what may be excessive or disproportionate to this ideal outcome.[2] The notion of over-identification serves to capture what may be too risky, too threatening to a practice that sees itself as eminently reasonable and which aims to bring its patients into line with its image of what a reasonable individual subject should be like.

The 'truth' of such an approach is the ideal of adaptation and integration, one most avidly embraced by New Age therapies which declare that 'feeling and integrating resides between ignoring and over-identification'; the task of identifying and assimilating what is irrational to a stable rational core of the self is quite explicit. The focus on 'feelings' and 'feelings beneath your feelings' in this explicitly humanistic and integrative work is the diametric opposite of Lacanian psychoanalysis, as is the notion that there is an 'innate okayness' about these things so that it does make sense to ask questions like 'Feeling old pal – what do you want' (Mensing n.d.). Here the ego is represented as able to access what lies outside the better to strengthen itself so that the end of this 'analysis' is one in which (in a well-known translation of Freud's formulation) 'Where id was, there ego shall be' (Freud 1933: 80). There is, of course, a connection with education again here, for the logic of this therapeutic intervention is to educate others so that they will be good self-governing subjects as reasonable as us, and then not liable to entangle us in over-identification with them.

OVER-IDENTIFICATION: A RESISTANT SUBVERSIVE PRACTICE

The 'work of culture' is viewed quite differently by Lacan, of course, and the ego is not hailed as the triumphal centre of the subject, so let us turn to the second way of conceptualizing over-identification.

This second way revels in over-identification and is a resistant subversive practice; it is directed against rational and irrational faces of authority, the reasonable calls for order and the obscene supplement of the law. Over-identification now operates as a strategy for making the conditions of possibility for the rule of the master visible in such a way as to make that rule impossible.

The concept of over-identification in this radical form originates from the punk movement in Ljubljana in the early 1980s, in a politically-charged punk scene that faced a peculiar combination of repression and tolerance in the last years of the Tito regime. The combination of surveillance that aimed to identify and isolate active dissidents, and indulgence that attempted to suffocate and recuperate the rest of the population, was but a particularly intense version of forms of ideological control in the rest of Europe. Art activists knew this, which is why the strategy of over-identification was ratcheted up a step when Slovenia broke from Yugoslavia in 1991 and was proclaimed as being at last a free and autonomous capitalist country.

The opposition to Tito–Stalinism in Slovenia began with punk, and a first step to a strategy of resistance organized around over-identification was the formation of NSK in 1984. Different components of NSK – the design group New Collectivism, the fine artist members of Irwin, and the band Laibach, for example – targeted the symbolic infrastructure of the regime, ridiculing and undermining it, but in such a way that it was difficult for the authorities to explicitly condemn or suppress it.[3] This political conceptual art practice is where Žižek is coming from, and it is crucial to take this into account if we want to grasp how and why he has used Lacanian theory to read Hegel upon a stage populated with Marxist categories; theory that was forged in and against a disintegrating regime that itself claimed allegiance to Marxism.[4]

Over-identification here takes the system at its word and takes the bizarre contradictory demands of the authorities more seriously than the system takes itself, so seriously that it cannot bear that knowing participation but cannot refuse it. This is not merely a parody of totalitarianism but functions as if it were an obsessive identification with it: it plays out exactly what a system of power demands of its supporters in its overt messages but what that system also needs to distance itself from, as part of its ameliorative attempts to buffer itself from criticism and to contain the criticism it must permit. For example, the New Collectivism design group submitted a poster for Yugoslavia's 'Youth Day' in 1987, the year when it was Slovenia's turn to come up with the main publicity for an event that also marked Tito's birthday. The panel of judges dutifully praised the design – a muscular figure leaning forward holding a torch out into the foreground – as embodying the spirit of Yugoslav socialist youth. It transpired that the original design was from 1936 German National Socialist propaganda. The resulting scandal raised questions about symbolic formations operating through the ideological state apparatuses, and that 'Youth Day' turned out to be the last (Stepančič 1994).

When Slovenia became an independent state in 1991, NSK's response was to form its own state apparatus, and so the 'NSK State in Time' set up its own consulates and embassies which issue passports that are fairly convincing, and enabled some people to flee Bosnia in 1995 when they were distributed in Sarajevo during the Laibach 'Occupied NATO Tour'. Žižek elaborated a theoretical rationale for NSK's restaging of a state apparatus: the state disintegrated in Yugoslavia, and NSK provided a symbolic form that rose above ethnic conflicts, a new state authority that was rooted in time rather than geographical territory (Žižek 1993a).

A key conceptual reference point for NSK state artists the Irwin group, a reference point that is echoed across the other components of NSK and through the work of its sympathizers, is that of Suprematism, a radical art movement that was established in 1915 and flourished in the aftermath of the Russian Revolution. Retrieved and remobilised from early Soviet history, Kazemir Malevich's 'black square' and 'black cross' function as forms that have become inert, that operate as if they are 'pure objects', and that can be resignified in and against Soviet realist and National Socialist art, over-identifying with those art traditions to explode them from within. The mixing of kitsch images like Landseer's antlered deer and reworking of Heartfield's anti-fascist photomontage turn this work from being merely parody into something that evokes and disintegrates the putative organic unity of cultural tradition (Mudrak 2001). As part of the iconography of NSK State in Time, Suprematism provides at once a triumphal and an empty symbolic system. Malevich's black square is still present in contemporary art practice from the former Yugoslavia. In feminist interventions at the 2001 Venice Biennale, for example, Tanja Ostojić shaved her pubic hair into a black square in an over-identification with the art establishment that played into and against the objectification of the female form: 'in between Ostojić's legs the real/impossible kernel of the art power capitalist machine received the only possible radical and critical appearance that is an appearance in flesh and blood' (Gržnić 2004: 30).

The most notorious members of the NSK state apparatus are its politicians, the band Laibach (see Parker 2005). Formed in the industrial coal-mining town of Trbovlje in 1980, the year Tito died, 'Laibach' is the German name for Ljubljana, and so the use of the name was already from the beginning a provocation. The music has mutated over the years as successive generations of communist, anti-communist, anti-fascist and neo-Nazi youth have rallied to support the band. The Malevich black cross and military uniforms pose a question to the audience about what lies behind their over-identification with the paraphernalia of the state. Žižek argues in his article, 'Why are Laibach and NSK not Fascists?', that they manipulate transference: 'their public (especially intellectuals) is obsessed with the "desire of the Other" – what is Laibach's actual position, are they truly totalitarian or not'. This audience expects an answer when actually what they are forced to work through is a question about desire and about where they, the audience, stand. So, with the dissolution of the transference, Žižek claims, 'Laibach here actually accomplishes the reversal that defines the end of the psychoanalytical cure' (Žižek 1993b).

Laibach saturates itself in totalitarian imagery of the state and with the theological apparatus that underpins it, and one can find many of the theoretical elements that structure Žižek's own writing. The deliberately tautological chant 'God is God' (on the album *Jesus Christ Superstars* [1996]) bears an uncanny resemblance to Hegel's invocation of the world spirit when read in the light of the description of God to be found on the NSK State Electronic Embassy website; there it is proclaimed that 'For God to be God, i.e., an absolute, infinite, self-referring, omnipotent Being, He can also be the substance of his own essence and the spirit of His own entity' (NSK 2002). Even something so close to one of Žižek's favourite Hegelian warrants for the peculiar version of 'materialism' – that for Hegel, '*Der Geist ist ein Knochen*' ('Spirit is a bone') – is to be found in the 'Admission Document' of the NSK 'Department of Pure and Applied Philosophy': 'The construction of Neue Slowenische Kunst (NSK) is therefore His scheme, penetrating into the pores of the nervous system, so that this penetration is work, the nature of which provokes reactions in the subject' (NSK Electronic Embassy 2002). What better way of summing up Žižek's turn to Christianity could there be than what Laibach–NSK State promise us there in their over-identification with it, as 'requited love from which we live and in which dogma is the tool' (NSK Electronic Embassy 2002).

As we have seen, Žižek has often been supportive of NSK, and the development of his work is rooted in the same constellation of problems and strategies that these art activists were elaborating. The squabble over whether NSK is a 'a kind of theatricalization of a few Zizek [*sic*!] theses', or whether Laibach were the first to use the 'method' of overidentification and that Žižek then theorized what they did, is beside the point (Richardson 2000). The ownership of ideas already displaces the question from the chain of signifiers to the domain of individual intentions. And that displacement would lead us away from a theoretical consideration of what Lacan has to say about identification and from a more serious question about what Žižek is up to. As we will see, Žižek's relation to the problematic of identification and over-identification is not so Lacanian and not as radical as he makes out.

IDENTIFICATION: FOR LACAN

Lacan focused on identification in Seminar IX (2002a), and from the start of the seminar he makes it clear that his elaboration of this concept is going to be very different from the too easy assimilation of it to internal mental processes in which one person is attached to the image of another. While that form of identification can be theorized with reference to the mirror stage and the imaginary, Seminar IX marks a shift of focus to symbolic identification. In the first session, Lacan sets up a series of oppositions – between recognition and conceptualization, between 'the small other and the big Other' – to emphasize that his main concern will be with identification as embedded within the realm of 'the signifier and its effects' (2002a).

The place of this seminar in the development of Lacan's work is important, and this is the case whether we view Lacan's work as necessarily contradictory, as tracing a logical succession of concepts or as unfolding a consistent position. Its immediate location is between Seminar VIII on transference (Lacan 2002), in which there is a focus on the 'agalma' that Alcibiades is drawn to as some hidden object inside Socrates, and Seminar X on anxiety (Lacan 2002b), in which the *objet petit a* is specified as that elusive object cause of desire that produces anxiety when it comes too close. So, there is an elaboration of agalma as *objet petit a* in the later seminar, and the position of the analyst in the place of the *objet petit a* is one way that transference will be explored further in Lacan's following seminars (2002c). However, Seminar IX elaborates a concept that will become important to later work on the analytic relation, even though it is not immediately related to transference at this point and is referred to as the guarantee of individual consciousness which we should 'learn at every moment to dispense with', this concept is the 'subject supposed to know' (Lacan 2002a: 4).

Broadening the scope a bit, this little group of seminars stands between Seminar VII on ethics, and Lacan makes reference to that seminar at the beginning of Seminar IX, and Seminar XI on four fundamental concepts (transference, unconscious, repetition, drive). We are therefore between two quite different accounts of the relation to what lies beyond signification: while the ethics seminar (Lacan 1992) – which Lacan viewed as one of the most important – discusses Antigone's step beyond the law into a region between two deaths to focus on the thing, the seminar on four fundamental concepts (Lacan 1979) focuses instead on this object in the real as the *objet petit a*, the object around which the drive moves without ever reaching it. In the wider temporal sweep of the seminars, there is, as Lacan notes, an alternation between a focus on the signifier from Seminar I and through the odd-numbered seminars and a focus on the subject in the even-numbered seminars. Seminar IX indeed focuses on the signifier, and this is particularly important as a corrective to the way identification is commonly understood, but it does something new to interrupt that sequence with an elaboration of the relation of the subject to the signifier, and there is repeated invocation of the definition of the signifier as opposed to a sign, as 'not what represents something for someone, it is what represents precisely the subject for another signifier' (Lacan 2002a: 12).

The formulations that Lacan provides in Seminar IX have a number of important consequences for political as well as clinical interventions, and regardless of who was actually responsible for the development of over-identification as a resistant subversive practice, it is a Lacanian conception of identification that underpins that practice. Without Lacan's particular return to Freud there would always be a risk that over-identification would slide from the realm of the symbolic into the imaginary, from a realm of properly political practice into the individually centred affective economy of love and hate (and appealing to humanist-integrative, ego-psychological, object-relations or Kleinian conceptions of the self).

It is significant that Freud's most detailed theoretical discussion of identification occurs in his text on collective activity, in a book that is given the rather misleading English title 'Group Psychology and the Analysis of the Ego' (1921). Here he outlines three modes of identification: there is a first tie with a love object; there are hysterical alliances with others in the same situation; and there is a third kind that may be important in the formation of a neurotic symptom which Freud describes as being 'a partial and extremely limited one' and which 'only borrows a single trait from the person who is its object' (1921: 107). This 'single trait' – the '*einziger Zug*' Freud specifies in the original German text – is taken up by Lacan, and is glossed as a first point of symbolic identification, as a 'sign' in the Seminar on transference (2002: 12) and then as a 'signifier' in the Seminar on identification (2002a: 1).

This crucial shift in Lacan's reading of Freud then revolves around the signifier as a point of identification rather than unification (2002a: 11): 'It is *qua* pure difference that the unit, in its signifying function, structures itself' (2002a: 10). This means that symbolic identification is with a signifier that will then repeat itself through the subject's life, and of course will do so in the course of the transference. It does not presuppose the internalization of an image, or indeed of any point of unification to define the consciousness of the subject to themselves. Lacan spends quite a lot of time tackling the underlying historically specific supposition of this view of consciousness, something which manifests itself in a 'subject supposed to know': there is in every self-identity the supposition that $A = A$ – 'A is A, has constituted, as I might say, the condition of a whole era of thought of which the Cartesian exploration with which I began [the seminar] is the term' (2002a: 10). Žižek endorses this critique of the Cartesian cogito, and emphasizes the historical location of it and of the practice of psychoanalysis when he draws attention to Lacan's corresponding argument that this cogito is actually 'the subject of the unconscious' (Žižek 1998: 6).

The repetition of signifiers, far from operating as a guarantee of self-identity, undermines it, and so symbolic identification should be treated as a practice within which there is always the possibility of over-identification. This Lacanian view of identification does not try to seal itself off from what is different or shut down what is different to itself, as is the case in the dominant clinical problematic, which views over-identification as something to be avoided. Instead, 'the signifier has a fecundity because it is never in any case identical to itself', and the repetition of signifiers – such as 'War is War' – produces difference rather than being simply tautology (Lacan 2002a: 4). If we consider, for a moment, Laibach's chant, 'God is God', we can see how this functions to disturb rather than fix the signified that is attached to the signifier 'God'. This identification of God is already an over-identification that breaks down its unity into non-sensical signifiers, something we could see as 'reducing the signifiers into their nonsensicality'.[5] Psychoanalytic practice, then, is always a cultural practice.

IDENTIFICATION: WITH ŽIŽEK

Over-identification is a crucial part of Žižek's rhetorical strategy, and his writing still has some power to disturb and oppose taken-for-granted ideological forms. At the moment he homes in on a text or cultural phenomenon to analyse it, for that moment of analysis it is as if he over-identifies with it. The symbolic effect is that writer and reader over-identify with the text or phenomenon in question, taking it extremely seriously to deconstruct it from within; to unravel the ways in which the artistic conventions of its formal construction, the ideological motifs of its explicit and implicit semiotic structure, and the fantasy elements that tie us to it as something enjoyable all function together. His best work produced during the period of cultural–political struggle in Slovenia at the end of the 1980s did provide a new way of reading Lacan and new strategies for tackling ideology (see Žižek 1989). However, the repetition of themes from those early texts has bit-by-bit accommodated some more dubious notions. We will emphasize here those that show the most striking departures from Lacanian psychoanalysis, particularly in relation to the problematic of identification.

Notice how the references to Lacan often embed him in a series of charismatic individuals who initiate or formalize systems of thought. There is already a telling slippage from the particular distinctive trait of the signifier 'Lacan' to the personal relations between leader and follower, a regression from the symbolic identification to the worst of imaginary effects that Freud described in *Group Psychology and the Analysis of the Ego* (1921). So, for example, Žižek argues that 'Lenin did not just adequately translate Marxist theory into political practice – rather, he "formalized" Marx by defining the Party as the political form of its historical intervention – just as Saint Paul "formalized" Christ, and Lacan "formalized" Freud' (2002a: 191). Once the sequence is set up in this way we are led to wonder about the position of the author who formalizes such a series. That issue is not to be settled so easily, for there is another figure inserted in the psychoanalytic series: Jacques-Alain Miller, Žižek says, 'exerted a retroactive influence on Lacan himself, forcing him to formulate his position in a much more concise way', and he did this by 'introducing the reign of institutional terror' (2002a: 316). In response to ex-Millerians who accuse Miller of Stalinism, Žižek then shrugs it off: he is 'tempted to reply' – and he then does – 'why not?'; this is not 'self-destructive terror' but something 'of a totally different order in the psychoanalytic community – here the Stalin figure is a "good" one' (2002a: 316).

Here a political battle is displaced into the squabbles between psychoanalytic traditions, and his identification with the cause is as a member of a group, the loyal follower of a leader with whom he evidently identifies. This is why, for example, he repeats almost word for word Jacques-Alain Miller's own calls to battle with the International Psychoanalytic Association (IPA): 'we Lacanians are, on the contrary, the psychoanalytic army, a combative group working towards an aggressive re-conquest defined by the antagonism between us and them, avoiding, rejecting even the tolerant olive branch of the IPA' (Žižek 1999a). There are certainly serious differences between IPA tradition and Lacanian psychoanalysis, as can be seen in the opposition we rehearsed between over-identification in the dominant clinical problematic in that tradition and resistant subversive over-identification. But to pose the question in terms of battles of conquest and re-conquest is to fall straight into the domain of imaginary identification. Anecdotes about rivalrous Slovene peasants are designed to drum home the message that there would be 'an uncontrolled explosion of resentment' if there was an equal society; symptomatically, this kind of appeal to underlying love–hate relations is replicated in humorous asides during polemical attacks on colleagues of the form, 'Now we come to the bad part, bad for him, good for me, ha ha'.[6]

The fixation on great individuals rests on the assumption of self-identity (that A = A), and so Žižek is drawn ineluctably into attempting to advise those he appears to identify with. One striking characteristic of Žižek's politics is his oscillation between an enthusiastic embrace of a system of ideas or structure of authority and an attempt to escape from that embrace by way of an utter refusal which he tries to justify with reference to Lacan's notion of the psychoanalytic 'act' (see Parker 2004a). His concern with the predicament of Pope John-Paul II faced with the historically accumulated institutional problems of the Catholic Church (sexual molestation of children by priests, the activities of Opus Dei, and so on) is indicative: Vatican officials are concerned with a neutral stance that will pander to liberal sensibilities and they betray, as one example, the pope's 'spontaneous reaction' to the film *The Passion of the Christ* as truly showing the passion as it was. The pope is thus singled out by Žižek and identified as the figure who is struggling against those who betray him, and while he may ultimately have been an 'ethical failure', there still remains an admiration for this lone individual and the judgment that 'what was best in the late pope' was 'his *intractable* ethical stance' (Žižek 2005c).[7]

Admiration of and advice for strong leaders may be a function of the position of our author, now abstracted from collective political practice and formulating political proposals that do presuppose conscious individual appraisal and action. In this sense, Lacan's warnings about the lures of unitary consciousness and of the fiction that there is a 'subject supposed to know' seem quite apt. The appeal to psychoanalytic clinical categories from this individualized position then serves to buttress an ultimately conservative politics, even if it is occasionally given an ultra-leftist twist. Žižek's characterizations of psychoanalytic practice also often seem designed to frighten liberals, and they do not do analysts any favours. To defend Laibach on the grounds that they manipulate transference and force the audience to give up looking to them for answers, for example, risks importing a particular process from the clinic into cultural practice and ends up reducing politics to psychoanalysis.

Laibach are quite happy to play with psychoanalytic imagery, and to taunt their audience with the idea that they might bring them happiness or knowledge. The title track on the 2003 album, *WAT* (the title letters stand for 'We Are Time'), makes this clear: 'We have no answers to your questions / Yet we can question your demands / We don't intend to save your souls / Suspense is our device' (Laibach 2003). However, the interventions of NSK have always been attuned to precise political circumstances, and as collective practices (see Monroe 2005). Contemporary feminist discussion of Tanja Ostojić – of the pubic-hair black square, for example – is still quite happy to refer to Žižek's 1993 defence of Laibach, but also addresses the role of strategic essentialism and critical distance in practices of over-identification. Ostojić's 'Looking for a Husband with EU Passport' also tackles head-on the intersection between gender and cultural oppression, and navigates rather than simply refuses the ideological contours of liberal multiculturalism (Milevska 2005).

Whereas Lacan is careful to locate the 'permanent metaphor' of the self upon which psychoanalysis operates historically (2002a: 4), Žižek treats psychoanalysis as if it must be permanent, available as a point from which to offer diagnoses of other cultures. In this respect he is quite a psychoanalytic fundamentalist, something which should be distinguished from psychoanalytic practice as such. Perhaps this is why he urges 'radical leftists' (among whom he counts himself for these rhetorical purposes) never to forget that:

> It is the populist fundamentalist, not the liberal, who is, in the long term, their ally. For all their anger, the populists are not angry enough – not radical enough to perceive the link between capitalism and the moral decay they deplore (Žižek 2004c: 20).

Presumably the role that psychoanalysis has traditionally played in the struggle against 'moral decay' should be seen as radical, or made more radical still.[8]

Lacan was only ever useful for Žižek as a grid through which to read the German idealists, among which Hegel is the most prominent but Schelling is the touchstone. Despite the tendentious references to the 'act' in Lacan's work, what Žižek is really interested in is an 'act of free self-positing by means of which man tears the chain of causal necessity asunder, he touches the Absolute itself as the primordial abyss-origin of all things' (1996: 19). This should also dispel any illusions about Žižek's supposed 'Marxism', as should the assertion that the decision of the Vietcong to cut off the left arm of vaccinated children when they retook a village was part of a revolutionary strategy: 'this thorough rejection of the Enemy precisely in its helping "humanitarian" aspect, no matter what the costs, has to be endorsed in its basic intention' (2005a: 147).

Žižek's trajectory is away from Marxism toward fake-leftist individualism, of the kind trumpeted after the First World War by Renzo Novatore in his 'anarchist' text *Toward the Creative Nothing* (in which we will find more than a shade of Žižek's Schelling):

> Now more than ever we need an anti-democratic, anti-capitalist, anti-state revolutionary movement which aims at the total liberation of every individual from all that prevents her from living his life in terms of her most beautiful dreams – dreams freed from the limits of the market (Anonymous 2003).

There are serious consequences for those who would still like to see Žižek as a 'Marxist', and equally so for those who would still claim him as a 'Lacanian'. It is surely only a matter of time before Žižek arrives at the point where apparently dogmatic fidelity to psychoanalysis is abandoned and loving adoration is replaced with avid hatred; in the domain of imaginary identification and over-identification his first objections to Seminar VII – the ethics seminar – will undoubtedly spiral away from Lacan, perhaps into fully fledged anti-Lacanian fervour.[9]

When Slovenia joined the European Union in 2004, Žižek wrote a brief newspaper article to explain to readers what these 2 million or so people might have to offer the new Europe (see Žižek 2004d).[10] Europe has, of course, been a favourite reference point for Žižek as the locus of revolutionary struggle: 'The third world cannot generate a strong enough resistance to the ideology of the American dream. In the present world constellation, it is only Europe that can do it' (2005e). He had already been asked by the Slovenian government for advice during its successful referendum campaign to join NATO, and after that it would seem that his account of Slovenia's contribution should be taken very seriously. Now we are far away from the gently self-ironizing material produced by the 'Slovene Space Agency' circulating at NSK Cosmokinetic Theatre Noordung events in 2004, or other NSK 'transnational' initiatives that key into alternative networks across former Yugoslavia opposing geographically delimited state apparatuses (Jeffs 1995). Instead, we are in the world of European state power and the NATO bombing of Belgrade, which Žižek endorsed (even if the phrase from the email version which declared that 'not yet ENOUGH bombs, and they are TOO LATE' was deleted before publication for a Left readership).[11]

At a moment when NSK 'State in Time' could provide an antidote to the pretensions of Europe and each national component, Žižek neglected even to mention his former comrades. One conclusion would be that too close identification with state power, or an 'over-identification' that is bewitched with access to power has taken the place of resistant subversive over-identification. Žižek has travelled a long way from the most radical readings of Lacan and is mired in the worst forms of identification with authority and of hysterical complaint that glues him all the more closely to it. This is the unfortunate message in reverse true form sent back to him about the functional place of his radical posturing, the truth about over-identification in Žižek.

NOTES

1 For an example of an approach to this that does also conceptualize the problems over-identification entails for the analysand, see Mendelsohn 2002.
2 For an example of this problematic, see Hartmann 1958.
3 For a detailed history and analysis, see Monroe 2005.
4 For an account that shows the distance between Žižek's Hegelian Lacan and revolutionary Marxism, see Parker 2004.
5 This is a modified translation by Dany Nobus and Malcolm Quinn of the Alan Sheridan translation of Lacan (1979) – which is: 'reducing the non-meaning of the signifiers'. See Nobus and Quinn 2005: 189.
6 The colleague in question here was Ernesto Laclau, and the comments were made during Žižek's intervention 'Against the Populist Temptation' at the November 2005 London conference, 'Is the Politics of *Truth* Still Thinkable?' The intervention consisted mainly of pieces read out from published material on the French street protests, in which the anecdotes about the Slovene peasant appears – 'the witch tells him: "I will do to you whatever you ask, but I warn you, I will do it to your neighbour twice!" The peasant, with a cunning smile, asks her: "Take one of my eyes!"' (Žižek 2005b).
7 Note that he appears to commend the Pope's positive response to *The Passion of the Christ* and then later slips in the tendentious comment that 'the modern topic of human rights is ultimately grounded in the Jewish notion of the love for one's neighbor' (Žižek 2005c). Elsewhere, he claims that the book of Job provides 'the first exemplary case of the critique of ideology in the human history', and – in a comment that is directly relevant to over-identification – Christianity is 'the first (and only) religion to radically leave behind the split between the official/public text and its

obscene initiatic supplement' (Žižek 2005d). Praise for Christianity and disparagement of Judaism is a running theme in his work (see Parker 2004).

8 See, for example, the account of the relation of lesbianism and psycho-analysis in O'Connor and Ryan 1993. For Žižek's own uneasy comments on lesbianism, see Žižek 2002a: 323.

9 In a talk advertized as 'Slavoj Žižek's sermon defends the Judaeo-Christian heritage' – given at King's College Chapel, London, 8 December 2004 – Žižek commented that the ethics seminar is 'not my Lacan' because it allegedly endorses resignation to fate, a politics of acceptance, as opposed to an 'act' that will shake up the symbolic.

10 An extended version was published in *In These Times* on the same day under a different title (see Žižek 2004e). Nevertheless, in a foreword to a new book on NSK, he still declares that 'the lesson of Laibach is more pertinent than ever' (Žižek 2005).

11 See Žižek 1999b, and the discussion of the different versions of this article on the NATO bombing in Homer 2001.

'ANOTHER EXEMPLARY CASE': ŽIŽEK'S LOGIC OF EXAMPLES

Richard Stamp

Tout exemple cloche.
(Montaigne 2004)[1]

When asked (or asking himself) about his use of examples from popular culture, Slavoj Žižek adopts one of a number of possible personae: either the cold, 'machinic' theorist who proclaims utter indifference to his examples, liable to reverse his opinions about a given film should he chance upon a 'good theory'; or the obsessive neurotic who claims he can only begin to write when he is presented with an example, *any* example; or the fanatically faithful adherent for whom the same writers, filmmakers and composers will provide the 'exemplary case' of *any* conceptual theme; or the cynical ironist who happily repeats the same examples and verbatim passages of analysis in text after text, sometimes even openly acknowledging this fact to his readers; or even the perplexed, misunderstood author who feels his popularity to detract from his more 'substantial' work; or the self-confessed 'idiot' for whom the *failure* of every example yields the only proper relation of 'looking awry' at a properly universal Truth.[2] The argument of this present chapter is that the latter persona certainly provides Žižek's most consistent account of his use of examples; but by the same token, it disables in advance the certainty and coherence he accords to his own logic of examples.

But *is* Žižek being inconsistent here? Or, according to a tropism that he has made his very own, is not this inconsistency 'precisely' the most fanatically consistent feature of his prodigious published output? However, claims and counter-claims of consistency and inconsistency are, as Ian Parker notes, equally misplaced responses to Žižek's oeuvre: 'Every attempt to capture what he is really doing, as if it were possible for someone else to be a "Žižekian", will fail' (2004: 114). This is not least because these contradictory personae sign texts which similarly oscillate between a rigid, inflexible theoretical framework and a repetitive, quicksilver proliferation of examples. Indeed, this oscillation constitutes what is most distinctive, entertaining and not least *marketable* about Žižek's writing – his now well-established brand profile as 'the high theorist of pop culture', which is reiterated and reinforced in most of the available introductions to his work.[3] Yet this formal conjunction also poses particular problems for any attempt to define what is distinctive about 'Žižekian' discourse. Let us take, although not merely for example, Sarah Kay's '*Critical Introduction*' to Žižek, in which reading his books is analogized as 'an exhilarating ride on a rollercoaster' through a list of assembled categories, genres and proper names, 'etc. etc.' (2003: 1). In the repetition of this 'etc. etc.' lies the challenge of summarizing and introducing Žižek, which Kay makes clear in her pertinent observation that Žižek's books at once appear to be 'so carefully orchestrated' and yet 'so utterly shapeless' (2003: 7).[4] This latter point might be addressed by any number of sequences from Žižek's books. Again not merely for example, there is the opening chapter of *For They Know Not What They Do: Enjoyment as a Political Factor* (2002b), in which Žižek circles around Lacan's notion of the master signifier, or 'quilting point' (*point de caption*), via a seemingly endless series of examples: beginning with what he claims to be Freud's sole extant reference to Slovenia (Žižek's own 'place of enunciation' in this book, which originated as a series of lectures given in Ljubljana in 1989–90); Monty Python; Hegel's *Phenomenology*; *Gulliver's Travels*; Hans Christian Anderson; a short story by Ring Lardner; inversion in Marx and Adorno; G.K. Chesterton; *Vertigo*; Feuerbach; *Mein Kampf* and anti-Semitism; Frederic Jameson on *Don Quixote*; *The Ambassadors*; *Psycho*; the Hegelian monarch; the paradox of *bodhisattva*; the Dreyfus affair; Saint Paul. . . (2002b: 7–31). *Etcetera*. Whilst this is doubtless an eclectic mix, it is not as provocative or as obscene as other possible cases, and it should also be noted that not all of these examples will have been given equal weight. Žižek repeatedly returns to a number of them throughout this and subsequent books – indeed some are already repeated from his previous book, *The Sublime Object of Ideology* (1989).[5] So it already seems that there might be method in this 'apparent' madness. This is Kay's claim. She reads the characteristic shapelessness of such sequences in terms of an 'excess in examples', in which the 'seemingly' trivial illustration of an argument is that which opens up 'unexpected departures' in the attempt to 'write around' the real, that impossible element which each example in turn necessarily fails to grasp or effectively illustrate (Kay 2003: 9).[6] The sequential *form* of those examples just cited might therefore count for more than the examples themselves, insofar as each necessarily fails to embody that impossible exceptionality of the master signifier. This necessary failure to illustrate allows Kay to write off any 'misfit' between (high) theory and (popular) example as only ever 'apparent', insofar as the lack of 'fit' only ever exists *in order to* draw attention to Žižek's core problematic of the relation to the real, which is 'conjured' for the reader in his or her own labour of reading (Kay 2003: 11). The apparent lack of formal coherence, it is claimed, is the very form of 'Truth'. If this line of argument indicates the structural openness of the act of interpretation, by the same gesture it moves to shut down the possibility of reading. From the very beginning, Kay posits the final point of concordance of every example in the real, so that whatever meandering route such digressions may take, each and every example is *destined* for the real.[7] We can rest assured that it will all fit together as a whole in the end.

Admittedly, the attribution of teleological argument is strenuously denied by Žižek's own characterizations of his argument by examples. As we shall see, this 'excess in examples' thus attains a certain exemplary performative status in Žižek's Lacanian reframing of the status of exception in Hegelian 'concrete universality'. Indeed, the logic of Kay's argument echoes that of Žižek's own characterizations of a certain Hegelian 'failure' to realize the truth of the matter in hand itself being the Truth. This brings us back to Kay's other half of Žižek's 'style': its formal orchestration. It is, of course, this very *absence* of coherence in the sheer profusion of examples that *points to* Žižek's true, substantial 'point' – the thought of 'the "unassimilable [*sic*.] kernel" of the real' (Kay 2003: 15) as the very *form* of formlessness as such. In other words, it is the ultimate failure of any example that allows it to exemplify the real. This would mean that, in that sequence from *For They Know Not*, what matters for Žižek is not the examples as such, but that *excess* 'in them' which is in and of itself indicative of the operation of a logic of the master signifier, or quilting point: each and every example is understood as *always already* that exceptional, superfluous element ('the One') which sutures the entire symbolic field by becoming the *'general equivalent'* of all other elements therein (Žižek 2002: 21). This is why Ernesto Laclau could declare that *The Sublime Object of Ideology* 'is not a book in the classical sense', since its unity is derived neither from a 'pre-determined plan' nor a 'thematic discussion of a common problem', but from the *'reiteration* of [an argument] in different discursive contexts' (Laclau, in Žižek 1989: xii). The series of these reiterations cannot be understood in the sense of a *'progression'* (from point A to point B), but as a 'whole series of equivalences' (Myers 2003: 6) in which each new example reframes the concept being applied to it. One can begin to see Laclau's attraction to this hegemonizing logic of examples.

However, Žižek's logic of examples is both more extreme and less radical than Myers' phrase, 'series of equivalences', might suggest. This is because whilst it explicitly challenges Laclau's assumption of a panlogist Hegel, it also relies almost entirely upon the rhetorical operation of analogy and homology in the positing of the series (A is B is C, etc.).[8] It is the certainty of continuity provided by Kay's assurance of the only 'apparent' disjunction between theory and example that alerts us to the problem with examples and exemplarity in Žižek. Ultimately, there can be *no possibility* of a misfit, insofar as the exact same categorical register (such as R-I-S) or conceptual framework (such as *point de caption*) is read into *every* example as its truth. Even their common failure to capture the matter in hand is redeemed as proper to their impossible 'object'. This argument-by-homology has two consequences: *first*, these examples present no resistance to theory; and *second*, therefore, there is (paradoxically) no need for examples. Does this mean, then, that there are no examples *as such* in Žižek's work? The critical intent of these questions finds its strongest exponent, however, in Žižek himself. As already indicated, he gleefully admits to (ab)using his many examples: they are just so much grist to his theoretical mill. This is because the 'main attraction' of his writing 'for many a reader', he claims in his foreword to *The Žižek Reader*, is the way that 'the theoretical line is sustained by numerous examples from cinema and popular culture' (Wright & Wright 1999: viii). It is this 'apparently postmodern' style that serves as a 'proper symbolic lure', in which the appearance of an ebullient and 'compulsive' wittiness masks 'a fundamental *coldness'* and 'utter *indifference'* (Wright & Wright 1999: viii). Every posited example, for Žižek, is the displacement 'from an initial gap to the assertion of an unexpected continuity' of a properly philosophical position, which is the 'true focus' of his work (Wright & Wright 1999: viii). Thus, Žižek's gesture here is intended to situate *himself* as always a point of philosophical continuity in opposition to what he sees as the contemporary theoretical 'commonplace'; against the doxa of the 'proponents of contingency and finitude', he portrays himself as 'adher[ing] to the emancipatory pathos of universal Truth', standing alone (in not-so-mock heroic pose) against 'any reduction of the proper philosophical stance to a form of social or cultural criticism' (Wright & Wright 1999: ix–x). What is important to note here is the performative linkage between a homologizing exemplarity and a 'faithful' adherence to the philosophical propriety of the universal as it is in turn exemplified in repeated gestures of 'resisting the commonplace'. One might wonder whether the particular specificity of Žižek's examples count for anything at all.

This ambivalence towards his examples becomes all the more paradoxical in his foreword to the second edition of *For They Know Not*. When he retrospectively judges his 1991 book to have been 'a more substantial achievement' than the more successful *The Sublime Object of Ideology* (1989), it is because, he claims, the former is 'a book of theoretical *work*, in contrast to the succession of anecdotes and cinema references' that made the latter so popular (Žižek 2002b: xi). Žižek's confession of disappointment is staged in reaction to readers who admitted to finding *For They Know Not* 'a little bit boring after all the firecrackers of *The Sublime Object*' (2002b: xi). If we suspend any initial suspicion that this kind of 'confession' is self-serving justification for a reissue (since it is not as though he had much problem getting published in the meantime!), we might take it seriously enough to raise questions about the strategic importance of Žižek's rhetoric of exemplarity.

We might well ask: why was Žižek's first book in English so much more popular than his second? It cannot be a simple case of an opposition between 'theoretical *work*' and the more spectacular display of 'anecdotes and cinema references' because, as we have already seen, *For They Know Not* does not dispense with Žižek's trademark exemplarity – nor, as we shall see in the following section, is it possible for *any* philosophical argument to proceed without a practice of exemplarity. Addressing his readers in the first edition of this book, Žižek defines a certain *shared* enjoyment of popular culture as the 'place' or the 'symptom' for drawing out his three theoretical foci: Hegelian dialectics, Lacanian psychoanalysis and ideology (2002b: 2). The position and persona of analyst and analysand is far more undecided in this book than it is in *The Sublime Object*. The difference lies not merely in a shift of authorial position or persona, but in the fact that it is in this book that Žižek first begins to explicitly *work through* his ('Hegelian') logic of exemplarity. The point is that, as Žižek writes in his 2002 foreword, *For They Know Not* was already marked by a certain critical distance towards what he acknowledges to be the 'quasi-transcendental' arguments for a substantive Real put forward in the earlier book (2002b: xii). In other words, it is in part by turning to address for itself the logic of his use of examples that Žižek endeavours not only to explicate but to redraw his conception of universality. And as we shall see, this logic is not only built upon a particular reading of the operation of exemplarity in Hegel – particularly in the undoing of any rigid ontological division of universal–particular in *Phenomenology of Spirit* (1977) – but in being made to bear the entire weight of this operation, is parasitical upon a fetishistic disavowal of a certain 'deconstructivist' reading of the example in Hegel.

EXAMPLES FOR IDIOTS

Doesn't this discourse hang together (*se tient*) by basing itself on the dimension of stupidity?

(Lacan 1998: 12)

Žižek's preceding statements about his use of examples – as the 'symbolic lure' intended to draw readers into the true 'theoretical work' of mapping the disturbance of the impossible, traumatic kernel of the real – might lead his readers to suspect that they are being taken for idiots. Indeed, hyperbolic attributions of 'stupidity', 'idiocy' or 'imbecility' are key tropes in Žižek's descriptions of popular culture examples – but to *whom* or to *what* is such stupidity attributed? Žižek is adamant that the idiot is ('ultimately') *himself*:

Why do I resort so often to examples from popular culture? The simple answer is in order to avoid a kind of jargon, and to achieve the greatest possible clarity, not only for my readers but also for myself. That is to say, the idiot for whom I endeavour to formulate a theoretical point as clearly as possible is ultimately myself: I am not patronizing my readers. (2005: 59)

Žižek's explanation here rests upon a further analogy with the Lacanian notion of *passe*, the passage from analysand to analyst which requires the surrender of all mastery in the mediating process of translation and transference, giving oneself up to a loss of any final word (or meta-discourse) on the signifying process. Hence, for Žižek, it is as a stubborn element of idiocy that popular culture matters, making it the most appropriate medium for the requisite 'full acceptance of externalisation' of *passe*: 'I am convinced of my proper grasp of a Lacanian concept only when I can translate it successfully into the inherent imbecility of popular culture' (1994: 175). Yet this analogy results in a further ambiguity: Žižek's self-avowed (Socratic) idiocy lies in his 'inherent necessity to clarify things', which entails a repetition motivated by a failure to grasp the point of his example the first time around – 'I am not yet at the level of this example' (Žižek & Daly 2004: 43–44). We should not miss Žižek's game here: he claims that he is not patronizing his readers, that he himself is the idiot he's addressing; and yet popular culture is valuable precisely because of its '*inherent* imbecility'. This leads to a hypostasization of stupidity, whereby Žižek declares himself to be 'too stupid' to reach the level of 'inherent imbecility' in his example, as it is played off vertiginously against some projected point of 'full' understanding, development, or acceptance. Yet the repetition of the 'same' examples in subsequent texts – such as the shark in *Jaws*, the monster(s) of *Alien*, the joke about Rabinovitch, 'etc. etc.' – may or may not bring about variation in interpretation, let alone this certainty of 'fully develop[ing] its potential' (Žižek & Daly 2004: 43). Just who or what is being idiotic here becomes unclear: is the idiot really himself? Or is it rather the 'imbecilic' medium of the popular culture example in itself? And what of the reader who enjoys the 'fireworks' of *The Sublime Object* more than the 'boring' 'theoretical work' of *For They Know Not*? Once again, it is worth examining the rhetorical operation of exemplarity.

In declaring himself the idiot, Žižek takes up an ironic relation to a Kantian inheritance. According to Kant – in the *Critique of Pure Reason* (1958), at least – examples are at best learning aids for the intellectually infirm, for those who lack any 'natural talent' for judgment as the proper application of universal concepts to the particularity of experience.[9] Insofar as an example is something taken to stand for something else, it serves to illustrate an argument or principle by serving as a particular instance, or case, of the universal law (*qua* principle, idea, concept). But this is also why Kant is wary of examples, as he is of all representational thought: if thinking were to become reliant upon its examples, unable to proceed without their aid, it would never escape the particular. Indeed, this proves most worrisome for Kant when he comes to define the operation of 'transcendental judgment in general' at the start of the 'Analytic of Principles':

> Such sharpening of the judgment is indeed the one great benefit of examples. Correctness and precision of intellectual insight, on the other hand, they more usually somewhat impair. For only very seldom do they adequately fulfil the requirements of the rule (as *casus in terminis*). Besides, they often weaken that effort which is required of the understanding to comprehend properly the rules in their universality, in independence of the particular circumstances of experience, and so accustom us to use rules rather as formulas than as principles. Examples are thus the go-karts [*Gängelwagen*] of judgment; and those who are lacking in the natural talent can never dispense with them. (1958: 178)[10]

Examples may 'sharpen' the practice of judgment, but it is more usual that they blunt it by 'weakening', or even demolishing [*tun sie. . .einigen Abbruch*], the proper hold of the universal. Although the exercise of judgment may be benefited by the use of examples, it cannot and should never be allowed to rely upon them, since for Kant there can be no (teachable) rule for the *application* of a rule, for subsuming the particular case under the universal law. This is why 'judgment is a peculiar talent which can be practised only, and cannot be taught', whereas the understanding can always be instructed and equipped with rules (Kant 1958: 177). For Kant, the power of judgment is thus a 'gift' from nature – the 'so-called mother-wit [*Mutterwitz*]' – whose equally natural deficiency 'is just what is ordinarily called *stupidity* [Dummheit]' (1958: 177, 178 n. a [B173]). No example can overcome this 'inherent imbecility'. One may be able to teach others about the meaning of a rule, but a different talent is required to apply one. Thus, idiots in all professions – Kant mentions 'physicians', 'judges' and 'rulers' (!) – all rely upon examples because, although they may grasp a rule '*in abstracto*', they are 'unable to determine' whether a case ('*in concreto*') comes under it (Kant 1958: 178). The danger here is that of mixing, or confusing, the finite case with the properly infinite principle, of being 'unable to determine' the *proper boundaries* of and between the empirical and the transcendental. The stupidity of examples is to endanger what Kant considers to be the properly philosophical distinction of particular and universal.

Derrida identifies this dangerous instability of the example in Kant's text more precisely when he translates '*Gängelwagen*' as 'wheelchairs' [*roulettes*], which captures the sense of 'invalidity' of Kant's original term. It is a prosthetic device rather than a plaything, one that Kant has to withdraw at the very moment he leans upon it:

> The exemplary wheelchairs are thus prostheses which replace nothing. But like all examples (*Beispielen*), as Hegel will have pointed out, they play, there is play in them, they give room to play. To the essence, beside the essence (*beiher*), Hegel goes on to make clear. Thus they can invert, unbalance, incline the natural movement into a parergonal movement, divert the energy of the *ergon*, introduce chance and the abyss into the necessity of the *Mutterwitz*. (Derrida 1987b: 79)

Kant realizes that philosophy cannot dispense with the use of examples, but this supplementary role must be limited to providing 'adequate training', it cannot be allowed to replace the very thing it illustrates. Both 'sharpening' the intellect *and* 'dulling' the 'natural gift' of judgment, it is a dangerous supplement indeed. If reliance upon examples, for Kant, is certain sign of intellectual infirmity – that one is lacking in the 'natural power' of properly subsuming the particular case under the general law – then it is this parergonal *by-play* of the example [*Bei-spiel*] that drives Hegel's attempt in the *Phenomenology of Spirit* to unravel this formalisation of the distinction between universal and particular in the 'unrest' of determinate negation (Hegel 1977: 51 [§80]). It is in this sense that the *Phenomenology* is structurally overdetermined by the parergonal instability of its examples, those figures of consciousness which are staged by Hegel as a series of 'provisional scenes', each of which proves 'too limited to satisfy the subject's desire to discover itself as substance' (Butler 1987: 21). For Butler, as for Žižek after her, the necessary and repeated *failure* of these figures is the 'lesson' of Hegel's text.[11]

The restless procession of examples in the *Phenomenology* begins, of course, with the dialectic of sensuous certainty. Hegel famously draws attention to the way in which the simplest claim to the immediacy of truth necessarily involves the *play* of the example alongside the very 'essence' of which it is an instance. So that when we examine more closely the truth of pure immediacy claimed by consciousness of '*this*' particular phenomenon, we find that 'much more is involved [*spielt*]' insofar as 'actual sensuous certainty is not merely this pure immediacy, but an example [*Beispiel*] of it' (Hegel 1977: 59 [§92]; 1970: 83). It is in this sense that what is apparently the most simple act of knowing – such as apprehending this object before me – already installs, behind its own back, a 'distinction between essence and example', between immediacy and mediation (Hegel 1977: 59 [§93]). In other words, by looking 'around the back' of this performance, 'we' (Hegel and his reader) can see how the very immediacy of '*this* case' – that is, the truth of '*this* example' – is always already split into 'two "thises"': this *I* and this *object*, neither of which can be said to be '*immediately* present', since each one 'is at the same time *mediated*' by the other (1977: 59 [§92]). Insofar as it is only by passing through one another that the 'I' and the 'object' take on their truth for the consciousness, this mediation of 'I' and 'object' reveals the restless, performative 'play' between (universal) essence and (particular) example, *Wesen* and *Beispiel*. Hegel, as Derrida suggests, sets the example in play, always 'to the essence, beside the essence'.

Each figure in the *Phenomenology*, for Žižek, thus 'implies a kind of hysterical theatre' (2002: 143) insofar as it stages or reflects the very condition of a theoretical 'position' which must remain hidden or unspoken to retain its consistency. But it is this consistency that is lacking. It is in this respect that Žižek himself defines this 'restlessness' of Hegelian examples in terms of a certain *failure*: 'an example never simply exemplifies a notion; it usually tells you what is wrong with this notion' (Žižek & Daly 2004: 44). Hegel's *Phenomenology* is the 'exemplary' case of the putting-to-work of such failure in that it shows ('again and again') how 'the very staging actualisation' of a notion, of an 'existential stance' or attitude, always produces 'something more which undermines it' (Žižek & Daly 2004: 44). Indeed, Žižek's reading of *concrete universality* is itself staged in the context of a strategic reading of 'Derridean "deconstruction"', in which he chides critics of Hegelian dialectics for missing the point: what they take to be an exception, a remainder or an anomaly of the dialectic is, in fact, a basic feature of Hegelian thought (2002: 37).

MAKING AN EXAMPLE OF DECONSTRUCTION

An example always carries beyond itself: it thereby opens up a testamentary dimension. The example is first of all for others, and beyond the self.

(Derrida 1994: 34)

And yet Žižek does not *read* Derrida's text at all. His strategy is bound, once again, by the terms of a certain logic of exemplarity. Žižek first develops this logic in *For They Know Not* under the rubric of 'A "chiasmic exchange of properties"', a phrase borrowed from Andrzej Warminski's essay on the example in Hegel, 'Pre-Propositional By-Play': 'Hegel's difference between an exterior and passive *Beispiel* and an interior and active thought is more problematic than mere (sublatable) opposition, for the two sides contaminate one another by means of an (chiasmic) exchange of properties' (Warminski 1987: 110). But if this 'chiasmic' exchange between thought and example remains an 'undecidable' difference, what is the status of the example as such? Žižek appropriates Warminski's argument without acknowledging the particularity of his argument, or its context, which is about the act of *reading for examples*. Indeed, it is evident that Žižek is not all that interested in the rhetorical operation of the example *as such*, but in extracting from it the general law of the 'subject' *qua* the operation of reflexive negativity:

We could even say that this 'chiasmic exchange of properties' defines the very status of subject in Hegel's philosophy: 'substance becomes subject' by means of such an exchange of their respective 'properties' – the subject which is at first caught in its substantial presuppositions, 'embedded' in them – which is their passive attribute – retroactively 'posits' them, subordinates them to its form, makes them its own passive object. (Žižek 2002: 42)

Warminski's reading of the undecidability of the chiasmic exchange between thought and example, and their predicates (interior/active vs. external/passive), is recast by Žižek as 'the elementary matrix of the dialectical process' (2002: 42). Moreover, this very undecidability is 'resolved' in the form of (in Hegel's phrase) 'the most sublime example': the figure of Christ, in whom the properties of the human (example) and the divine (Idea) become 'indistinguishable', is the 'reflective "example of the example", the exemplification of the very principle of example)' (Žižek 2002: 42). Yet, as Warminski had already pointed out earlier in his essay, Hegel's 'most sublime example' is *no longer* an example – and brings an end to the very same restless movement between thought and example that Žižek is drawing upon. It whisks away the example when 'what "we" want. . .would be precisely the *Beispiel* of the meaning of meaning. . .that is still an example' (Warminski 1987: 100). What 'we' want, then, is the impossible: another thinking of the example, which cannot be subsumed under the law. For Warminski, it is only possible to ask: 'What would it be like, such an other *Beispiel* and its other temporality?' (1987: 100). An impossible question, perhaps.

Following Žižek's own logic of examples – that is, by following his example – it becomes possible to discern the extent to which the repeated denunciations of Derrida and deconstruction (through avatars such as Warminski) effectively install the 'unexpected continuity' of Žižek with the very thing he fights so hard against: the thing he names 'deconstructionism'.[12]

If thought, or at least the pedagogy of philosophical thinking, cannot proceed without examples, neither can it allow itself to rest upon them; nor can the singularity of any example remain outside relations of substitutability. If every example is singular, more than or other than simply 'an instance of. . .', it is at the same time *as* 'this' or 'that' example that it becomes open to reading. *Every example necessarily fails to do its job.* According to Derrida, such would be the aporia of exemplarity: 'The example is not substitutable; but at the same time the same aporia always remains: this irreplaceability must be exemplary, that is, replaceable. The irreplaceable must allow itself to be replaced on the spot' (Derrida 1998: 47). If, for Žižek, Warminski's reading of Hegelian *Beispiel* is exemplary of the logic of the subject – *qua* 'chiasmic exchange of value' – he can only subscribe to it insofar as he identifies a Hegelian anticipation (and therefore, inoculation) of this contaminative aporia. So why is it that Žižek takes Warminski's 'chiasmic reading' of Hegel's *Beispiel* to be exemplary of a 'deconstructive' approach to the Hegelian dialectic?

Equally, we might ask why it is that his preceding critique of Gasché's account of the operation of an infrastructural 're-mark' in Hegel's notion of reflection is held up as 'the clearest example' for a refutation of 'Derridean "deconstruction"' (Žižek 2002: 74). Why is it, in other words, that Žižek can only *make an example of* 'deconstruction(ism)' by *not* reading Derrida's texts?

It would be tempting to answer that Žižek reproduces in his own thinking the very 'style' of thought against which he works so hard to differentiate himself: to turn his own characterization of 'Derrida' and 'deconstructionist' readings of Hegel back upon himself – and thus to produce the neat conclusion that Žižek himself *is the exemplary case of what he criticizes, rejects, disavows*, etc.[13] Such a conclusion, however formally satisfying, must be resisted. Not least because it all too easily overcomes (by disavowing) the constitutive resistance provoked by 'taking precisely *this* example. . .'. This is more or less where we came in. We are back again with the performative 'idiocy' of Žižek's examples – and, as we have seen, these are all examples (or personae) *of* Žižek: 'the idiot. . .is ultimately *myself*'. But we are also always already circulating within the terms of what Derrida calls a 'very old children's game': every time I utter, 'Now take precisely *this* example. . .', I set in motion a 'performative fiction' which signifies *at once* the absolute singularity of this example *and* its general exchangeability for every other example in a signifying chain (Derrida 1995: 18). *Is this not precisely* the logic of Žižek's examples?

Furthermore, Žižek's 'will to exemplify', his drive for examples, installs him all the more securely within the very apparatus of liberal pedagogy he claims to eschew; exemplarity as a rhetorical practice secured by the performative linkages of irony, ideology and institution. Even when he is careful to distance his (Hegelian) logic of examples from that (Kantian) understanding of every example as ultimately inadequate to the ideal it represents, it is still the case in his counter-conception that it is he/we (idiots all!) who fail to grasp the full import of the example until afterwards (*après-coup*), 'in the next book'. Thus, the narrative unfolding of this logic of examples remains rooted in Kant's liberal pedagogy of the first and third critiques (see Lloyd 1995). It is in this sense that Žižek's examples are, in fact, incidental illustrations of an already installed machine. For all the quasi-Hegelian bluster about 'concrete universality', he *does not need* the examples he proclaims as his symptom/*sinthome*. In a certain sense, nothing need be added for it to work. This peculiar theoretical self-sufficiency might be contrasted to deconstruction, which is nothing without an '*and*', almost nothing but its examples in their aporetic singularity (Derrida 2000). Žižek's almost absolute proximity to those 'Derridean' or 'deconstructionist' readings of Hegel – which are never 'Derrida's', of course, but those of Warminski and Gasché – might prompt us to read him as a 'deconstructionist-in-disavowal'; a disavowal that Žižek himself would have to call *fetishistic*. Certainly, he performs his now customary disavowal of a given 'deconstructive' reading by always countering that what it states as a criticism of Hegel is already anticipated, taken up and affirmed by Hegel himself.[14] This is a serious failure to understand the precise sense in which deconstruction is not reducible to a method, a theory or, indeed, a 'philosophy'. Indeed, it is nothing without its *examples*; it takes place at/as the very limit of every gesture of 'taking *this* example. . .' On the other hand, however, we must not cede Hegel to Žižek's reading either: it is not simply that Žižek gets Derrida wrong, but that he cannot read Hegel's text without reducing it to a set of formalizable principles; nor without losing sight of that aporetic logic of examples which, *only after* Derrida and Warminski, he locates in the Hegelian text.

So what, after all, is an example? As we have seen, Žižek's focus on the logic of examples in Hegel's *Phenomenology* (and elsewhere) sparks questions about the metaphysical grammar of exemplarity: is it possible to think the example otherwise than as the illustration of a pre-established universal concept? What would an example that was not subsumable under such a general law (of the concept) look like? Is it even possible for examples to resist their subsumptive incorporation by concepts? What thinking of singularity would this exemplary resistance (if there is any) produce? Yet Žižek asks none of these questions. Nor could he, since he already has his answers.

NOTES

1 Translation: 'Every example is lame'. Or, more appropriately in the present context: 'Every example goes awry'. Removed from the context of Montaigne's seventeenth-century French, the verb *clocher* is now less often used to refer to possessing a limp, but more to convey a sense of something (or someone) being defective: *il y a quelque chose qui cloche* is used to convey the sense that 'something is up', 'doesn't fit', 'goes wrong'

or 'is not quite right'. As a noun, *la cloche* is not only a 'bell', but also an 'idiot': as we shall see, the idiocy or stupidity of examples is central to Žižek's inheritance of a Kantian discourse of exemplarity as a dangerous supplement to properly philosophical thinking.

2 These personae are deployed respectively in: Wright & Wright 1999; Boynton 1998 ('For me, life exists only insofar as I can theorize it'); Žižek & Daly 2004; Patricia Highsmith, to give but one example, is 'the One' (see Žižek 2003); too numerous to list, but one might track the Rabinovitch joke(s) from Žižek 1989 to Žižek 1999 (and many points in-between); Žižek 2002; Žižek 1994, 2005.

3 See the introductions to 'Introductions' by Kay (2003), Myers (2003) and Butler (2005), all of whom begin from the positing of just such a signature. As will become clear, such is that contradictory nature of this discourse that any attribution of a systematic 'logic' is doomed to delude. See the cogent deduction of the absence of *any* Žižekian system in Parker 2004.

4 In fact, *Žižek: A Critical Introduction* is notable for its *lack* of criticism of its subject. Critical engagement is also scarce in Butler 2005 and Žižek and Daly 2004, both of which involve Žižek's direct participation. Leaving aside Tony Myers' useful introduction for Routledge (2003), we are left with Ian Parker's book for Pluto which, as Yannis Stavrakakis rightly points out, represents 'the *only* critical introduction to Žižek' (2004, front jacket blurb).

5 Indeed, as we shall see, Žižek himself insists on the dissimilarity of these two books. Žižek's 'cut-and-paste' methodology is adeptly diagnosed in Mowitt 2002.

6 Kay lists three altogether, the other two features being 'obliqueness' (formal analogy) and 'personal style' (humour) (2003: 8–12).

7 The question here is, of course, whether 'the letter always arrives at its destination', that dispute between Lacan and Derrida which stemmed from Derrida's critical response to Lacan's symptomatic reading of literature in '*Le facteur de la vérité*': 'From the outset, we recognise the classical landscape of applied psychoanalysis. . .An example destined to "illustrate," in a didactic procedure, a law and a truth forming the proper object of a seminar' (Derrida 1987a: 425–26). See also those texts assembled in Muller & Richardson 1988.

8 This exchange is played out most directly in both Butler and Laclau's opening salvoes in *Contingency, Hegemony, Universality* (Butler at al. 2000) – 'Restaging the Universal' and 'Identity and Hegemony', respectively – with Žižek's response in '*Da Capo senza Fine*'.

9 In the *Critique of Judgment*, the role of examples and the exemplary will occupy a central and (importantly) paradoxical role in Kant's analysis of judgments of taste, although it preserves his essential suspicion that over-reliance upon examples constrains and cripples the power of judgment. Hence, in the case of genius, examples are for 'following' [*Nachahmung*] not 'imitation' [*Nachmachung*] (1987: §47). For a detailed contextualized analysis of Kantian exemplarity in relation to taste and genius, see Lloyd 1995.

10 Joan Copjec is alluding to this passage, of course, in her blurb for *Enjoy Your Symptom!*: 'Kant called example the "go-kart of judgment". His description can now be described as pre-Žižekian. This [book] updates Kant, turning example into a whirling, dizzying, linear-logic defying turbo-jet of judgment' (Žižek 2001, rear jacket blurb).

11 In what we might read as a '*proto*-Žižekian' gesture, Butler analogizes the relentless mishaps of Hegel's 'instructive fiction' with the cartoon misadventures of Mr Magoo (!): 'Like the miraculously resilient characters of the Saturday-morning cartoon, Hegel's protagonists always reassemble themselves, prepare a new scene, enter the stage armed with a new set of ontological insights – and fail again' (1987: 21).

12 It is difficult to think of any commentator on that awkward thing, 'deconstruction', who so deliberately and mockingly utilizes the terms 'deconstruction*ism*' or 'deconstruction*ist*'. As I have noted elsewhere (Stamp 2003), no one ever uses this term to be nice!

13 As Barbara Johnson notes (before going on to repeat it herself!) this strategic game of textual 'one-upmanship [and] inevitable one-downmanship' is, well, exemplary of the relations between (Derridean) deconstruction and (Lacanian) psychoanalysis (Muller & Richardson 1988: 218). There is much wrong with this picture, and so much to do to correct it – insofar as attempts at correction, like Irene Harvey's short survey of the 'unthought' structures of exemplarity in these interpretations and counter-interpretations of Poe's 'Purloined Letter', merely repeat the problem – that a reference here to Geoff Bennington's 'Circanalysis (The Thing Itself)' will have to stand as an indication of the scope of the task to be undertaken: to (re-)read Freud and Lacan with a view to picking up 'the trace of a singular, original, nervous relation between psychoanalysis and deconstruction' (Bennington 1998: 107).

14 Geoff Bennington has noted the familiar rhetoric of such disavowal not only in the work of Žižek with regard to Hegel, but also in the work of Gillian Rose (on Hegel, again), Barbara Johnson (on Lacan) and others: 'This type of reading', he states, 'has the merit of bringing out, negatively, a certain negative truth of deconstruction' – that is, the sense in which deconstruction is *not* a theory to be applied to a given text, but is always 'already-there' in Hegel, Lacan, etc. (Bennington 1998: 106). It is in this sense that the different halves of Butler's and Laclau's partially successful critiques of Žižek's 'Hegelian' 'concrete universal' find their target. See their initial contributions to Butler et al. 2000.

DENIAL, ANGER AND RESENTMENT

Jeremy Valentine

> No one has ever died from contradictions.
> (Deleuze & Guattari 1977: 151)

LEFT-WING FOGEYISM: A MENOPAUSAL DISORDER

Let's start with the good news. According to Buchanan (2005), socialism will survive and expand in the twenty-first century. The prediction is significant because Buchanan is one of the major advocates of Public Choice Theory (PCT), a political project that stands in relation to mainstream Rational Choice Theory in political economy as al-Qaeda does to the Taliban in monotheism. It is the economic theory which has probably had most influence on the policies and actions of governments since the 1970s, and which is distinguished by pushing the behavioural assumption that people are basically lazy and will try to get what they want with the least inconvenience to themselves, despite what they say otherwise (Valentine 2005). Thus, the real reason a beggar who self-amputates in order to receive alms does so is because the benefit is greater than cost of the loss of the limb and easier than working. For PCT the only role of government is to create and maintain the circumstances where this will not be the case, but not by redistributing wealth to those in need, as doing so will provide a further 'perverse incentive' to be needy. And nor by the al-Qaeda solution, which is to amputate everyone, because of the expense of subsidizing an economy in which wealth derives from status. In fact, what governments should do is abolish themselves as much as possible as not only do they produce nothing but simply ponce off the wealth produced by others through taxation, they also provide a risk-free career opportunity for those who prefer to sit back and live off the fat of land. All government is gang-sterism, all politicians are pimps. So by applying the lessons of PCT we will stop hanging around outside Tesco Metro singing the more inane selections from the Bob Marley songbook, or getting pregnant at 12, or working in the 'public sector', and turn into dynamic self-staring entrepreneurs who 'embrace risk'. Yeah, right.

Buchanan's prediction means that the PCT project has failed. Do not get too excited though, as by socialism PCT means nothing more than 'collectivized controls over individual liberty of actions' and not 'collective ownership and control of the means of production', which is dead and buried (Buchanan 2005: 19–20). Neither is socialism about elites deciding the best interests of the masses, although this is still alive in unpopular health and environmental crusades, and re-distribution according to Rawlsian liberal-democratic principles of fairness is on its last legs. Rather, socialism is now 'parental', the triumph of 'the attitudes of persons who seek *to have values imposed upon them* by other persons, by the state or by transcendent forces' (Buchanan 2005: 23). According to PCT, what has gone wrong is that people prefer subjection, and thus prefer dependency to freedom, of which they are afraid. They prefer it because it allows them to 'escape, evade and even deny personal responsibilities' (Buchanan 2005: 19) because most of them are too weak to accept them. Socialism is thus 'bottom up'.

PCT underpins this approach with the economic category of 'rent-seeking', that is, the attempt to establish a source of wealth that is non-productive and thus 'unearned', and over which ownership guarantees exclusive use. Rent is just the general term for unearned income and greater reliance on it decreases the aggregate production of wealth and should therefore be eliminated. Because of their past dependency on the outcomes of feudal gang wars, governments are the biggest rent-seekers in the game and spend the income they get from taxation trying to protect themselves and their cronies from 'free-market' competition. But the explanation reveals a fundamental flaw in PCT – albeit one of many – which is its dependence on a prior assumption of subjective moral consistency and absence of contradiction as the ground of economic action. This dependence takes the form of a prior commitment to the moral desirability of some economic activities over others, located at the level of the sub-jectivity of economic agents themselves. The moral assumption is necessary to the PCT project because, as Hindmoor (1999) points out, the distinction between 'rent-seeking' and 'profit-seeking' activity is the expression of a purely subjective preference, since the economic consequences of economic activities are uncertain at 'T1' (the point in time when they are considered), and can only be identified retrospectively at 'T3' (the point in time when they are realized), where 'T2' constitutes the economic action itself. Therefore: 'To accuse someone of rent seeking is to say simply that you do not approve of what it is their investment is intended to achieve' (Hindmoor 1999: 440). Rent-seeking is therefore not a sufficient explanation of the types of economic behaviour that PCT wants eliminated. Thus for PCT the moral desirability of the economic agent is secured by a categorical imperative, even if its content is not Kantian; a hidden transcendental, invented in order to eliminate the uncertainty that economic activity relies on by identifying the economic agent with the resources of moral purity. Be productive!

Unfortunately, this moral supplement undermines the behavioural assumption that makes the explanation possible, since both rent-seeking and wealth-producing can only derive from the same propensity to self-interest maximization, and are thus undecidable. That is why PCT's confidence in the persistence of a form of socialism is misplaced because, on Buchanan's account, it is likely that everyone will simply evade the values which they allegedly want to have imposed on them in order to maximize their self-interest. That explains why the more recognizable versions of socialism have evaporated as they entail a commitment to restraining the pursuit of self-interest. But it also explains why it has not been replaced by a universal desire for self-reliance, and why what Buchanan calls 'parental' socialism will suffer the same fate. It does not follow from a requirement that the state provide free medical care that its recipients will do anything in return. That is why the middle classes in welfare states milk the system for all they can get out of it. Evidence of the force of moral inconsistency is regularly provided by opinion polls where, typically, people will say that they want less traffic on roads, and will explain their preference in terms of the opportunities it will provide for them to drive faster. After all, there is no reason why one should not say one thing and do another. By assuming that there is, Buchanan mistakenly assumes the consistency of the problem, as if everyone is in reality a timid university student who does not want the shame of being caught in a contradiction through 'dialogue' with a lecturer in a class.[1] Just because people may want some controlling authority it does not follow that they will be controlled, and even less be prepared to pay for it, unless they are already morally consistent in the way that Buchanan thinks they ought to be. But if they were, they would not do the things of which Buchanan disapproves. Through such inconsistencies people preserve their liberty without the burden of responsibility and escape the state's attempt to take it away, even if formally they have provided the legitimacy for it to do so.

There is, of course, a more substantial criticism of PCT that links the interminable psycho-babble of individual motivation with a rational account of political economy. An elementary psycho-Marxist interpretation of Buchanan's argument would conclude that it is in denial about contemporary economic reality. This is because it disavows the existence of capitalism. Capitalism is 'an unfortunate and widely used term'; '("free enterprise" would be a much better term here)' (Buchanan 2005: 20, 28). That is, Buchanan is deliberately ignorant of the fact that economic exchanges are determined by capitalism, particularly the market in 'free' labour, and cannot be abstracted as an autonomous cause. You would think that a Professor of Economics who works in a building named after himself at George Mason University had heard of Adam Smith! Free enterprise would not survive for one second without state regulation.[2]

One should not be surprised by Buchanan's coyness about capitalism, as it is consistent with an epistemological argument provided by another PCT advocate to explain the alleged return of mass dependency on transcendental authority. According to Cowen (2005), the persistence of the state is a consequence of a mass self-deception or 'confirmation bias' in which people ignore the evidence of the superiority of the free-market in order to preserve their own prejudices, or 'pride goods'. Thus, in order to maximize the utility of feeling good about themselves and avoid the dis-utility of thinking hard about a difficult decision, people prefer ignorance of the facts, especially since, apparently, 'lack of self-deception, in fact, is a strong sign of depression' (Cowen 2005: 440). Physician heal thyself! The PCT project is just a colossal case of resistance and transference, one symptom of which is Buchanan's proposal simply to educate people about 'the spontaneous order of the market', so that they will see that its benefits outweigh the costs of dependency (2005: 27). The assumption is that people will pay for the privilege of this experience; an expectation that has re-structured the institutions of education globally. Freedom is responsibility. Yeah, right. If economic agents had absolute knowledge the market would be eliminated either by the disaster of monopoly or the catastrophe of perfect equilibrium. Morally upright entrepreneurs have to be a bit stupid in order to get up in the morning and go out and 'grow' their businesses because if they knew the truth, the statistical likelihood of failure, they would stay in bed, which probably explains why workers in corporate America 'go postal' at the slightest hint that someone will rain on their parade. The PCT project is nothing more than a massive dose of pseudo-intellectual Prozac to remedy the serotonin deficiency of individual capitalists as a consequence of their experience of the reality of capitalism. Never mind touchy-feely therapy, what PCT needs is a good dose of old-fashioned, no-nonsense ECT.

But now the bad news. Žižek wants to provide capitalism with moral consistency by denouncing the fact that it lacks it and thus, amongst other things, to put people like Buchanan back into the security of their fantasy in order to expose it as a contradiction. Žižek argues this in the midst of the creative destruction of contemporary capitalism, concluding that the revolutionary exception would be a ' "stable" ethical position' that would 'revolutionize an order whose very principle is constant self-revolutionizing' (2004a: 213). That is to say, the revolution would simply mirror what capitalism does not have and thus provide the supplement of stability. For Žižek, when capitalism realizes its stability is illusory, it will collapse. Or, as he explains in a response to some rather feeble feminist criticisms: 'It is not I who am to be deposed; it is they who fear their own deposition' (Žižek 1999c: 96). Hence, Žižek's notion of revolution is essentially conservative, since it aims to replace something that capitalism has destroyed. In doing so it converges with the Right-wing and conservative reaction to the loss of its own certainties about capitalism, such as with PCT, and can be objectively described as a sort of 'Left-wing fogeyism' – a menopausal disorder that mirrors the infantile communist one. It is designed to appeal to the same individual capitalists that constitute PCT's constituency, who cannot understand that no matter how much hard work they put in, they still cannot rely on any guarantees. So let's just sit back and have a laugh at the way that Žižek invents the necessity of an ethical position through which everyone will be constrained.

ŽIŽEK'S ENORMOUS DIALECTICAL DILDO

As is obvious to everyone, Žižek's strategy is to target radical accounts of capitalism that locate its agency in its destructive power through which the force of contingency is universalized. Following Marx and Engels's *Manifesto* (1967), this aspect of capitalism is a good thing because – all together now – 'man is at last compelled to face with sober senses, his real conditions of life, and his relations with his kind', although it is unlikely that one would be entirely sober in such circumstances. Against Marxist radical materialism, Žižek wants to see the recreation of the transcendental illusions that capitalism profaned and, no doubt, guaranteed salaries for people to establish and maintain them, as appointed by himself. One of the ways that he does this is by trying to show that everything radical materialism affirms is already comprehended by its intellectual opponent: the Hegelian dialectic. Thus, for Žižek, Hardt and Negri's 'multitude' is in fact simply the dialectical other of centralized state power and, following Laclau, is just another charismatic populism (Žižek 2004a: 197–98). Except, of course, that for Hardt and Negri 'multitude' is everything that the defence of particularities through their universalization is not. Žižek's deflationary ambition is assisted by reference to a Hegelianized Lacan, which derives its authority from the structure of the Oedipus complex in order to show that absolute knowledge is the realization that you are more fucked-up than you thought you were, for systemic reasons that condition your ability to think anything at all. For Žižek, these systemic reasons are the properties of the symbolic in and through which all thought takes place and which can only be understood with the aid of what he calls 'dialectical materialism'.

For Žižek, the ringleaders of contemporary radical materialism are Deleuze and Guattari, and the tool of their trade is their book, *Anti-Oedipus* (1977). Žižek was so incensed about it that he wrote a book denouncing it, *Organs without Bodies* (2004a), which title puns on 'bodies without organs', one of the key phrases in *Anti-Oedipus* which they took from Artaud. The point of the exercise is to rescue a Deleuze who allegedly is much closer to psychoanalysis and Hegel, and thus on Žižek's home turf, from a Deleuze who (with Guattari) is simply an ideologist of digital capitalism passed off as its radical critique; 'the ideology of the newly emerging ruling class' (2004a: 193) or 'netocracy'. Although it is true that many recent cyber-gurus cite Deleuze and Guattari as an authority, the basis of the allegation is Deleuze and Guattari's constant affirmation of any forms of instability that they can think of as radical anti-status quo forces for the better. Hence, one could not get a Rizla paper between Deleuze and Guattari's notions of de-territorialization and de-coding and the dislocatory force of capitalism. The advantage of the terms in which Žižek establishes a critical framework is that they slander the anti-psychoanalytical and anti-Hegelian basis of Deleuze's radical reputation in order to rescue him from the 'bad influence' of Guattari, thus isolating the real troublemaker. According to Žižek, Deleuze is 'Guattarized' because Guattari provides him with an alibi with which to escape from the deadlock of the duality of the disruption of the event and the immanence of becoming that arises in Deleuze's single-authored works, principally in *The Logic of Sense* (1990) and *Difference and Repetition* (1994) respectively, which are elevated over the books co-written with Guattari. The alibi is just an arbitrary decision to elevate one term of the opposition, the destabilizing one, over the other on the grounds that the former is good and the latter is bad. Although such a decision is perfectly consistent with Marx's emphasis on revolutionary capitalism, for Žižek the correct dialectical-materialist approach to the problem is that event cannot be reconciled with either becoming or being, but is that which emerges from becoming to unify the irreducible 'multitude of particularities' as being (2004a: 28). The event is Žižek's new moral order which stabilizes the becoming of capitalism by overturning it, replacing it with what it cannot be, and which is, of course, only capitalism stabilized. Despite the fact that this approach is merely a crude instrumentalization of Heidegger's non-Hegelian research on the historicity of being, Žižek's hope is that some sort of *ereignis* in which *princeps* and *principium* coincide will happen as a position from which to depose the existing order through establishing a new one. Žižek's word for this order is symbolic.

In order to universalize the symbolic in which everything is in its proper place, Žižek emphasizes the difference between the status of rupture in Deleuze and Guattari and in Hegel. For Žižek, Deleuze is split metaphysically and politically between leftist self-organization as continuity with becoming, and the 'sense-event' that transforms reality by establishing a new order. For Žižek, only Hegel's dialectic can give a consistent account of change and newness, which is universal because it reconciles contingency with the necessity of the thought that thinks it, whereas for Deleuze and Guattari it is simply a matter of immanence which does not require the mediation of self-consciousness. In fact, the differences between Hegel and Deleuze and Guattari boil down to those between their apparently rival explanations of how the stability of being can emerge from the flux of becoming. According to Žižek, for Hegel 'immanence generates the spectre of transcendence because it is already inconsistent in itself' (2004a: 61). But this is exactly what Deleuze and Guattari affirm, and in doing so emphasize the illusory nature of transcendence. The real difference is that for Deleuze and Guattari there is nothing necessary about such an illusion, as it is itself inconsistent; or, to put the same thing differently, the illusion is necessary only because everything that is is necessarily so. Consistency is the illusion that what is is everything that is, whereas for Žižek and Žižek's version of Hegel it is the ground of reason itself from which the necessary and contingent can be distinguished. Hence, in principle, the symbolic is necessary.

Of course, as this lapse into the complications of the distinction between necessary and contingent suggests, the real disagreement is not between Žižek's Hegel and Deleuze and Guattari, but between Hegel and Spinoza. Hence, Deleuze and Guattari's term for Spinoza's joy is schizophrenia, in which the uncertainty of infinity is embraced at the cost of abandoning the deceptions of illusory and finite certainty, and which is derived from typically Spinozist formulations such as the distinction between *natura naturans* – nature viewed as active, the dimension of contingency – and *natura naturata* – nature viewed as passive, the dimension of necessity – with all the permutations that derive from whether it is God or nature or humans that are doing the viewing. Deleuze and Guattari improvise on the Latin of Spinoza's perspectivism in the following explanation, in which history stands for active contingency, and through which the duality of necessity and contingency is preserved. Thus:

> We can say that social production, under determinate conditions, derives primarily from desiring-production: which is to say that *Homo naturata* comes first. But we must also say, more accurately, that desiring production is first and foremost social in nature, and tends to free itself only at the end: which is to say that *Homo historia* comes first. (Deleuze & Guattari 1977: 33)

The topic concerns the basic materialist premise that whatever is is in a particular case, or 'determinate conditions'. To be sure, change happens, and is understood as catastrophic and without reason or ground, as the mark of the finitude of human understanding of its necessity, since determination is infinite and can only be grasped through the necessarily limited historical circumstances in which it exists. Hence the priority of the historical–social. Crucially, the same principle applies to the catastrophe of transcendence and its illusions. But Žižek does not show how Hegel can explain this phenomenon either, only positing the necessity of its effects which are in reality contingent. It is those effects that Deleuze and Guattari oppose precisely because they masquerade as necessary, hence the radical nature of their position. So when Žižek concedes that 'the Event is *nothing but* its own inscription into the order of Being, a cut/rupture in the order of Being on account of which Being cannot ever form a consistent all' (2004a: 107), he affirms as a breakthrough the very impasse that his critique of Deleuze and Guattari was supposed to overcome, despite persistently grounding freedom retroactively in a subject constituted as the ground and failure of the symbolic. In contrast, for Deleuze and Guattari, being is all there is and all there is is neither closed nor complete. There is no opposition between being and becoming because becoming is being. So the difference between Žižek's Hegel and Deleuze and Guattari's Spinoza is simply one of pedagogical strategy and the ends to which it is put. For Žižek, these ends are clear: it is better to believe in transcendence for political reasons because it provides a position from which society can be ordered.

One symptom of Žižek's failure to defeat Deleuze and Guattari with Hegel is the failure of what is normally the canny t'ai chi tactic of using the strength of your enemy to defeat your enemy. Thus, in order to subvert Deleuze and Guattari, Žižek adopts one of Deleuze's methodological innovations: he proposes to bugger Deleuze in the same way that Deleuze argues that the correct approach to philosophy is buggery. But in fact Žižek immediately announces that Hegel will do it with some sort of monstrous strap-on dildo with which he is able to bugger himself, and which summarizes the movement of the dialectic itself (2004a: 48) – precisely, up its own arse.[3] So the method is applied by proxy.[4] Žižek arranges this scene in order to correct a lapse in Deleuze's application of his method whereby, allegedly, Hegel and Oedipus are simply the opposite of everything that Deleuze affirms – 'them' to Deleuze's 'us'. Žižek thus introduces antagonism and duality into Deleuze's positive monism in order to show that Hegel and Oedipus are already within Deleuze; with Deleuze as passive receptor, femme to Hegel and Lacan's butch – or '2 up', if you will. We will consider the relation between Deleuze and Guattari and Lacan in more detail in the next section. Here we can simply note the consequences of the fact that any opposition between Deleuze and Guattari and Hegel is not of the order of contradiction, and is therefore not governed by Hegel's dialectic. Instead, it is antagonistic in the sense that it does not occur on the ground of objective differences.[5] Yet for some reason, Žižek prematurely withdraws from the conclusion that since the relation between Deleuze and Hegel and Oedipus is antagonistic, this can only be a consequence of the ultimate impossibility of distinguishing them.

In this respect, we are already witnesses to the typical hardcore pornography scene Žižek refers to where 'the very unity of the bodily self-experience is magically dissolved, so that the spectator perceives the bodies as a kind of vaguely coordinated agglomerate of partial objects', and which for Žižek is exemplary of the notions of a multiplicity of intensities and desiring machines introduced in *Anti-Oedipus* (2004a: 184). Thus, hardcore – antagonism – becomes the collapse of the symbolic, which in Žižek's anthropology is a structured hierarchy of places and positions that individuals occupy in order to become subjects, exercising the power, but also duties, that the place somehow provides. Although this explanation of the symbolic is supposed to explain the necessity of the phallic signifier, it does not happen. Žižek simply proceeds to illustrate the use of the phallus as an organ without a body, one 'that I put on, which gets attached to my body, without ever becoming its "organic part", namely, forever sticking out as its incoherent, excessive supplement' (2004a: 87). The choice is clear: either the Viagra of the organic phallus; or the performance of the strap-on signifier. Žižek prefers the latter option and in that respect occupies the imaginary position of the 'butch lesbian' because – *pace* Butler (1993: 127) – the 'lesbian phallus' is the phallus *tout court* (Žižek 2004a: 99). Hence the emphasis on the symbolic as free of the bodily drives, although one would not rely on Žižek's knowledge of it. After all, he's a man who thinks that a pearl symbolises 'the vagina'.

Žižek is thus trapped in the symbolic, gazing out at the real of sexuality, looking at himself in the bathroom mirror to admire his strap-on, like a bureaucrat, with Hegel up his arse. And that is nothing to be ashamed of. But it does make his explanation of the epistemological privilege of sexuality look a bit odd. Sexuality over-flows the symbolic so that finally everything symbolizes sex in a 'universal innuendo' (Žižek 2004a: 91) because sex always fails, and this excessive sexuality is lack. Surely this simply shows that the symbolic always fails to master sex, and that its lack is the fullness of sexuality, the excess of drive and desire which Deleuze and Guattari affirm any chance they can get? Although Žižek eventually concedes this point, characterizing both Deleuze and psychoanalysis in terms of a *'phenomenology without a subject'* (2004a: 96), it does not alter his assertion that 'an element is always logically preceded by the place in the structure it fills out' (2004a: 92). No surprise then that, for Žižek, 'the phallic element as the signifier of "castration" is the fundamental category of dialectical materialism' (2004a: 91); the non-sense that distributes sense. Yet he has not demonstrated the necessary character of the content of this event, and cannot do so from the spectator's side of the symbolic screen. It is merely the formal emptiness of non-sense, which can be designated only from within the symbolic – the strap-on. Consequently, Žižek's objective position is nothing more than that of a spectator at a sort of meta-physical dogging. All of which naturally brings us to the question of Deleuze and Guattari's alleged opposition to Lacan.

THEY FUCK YOU UP, ETC.

What really gets on Žižek's tits is the fact that Deleuze and Guattari are opposed to Lacan, which he then reverses by opposing the allegedly superior force of Lacan's dialectical materialism to Deleuze's 'empiriocriticism'. But is Deleuze and Guattari's anti-Lacan reputation warranted, or is it in actuality much more antag-onistic? Žižek insists that Deleuze presents 'an outright falsification, of Lacan's position' on Oedipus (2004a: 80), but he does not say what it is or where Deleuze does this. At the same time, he claims that Deleuze and Guattari desperately try to avoid a conclusion, which Žižek attributes to Lacan, wherein the 'obverse of the Oedipus' is 'the presubjective field of intensities and desiring machines' (2004a: 80). But this stark opposition weakens when Žižek speculates that Lacan enjoyed reading *The Logic of Sense* because its notion of pure transcendental affect over and above the necessarily incomplete chain of corporeal causality is 'the exact equivalent of Lacan's *objet petit a*' (2004a: 27). Žižek even goes on to concede that Deleuze adopts Lacan's notion of the pure signifier in *The Logic of Sense*, and is not opposed to structuralism; but then states as fact that all of this is erased in Deleuze's later thought – without saying how and where – simply because he is unable to face its full implications (2004a: 82–83). But perhaps the causality of these overlaps is unreliable because whilst Žižek admits that his argument, in addition to relying upon Badiou's Deleuze book (2004a: 20 n. 24), is derived from Flieger's critique of *Anti-Oedipus* – which claims that Deleuze and Guattari only grudgingly acknowledge their debts to Lacan in that book and that the category of the Real is entirely ignored there (Flieger 1999: 226) – he nonetheless agrees with Deleuze and Guattari that the unconscious does not lack anything (Žižek 2004a: 227). Hence, Žižek's argument is an attempt to prevent any contamination. Perhaps if he had bothered to read the bloody book, or just looked up 'Lacan' in the index, he might have found out that his 'discoveries' – through which he claims to demonstrate both the explanatory relevance of Lacan for reading Deleuze and Guattari, and their indebted opposition to him – are already there, fully acknowledged, in *Anti-Oedipus*. Instead, he arrives at a 'confirmation bias', or what he calls the fundamental desire '*not* to know too much' (Žižek 2004a: 128); or what is more usually called a complete load of bollocks.

If that had happened, then perhaps Žižek would have worked out (as opposed to acted out) the full consequences of conceding that Lacan recognised that 'the Name-of-the Father' is no longer the basis of the social (Žižek 2004a: 101), and that 'Oedipus' is a symptom to be interpreted. Indeed, his entire anti-Deleuze/Guattari argument is predicated on the assumption that this is *not* the case. Moreover, he himself had made exactly the same discovery in *The Ticklish Subject* (1999: 332), which formed the basis for his revisionist claim that all psychoanalysis has ever done is describe an anthropology of 'the unexpected consequences of the disintegration of traditional structures that regulated libidinal life' (1999: 341). At the same time, he could complain about the narcissism and immaturity of 'young people' in order to establish the moral desirability of 'traditional structures', if only as something to be against. In other words: Oedipus must be reinvented. How fucked up is that?[6] Correct me if I am wrong, but do not psychoanalysts call that 'disavowal'? But get this: in *Organs Without Bodies*, Žižek gets so completely tied-up in syllogistic knots with Oedipus and the relation that he thinks it enjoys with Lacan and Deleuze and Guattari that he goes on to maintain that the collapse of Oedipus means there is no link between revolution and *Anti-Oedipus*, as if Deleuze and Guattari ever claimed that there was. Moreover, according to Žižek, the abandonment of Oedipus and following the drives 'beyond castration' gives rise to a 'postdemocratic politics' (2004a: 102). This is exactly where Deleuze and Guattari are at because they worked out the consequences of all this, and they duly acknowledge their debt to Lacan in doing so. There is no opposition to Lacan in *Anti-Oedipus*, although there may be an antagonism involving Deleuze and Guattari and Lacan, according to Žižek's 'hardcore' model. The clue is in the title of the book. It is not called '*Anti-Lacan*'. It's called *Anti-Oedipus*. Like, duh!? In this case, the letter always arrives at its destination. It's called *Anti-Oedipus* because, for Deleuze and Guattari, Oedipus is the cornerstone of Freudian psychoanalysis, and a lot more besides, to which they are opposed. Perhaps there would be less confusion if it had been called '*Anti-Freudian-Psychoanalysis*'. The facts of the matter may well piss off Deleuzians as much as they may piss off Lacanians because they undermine the 'confirmation bias' of both. Here's why.

For Deleuze and Guattari, all that psychoanalysis affirms is simply the mechanisms by which desire is repressed, and which include the symbolic order itself. The main charge against psychoanalysis is that it represses desire through trying to reconcile patients with the problem from which they suffer, which is in essence the bourgeois family, rather than getting rid of the problem itself. The Oedipus complex is a tool in this conservative practice of psychoanalysis, which refuses to conceive of the independence and autonomy of the neuroses in order to implement 'daddy–mommy–me' by making its patients internalize it as their own and then projecting that onto 'social authority'. It is a swindle, a 'gigantic enterprise of absorption of surplus value' (Deleuze & Guattari 1977: 239). What Deleuze and Guattari reject in psychoanalysis is the classical distinction between production and acquisition – or consumption – which splits desire into both (*a*) desire for, and (*b*) lack of, the real object. The latter is the constitutive negative condition of desire through which the dialectic is thinkable. They also reject the epistemological dismissal of the positivity of desire as an attribute of the imaginary. Thus, Deleuze and Guattari reject the infinite regression of psychoanalysis in general, its '*anthropomorphic representation of sex*' (1977: 294) and its statistical order of the sexes in particular. The unconscious is a force *sui generis* and not the product of repression. Instead, 'Oedipus is a factitious product of psychic repression' (Deleuze & Guattari 1977: 115). 'The unconscious does not speak, it engineers. It is not expressive or representative, but productive' (1977: 180); it is 'matter itself' (1977: 283), which runs on libido. For Deleuze and Guattari, 'desiring-production is pure multiplicity; that is to say, an affirmation that is irreducible to any sort of unity' (1977: 42), without mediation or sublimation, representation or symbolization, both the 'impossible real' itself and its production. For its part, psychoanalysis is thus an attempt to explain what Deleuze and Guattari do not accept, but not their non-acceptance itself. Deleuze and Guattari do not 'resist' analysis. Thus, Deleuze and Guattari begin from a position inconceivable from within psychoanalysis except perhaps as pathology, and by equating it with materialist becoming they render that position as ontologically prior and politically superior.

The thing is that Deleuze and Guattari get all that from Lacan – or from what they think Lacan thinks. If Deleuze and Guattari's politics of pleasure owes its style to Laing and Reich and their followers, the terms that ground this politics are understood through the theoretical framework developed by Lacan, and takes the political opposition between Lacan and professional psychoanalysis as fact. Hence, in addition to Lacan's role 'in the beginning' of the formation of 'institutional analysis', with which Guattari was associated in the 1950s (1977: 30 n.), Deleuze and Guattari also acknowledge a debt to Lacan in their formulation of the operations of codes. In particular, they signal their debt in the 'discovery' of the 'signifying chains' that constitute 'the code of the unconscious', only to dwell upon its multiplicity and the polyvocality of the non-signifying function of the indifferent signs that compose them (1977: 38, 41). For Deleuze and Guattari, Lacan's notion of the real is precisely the signifying chain, or symbolic without foundation and thus without limit, so Žižek simply wastes his time by arguing against them that this is what they do not think (Žižek 2004a: 54). Importantly, Deleuze and Guattari do not think that Lacan can be subsumed by the Oedipalization project of psychoanalysis, even if his disciples can. On the contrary, Lacan schizophrenizes 'the analytic field, instead of oedipalizing the psychotic field' (Deleuze & Guattari 1977: 309, 363).[7] For Deleuze and Guattari, Oedipus is simply a synthesis wrongly elevated by psychoanalysis to the level of a transcendental condition and is in no way immanent to the unconscious itself. Hence the advice to 'heed Lacan's word of caution concerning the Freudian myth of Oedipus', which accepts that it is not viable in modern society because no one takes rituals seriously (Deleuze & Guattari 1977: 83).[8] No disavowal there, then. There is nothing necessary about Oedipus. As Deleuze and Guattari put it: 'Oedipus disintegrates because its very conditions have disintegrated' (1977: 105); even if 'Oedipus is always colonization pursued by other means' (1977: 170).

SHIT HAPPENS

So Žižek's claims that his analysis of Deleuze – but not Guattari – is a traumatic encounter, a rare event, as distinct from a dialogue or symbolic exchange (Žižek 2004: xi), is false. The encounter does not take place. Or rather: it has already taken place – but in *Anti-Oedipus* itself, right under Žižek's nose. Instead of buggering Deleuze, Žižek is simultaneously fucked by Deleuze and Lacan – a 'spit roast', if you will. So if Deleuze and Guattari are to be criticized for deriving two contrary phenomena from the same ground, then so is Lacan. For example: subjectivity and subjugation; subject of the enunciation and subject of the statement; 'small object a' and 'great Other', etc. This similarity derives from the fact that, both for Deleuze and Guattari and for Lacan, the unconscious is agency: it is distinct from the structure of 'belief' that it both produces and fucks up as the limit of the unconscious, and which is 'not even irrational, but on the contrary only too reasonable and consistent with the established order' (Deleuze & Guattari 1977: 61). Hence: 'the mechanisms of money remain totally unaffected by the anal projections of those who manipulate money' (1977: 28). For Deleuze and Guattari, desire produces the real. At the same time, they do not deny the existence of lack, but locate it at the level of historically determined effect of organized social production. Whether such a reference to historical materialism is compatible with Lacan is a moot point, but it allows Deleuze and Guattari to attach their plenism to Marxism, and to the Althusserian approach in particular and its cause in the *Grundrisse*. That's why the subtitle of *Anti-Oedipus* is 'Capitalism and Schizophrenia'. Lack is simply Lacan's word for the production of scarcity in the midst of the production of the plenitude of abundance in which objective reality is inverted through the appropriation of the surplus. 'The truth of the matter is that *social production is purely and simply desiring-production itself under determinate conditions*' (Deleuze & Guattari 1977: 29). There is no society which does not produce lack, albeit under determinate conditions (1977: 342). Thus: '*There is only desire and the social, and nothing else*' (1977: 29).

However, history and determination only go so far in *Anti-Oedipus*, since they are only the contingent expression of the unfolding of the absolute immanence of necessity. But how is the possibility of these determinate 'social conditions' explained if the 'capitalist machine is incapable of providing a code that will apply to the whole of the social field' (Deleuze & Guattari 1977: 33)? For Deleuze and Guattari, it is because of another equivalent set of terms: the Asiatic despot, the state, repression, Oedipus. The point is that none of these terms refers to a fundamental cause, but to a determinate effect. Thus, nothing necessarily follows from the collapse of Oedipus, nor from the effects of attempts to pretend that it still produces effects. Despotism persists because of the necessary incompletion of capitalism; its non-totalizable, infinite nature; the immanent displacement of its own limits through the crisis of appropriation. The state persists as encoded desire (1977: 221), as a 'gigantic enterprise of anti-production, but at the heart of production itself, and conditioning this production' (1977: 235). Anti-production produces scarcity and lack, the price of the system integration on which capitalism depends. The state provides something for capitalism to exploit, what Buchanan calls rent. Hence banks create a debt that is owed to themselves. It is for this reason that Deleuze and Guattari see revolution as the deepening and acceleration of decoding and de-territorialization (1977: 339). Capitalism is anti-social in that it decodes and de-territorializes the flows of desire. It is the de-territorialized 'body without organs', the 'immanent substance' for which 'partial objects' are its ultimate 'attributes', motor and working parts (1977: 327), and not its contradictions as they are for Žižek. Following Marx, Deleuze and Guattari locate the basis of capitalism in the rupture of its very contingency, which is elevated to the level of universal history, decoding – or perhaps more accurately un-coding – prior inscriptions and marks, tattoos and scarifications, settled signifying chains, in order to establish equivalence and exchange over alliance and filiation, profit over debt, circulation over repetition (see Read 2003). It is in this sense that capitalism:

> Is the only social machine that is constructed on the basis of decoded flows, substituting for intrinsic codes an axiomatic of abstract quantities in the form of money. Capitalism therefore liberates the flows of desire, but under the social conditions that define its limit and the possibility of its own dissolution, so that it is constantly opposing with all its exasperated strength the movement that drives it towards its limit. (Deleuze & Guattari 1977: 140)

'WHAT I'M OUT FOR IS A GOOD TIME. ALL THE REST IS PROPAGANDA'

Most people will find this account of Deleuze and Guattari's position in *Anti-Oedipus* depressing since it challenges the 'confirmation bias' of both Lacanians and Deleuzians. But it would be a mistake to assume that just because Žižek's account of them is wrong, Deleuze and Guattari are right in their own terms. In fact, no one could argue with Žižek's judgment that *Anti-Oedipus* is Deleuze's worst book, although there is no evidence that Guattari is to blame for that. Who could put up with its tedious enthusiasm for its Heath Robinson 'desiring machines'? Who in their right mind thinks that D.H. Lawrence, of all people, is revolutionary?[9] And what about the embarrassing anthropology? Who, in this day and age, could tolerate the following prose where, speaking of 'the primitive territorial machine', Deleuze and Guattari describe how 'the full body of the goddess Earth gathers to itself the cultivable species, the agricultural implements, and the human organs' (1977: 142)? Creepy. On balance, the main weakness of the book is its overdetermination by a stereotypically Gaullist 'exceptionalism'.[10]

Yet one of Žižek's criticisms of Deleuze and Guattari is particularly weak. It is when Žižek opposes the allegedly elitist and indifferent character of Deleuze's own texts, which are not 'in any way directly political' (Žižek 2004: 20), to the political character of *Anti-Oedipus* – as if the two characteristics were mutually exclusive and as if elitism is absent from the latter – as a formal means of verifying the judgment and thus dividing Deleuze from Guattari. Nothing could be further from the truth. *Anti-Oedipus* is political because it is elitist in the sense that, on its account of politics, ordinary people are 'zombies' (Deleuze & Guattari 1977: 335) driven by the 'death drive'. Like, obviously. That's why – don't you see, you fools! – 'Everything in the system is insane' (Deleuze & Guattari 1977: 374). That's why Deleuze's positive term for elitism is 'becoming-minority'. Hippies to the core, Deleuze and Guattari cast the unconscious as repressed by 'the system' because 'every position of desire, no matter how small, is capable of calling into question the established order of a society', and thus 'desire is revolutionary in its essence' (1977: 116). There is no deontology in *Anti-Oedipus*, except in the sense of 'Do what thou wilt shall be the whole of the law'. So take your clothes off. Hence Deleuze & Guattari's celebration of 'men who know how to leave' (1977: 133), even if they fail against the weak, catatonic majority which prefers to 'fall back under the law of the signifier, marked by castration, triangulated in Oedipus' (1977: 135). You get the picture? It's the process of trying to 'break through the wall' that is noble; presumably through to what Jim Morrison called 'the other side' (see Deleuze and Guattari 1977: 277). Thus, Deleuze and Guattari's politics is one of beatniks versus squares. And in itself that opposition in no way undermines its radical and political character, and is not something to be opposed on principle. After all, why should everyone be condemned to the slave vices of work and misery, instead of enjoying the aristocratic virtues of leisure and enjoyment?

But perhaps the real virtue of *Anti-Oedipus* is that it does not produce a mythical subject that would reconcile the contradictions that exist as a consequence of the finite nature of human understanding. Deleuze and Guattari recognize that all revolutionary acts and positions are immediately co-opted, if not today then tomorrow, by virtue of the fact that they are merely representations, entities, and as such interruptions of the aimless revolutionary process (1977: 341); a 'rupture with causality' (1977: 377). The point is to have a go, simply to enjoy the buzz of violence. It is for this reason that the schizophrenic is not a revolutionary. In fact, no one is, insofar as one is the number of a subject. Schizophrenia is a product of the capitalist machine, just as 'manic-depression and paranoia are the product of the despotic machine, and hysteria the product of the territorial machine' (Deleuze & Guattari 1977: 33). The schizo is produced by capitalism in order to revolutionize it, to break the attempts of capitalism to recode the social which, for Deleuze and Guattari, arise from government, law and bureaucracy. This is because capitalism derives from its dependence on that which is coded and territorialized, its object for which it forms an internal limit. Schizophrenia is the exterior limit of this limit, which capitalism both requires and inhibits in order to have something to appropriate (Deleuze & Guattari 1977: 250). The stable ethical position simply causes the depression of PCT. Hence, Laclau's cheeky claim that Žižek is 'schizophrenically split between a highly sophisticated Lacanian analysis and an insufficiently deconstructed Marxism' (Laclau 2000: 205) is unfounded, since the entirety of Žižek's endeavour is directed to reconciling these two poles, but only insofar as the opposition is a consequence of the endeavour itself. One could even say the same thing about Laclau's split between reactionary populism and progressive liberal democracy. Both are depressed – but not depressive – positions in that each attempts to derive everything from a stable ground that is both cause and effect, and thus fully reconciled with itself. Perhaps the treatment is to enjoy the schizzes that the attempt produces. In that way, perhaps, as Deleuze and Guattari suggest, 'a little joy, a little discovery' might be returned to psychoanalysis (1977:113). Life is too short to worry about being right. It only leads to the downward spiral of self-deception. Just grab what you can.

NOTES

1 Of course, this scenario is idealistic. Most students will stare blankly and perform ignorance in response to a question and complain to university administrators that their 'feelings have not been respected'.

2 One might point to the narcotics market as a counter-example of a healthy free-market running without government regulation but, as Burroughs never tired of pointing out, it is the illegality of the commodity that determines its price as its prohibition creates artificial scarcity. Only morons think that people who sell narcotics are inherently 'evil'.

3 By advising that buggery is not to be thought obscene, Žižek does not tell us anything that we do not already know. Indeed, one thing is sure: anal sex is no longer the exclusive property of male homosexuals.

4 One might ask: What's the matter, Žižek, scared you might like it? Or do you just want to watch and wank yourself off? Nothing wrong with that of course. Indeed, why is it that the latest fashion in the London sex industry is for a group of men to hire a prostitute and another man to fuck her while they stand around and masturbate? Is it because it

reminds them of a time when sex was innocent; namely, before they had sexual intercourse with a woman and so had to rely on masturbation? Perhaps in this way they regain a sense of youth and vigour through a shared experience?

5 Here one should refer to Žižek's celebrated and useful distinction between 'antagonism as *real*' and 'the social *reality* of the antagonistic fight' (1990: 253). In this case the latter is overdetermined by the demands of Žižek's publishing schedule.

6 On the related matter of the incest taboo, recall the following joke popularized by Martin Amis in *London Fields*: 'How do you know if your sister is having a period? Your dad's cock tastes of blood'.

7 Deleuze and Guattari complain that 'even an attempt as profound as Lacan's at shaking loose from the yoke of Oedipus has been interpreted as an unhoped-for means of making it heavier still and of resecuring it on the baby and the schizo' (Deleuze & Guattari 1977: 175). And again, they praise 'the strength of Lacan' which 'saved psychoanalysis from the frenzied oedipalization to which it was linking its fate' (1977: 217 – see also 265, 268).

8 At this point, Deleuze and Guattari go on to say that Lacan asserts that the 'sole foundation for the society of brothers, for fraternity, is "segregation"', where they add parenthetically '(what does he mean here?)' Some 20 pages later, they claim that 'Lacan has demonstrated in a profound way the link between Oedipus and segregation' (Deleuze & Guattari 1977: 104). Make of that what you will; I call it sloppy thinking.

9 Deleuze and Guattari are like a couple of irritating French exchange students in Carnaby Street, overexcited by the fact that English girls do not live in constant fear of random sexual harassment, and thus have not learned any of the defences that French girls have had to invent. That is why French woman think that English woman are sluts. They cannot imagine that they do not have to put up with the constant sexual pleading and excruciating chat-up routines that they have to. If French women went about drunk, eating chips with hardly any clothes on like English women do they would be raped on the spot. For more on this topic, see Guiliano 2005.

10 Question: Why is it that in Deleuze and Guattari's other excruciatingly tedious and nerdy book, *A Thousand Plateaus* (1988), there is no mention of the electric guitar and Hendrix is not in the index? Answer: Name one French electric guitarist. 10,000 years of non-linear history as if Elvis Presley, the real 'sense event', never happened.

AFTERWORD: WITH DEFENDERS LIKE THESE, WHO NEEDS ATTACKERS?

Slavoj Žižek

In his 'Foreword' to the present volume, Simon Critchley claims that the severe criticism of my work which sets the tone of the contributions is really a defence of my work: a recognition that it should not be ignored, that it deserves a detailed reading and engagement. After reading the contributions themselves, I cannot but notice a profound objective cynicism to these words.

When we are avidly expecting the new book of an author, and this book, when it finally appears, turns out to be a disappointment, we can say: 'Although we were waiting for this book, this is not the book we were waiting for'. This, unfortunately, is also my impression apropos the texts in the present volume – not because it is highly critical of me, but because so many arguments in it are based on such a crude misreading of my position that, instead of confronting theoretical positions, I will have to spend way too much time just answering insinuations and untruths as well as setting straight the misunderstandings of my position – which is, for an author, one of the most boring exercises imaginable. In order to ease this burden, I will effectively do what I am often accused of (over)doing: cut and paste bits of my past texts where I already clarified the issues debated here. So let me begin with a brief digression apropos this cut-and-paste procedure: once, I repeated the same passage in the same book in order to make a theoretical point clear. In the introduction to my book *The Fright of Real Tears* (2001), I invoke an experience of mine in order to exemplify the sad state of cultural studies today:

> Some months ago, at an art round table, I was asked to comment on a painting I saw there for the first time. I did not have *any* idea about it, so I engaged in total bluff, which went on something like

this: the frame of the painting in front of us is not its true frame; there is another, invisible, frame, implied by the structure of the painting, the frame that enframes our perception of the painting, and these two frames do not overlap – there is an invisible gap separating the two. The pivotal content of the painting is not rendered in its visible part, but is located in this dis-location of the two frames, in the gap that separates them. Are we, today, in our postmodern madness, still able to discern the traces of this gap? Perhaps, more than the reading of a painting hinges on it; perhaps, the decisive dimension of humanity will be lost when we will lose the capacity to discern this gap. . . To my surprise, this brief intervention was a huge success, and many following participants referred to the dimension in-between-the-two-frames, elevating it into a term. This very success made me sad, really sad. What I encountered here was not only the efficiency of a bluff, but a much more radical apathy at the very heart of today's Cultural Studies.

A hundred and fifty pages later, in the book's last chapter, I bring in the same example of 'between-the-two-frames', this time without irony, as a straightforward theoretical concept:

> One of the minimal definitions of a modernist painting concerns the function of its frame. The frame of the painting in front of us is not its true frame; there is another, invisible, frame, the frame implied by the structure of the painting, the frame that enframes our perception of the painting, and these two frames by definition never overlap – there is an invisible gap separating them. The pivotal content of the painting is not rendered in its visible part, but is located in this dis-location of the two frames, in the gap that separates them.

Even some of my friends and followers missed the point – most of those who noticed this repetition read it either as a self-parodic indication of how I do not take my own theories seriously, or as a sign of my growing senility (I simply forgot towards the end of the book that I mocked the same notion in the introduction). Was it really so difficult to perceive how my procedure here perfectly illustrates the point I am trying to make repeatedly apropos of today's predominant attitude of cynicism and of not taking oneself seriously: even if the subject mocks a certain belief, this in no way undermines this belief's symbolic efficiency – the belief continues to determine the subject's activity. When we make fun of an attitude, the truth is often in this attitude, not in our distance towards it: I make fun of it to conceal from myself the fact that this attitude effectively determines my activity. (Say, someone who mocks his love for a woman often thereby expresses his uneasiness at the fact that he is deeply attached to her.) In this sense, irony is to be opposed to cynicism. If, to simplify it to the utmost, a cynic fakes a belief that he privately mocks (publicly you preach sacrifice for the fatherland, privately you amass profits), in irony, the subject takes things more seriously than he appears to – he secretly believes in what he publicly mocks. Irony confronts us with the embarrassing fact that – not in our interior, but in our acts themselves, in our social practice – we believe much more than we are aware of.

Since, in the chapters that comprise the present volume, there is often a question of (my) style, the first feature that should at least be noted is the frequent brutality of attacks – *anything goes*, from hints at my personal pathology and claims that my texts do not satisfy even the requirements of an undergraduate paper, up to lies pure and simple about my political engagements. (See, among others, Ian Parker's claim that I was 'asked by the Slovenian government for advice during its successful referendum campaign to join NATO' (above, p. 158) – a complete lie if there ever was one). The question to be asked here (but which I have no will or patience to engage in) is: why am I so often selected as a target about which one can write things that would otherwise immediately provoke an indignant politically correct rebuke? What amuses me is to imagine myself daring to treat in the same way and terms another publicly exposed figure of human and social sciences – say, can one sincerely imagine what would have been the reaction if I were to articulate hypotheses on Judith Butler's personal pathology (my personal friend and a very decent person, of course!) as part of a theoretical engagement with her work?

Before I throw myself *in medias res*, just two more general observations. The 'Editors' Introduction' makes the point how 'often, it seems, academics forget (or pretend to forget) that they speak and write from a position that is already situated within a complex set of apparatuses, which are not merely disciplinary and institutional but bound up with commercial and market-driven imperatives' (above, p. 6). The point of this point is clear enough: if we locate my pose of theoretical radicality within the existing academic-institutional and commercial constellation, it loses its radicality: that is, it becomes visible how my theory poses no threat to the existing power relations, how it even perfectly fits them. This is why 'Žižek very rarely takes cognizance of the institutional and commercial forces that act upon him and make his interventions possible' (above, pp. 6–7): the full cognizance of these forces would undermine my 'radical' theoretical claims. This thesis is further developed in Gilbert's contribution:

> What we see here is simply the logic of celebrity culture and deep commodification extended to the field of 'intellectual' publishing, and it is virtually a truism today to acknowledge that celebrity culture is one of the most striking manifestations of the commodifying and individualizing logics of neo-liberal capitalism, logics whose widespread operation is symptomatic of the secure hegemony of neo-liberalism almost throughout the non-Islamic world. (above, p. 68)

Are, however, things really so simple? What, if one discounts signs of superficial (and limited) 'popularity', is my status? (Incidentally, my very 'popularity', emphasized as a rule by my opponents, is evoked to undermine my status – 'pop-philosophy instead of serious analysis'.) In today's academia, the main indication of one's status is the influence one exerts on departmental politics and research grants; on who will be hired, etc. In this domain, my influence is not only minimal, but often even negative (a couple of times, I learned afterwards that people who asked me for a recommendation letter were not hired precisely because my name was associated with them). In comparison with other 'radical' or 'critical' orientations (deconstructionists, Foucauldians, Deleuzians, Habermasians), the institutional power of Lacanians is minimal – there is, to my best knowledge, in the entire English-speaking academia, not even one department dominated by Lacanians. As to 'commodifying and individualizing', I lag far behind people like Habermas (the European Union's de facto Staatsphilosoph) or Toni Negri. As for research grants: never in my life did I get a grant (or, for that matter, succeeded in helping a colleague of mine to get one). And even as to the access to public media and contacts with colleagues, my 'Leninist turn' cost me dearly (suffice it to mention the de facto Verbot to appear in German dailies and weeklies after the Lenin conference I organized in 2001 in Essen). So, when one speaks about institutional power, the only honest thing is to note my extreme marginalization: true, I enjoy a certain visibility, and I often give public lectures, because *this is all I have* – there is no institutional power behind.

Second general observation: I cannot but note how many texts in the present volume follow a similar argumentative strategy. First, they impute to me a ridiculously caricaturized position; then, when they are forced to admit that many passages in my work directly contradict the described position, they do not read this discrepancy as what, *prima facie*, it is, a sign of the inadequacy of *their* reading, but as *my own* inconsistency. This procedure reaches its apogee in the concluding 'Coda' of Gilbert's text:

> Immediately I had completed the final draft of this chapter, Žižek published an article in the *London Review of Books*, arguing that the apparent philanthropy of socially conscious liberal entrepreneurs such as Bill Gates – 'liberal communists' as Žižek calls them[1] – should be treated with circumspection by anyone concerned about the implication of neo-liberal capitalism in contemporary social problems. Žižek casually remarks that 'it may be necessary to enter into tactical alliances with liberal communists in order to fight racism, sexism, and religious obscurantism'. This is extraordinary. For if it is allowed that in the course of fighting a Gramscian 'war of position', it may be legitimate to enter into such tactical alliances, then every single one of Žižek's attacks on 'the academic Left' or 'radical chic' since the late 1980s is without foundation, and concepts such as 'revolutionary intolerance' and the philosophy of the 'act', are clearly illegitimate. So one really has to wonder if the whole business of reading and commenting on Žižek since 1989 has not been an enormous waste of time. (above, p. 81)

This really *is* extraordinary! As if I did not formulate the point which surprised Gilbert many times before – suffice it to quote a passage from my exchange with Ernesto Laclau:

> Far from compelling us to dismiss all the variety of anti-sexist, anti-racist, etc., the 'structuring role' of class struggle functions as a device which (1) enables us to account for the very changes in the focus of emancipatory struggles (in my view, the very shift from the central role of the 'classic' working-class economic

struggle to identity-politics of recognition should be explained through the dynamics of class struggle), and (2) which enables us to analyze and judge the concrete political content and stakes of different struggles. While professing their solidarity with the poor, liberals encode culture war with an opposed class message: more often than not, their fight for multicultural tolerance and women's rights marks the counter-position to the alleged intolerance, fundamentalism, and patriarchal sexism of the 'lower classes'. The paradox here is that it is the populist fundamentalism which retains this logic of antagonism, while the liberal Left follows the logic of recognition of differences, of 'defusing' antagonisms into co-existing differences: in their very form, the conservative-populist grass-roots campaigns took over the old Leftist-radical stance of the popular mobilization and struggle against upper-class exploitation. We should thus not only refuse the easy liberal contempt for the populist fundamentalists (or, even worse, the patronizing regret of how 'manipulated' they are); we should reject the very terms of the culture war. Although, of course, as to the positive content of most of the debated issues, a radical Leftist should support the liberal stance (for abortion, against racism and homophobia. . .), one should never forget that it is the populist fundamentalist, not the liberal, who is, in the long term, our ally. In all their anger, the populists are *not angry enough* – not radical enough to perceive the link between capitalism and the moral decay they deplore.

As to my 'injunctions to overthrow capitalism or to abolish liberal democracy, which have no meaning at all' – where did Laclau find them? Let me formulate my position as clearly as possible. Both Laclau and Mouffe and Hardt and Negri, although opposed theoretically, are basically optimists, propagating an enthusiastic message: the old oppressive times of 'essentialism' and centralized struggles for State power are over, we live in a new epoch in which the Left is given a chance to reinvent itself as occupying the field of multiple struggles (anti-sexist, anti-racist, ecological, civil rights, anti-globalization), new spaces of politicization and democratization of our daily lives are opening up . . . (Hardt and Negri nonetheless hold here one advantage over Laclau and Mouffe: they relate to – and are part of – an effective large-scale political movement (of anti-globalization), while Laclau provides just an empty 'transcendental' frame which does not echo with any determinate political movement or strategy – which is why Hardt and Negri's work also finds a much larger public.) In contrast to both of them, my stance is much more modest and – why not – pessimist: we effectively live in dark times for emancipatory politics . . . while one can discern the contours of the fateful limitation of the present global capitalist system, inclusive of its democratic form of political self-legitimization, while one can outline the self-destructive dynamics that propels its reproduction, and while one can perceive the insufficiency of all the forms of struggle at our disposal now (enumerated above by Laclau), one cannot formulate a clear project of global change. So, contrary to the cheap 'revolutionary' calls for a radical overthrow of capitalism and its democratic political form, my point is precisely that such calls, although necessary in the long run, are meaningless today. What I am *not* ready to do is, however, the standard 'postmodern' political solution to turn defeat into a blessing in disguise, i.e., to abandon the horizon of radical change in favor of the prospect of multiple local practices of resistance, etc. – today, it is more crucial than ever to continue to question the very foundations of capitalism as a global system, to clearly articulate the limitation of the democratic political project'.

This topic brings us to the first text in the present volume, Critchley's 'Foreword', which critically relates this what-follows-for-action reproach to my basic thesis on ideology:

> Reality is structured by belief, by a faith in fantasy that we know to be a fantasy yet we believe nonetheless. This is a stunning diagnostic insight, yet my question is and always has been: what does one *do* with this insight? What follows for action from this argument for the constitutive nature of ideological fantasy? Are we not eternally doomed to an unending plague of more fantasies that can in turn be criticized by Žižek and by generations of future Žižeks? Sometimes, I wonder. (Above, p. xv)

Well, I also wonder – about Critchley's strange conclusion: why on earth should the thesis on ideological fantasies as embodied in our social reality lead to being 'eternally doomed to an unending plague of more fantasies'? Why not read it in the exactly opposite way, the one proposed by me, as opening a new field of political intervention: insofar as social reality itself is sustained by fantasies, 'moving the underground' of fantasies is a key step in transforming reality itself? In other words, Critchley's reproach that, according to me, we are 'eternally doomed to an unending plague of more fantasies', precisely misses the point of fantasy as constitutive of social reality, and reintroduces underhand the standard opposition between 'mere fantasies' and 'true' reality external to them.

Here, then, is Critchley's conclusion:

> I remember asking Žižek years ago about the implications of his work for political action and he answered, characteristically, 'I have a hat, but I do not have a rabbit'. My question is: where is the rabbit? We need at least one rabbit, maybe more if we want them to breed. (above, p. xvi)

True enough, but my problem is precisely that I remain critical about rabbits being offered to us by today's Left, including Critchley himself: the true wishful 'whistling in the dark' is to take these rabbits seriously. What is needed is a concrete analysis of the rabbits breeding around, not cheap rhetorics on how it is better to have a rabbit than not to have it.

A detail from a public exchange between Critchley and me nonetheless remains stuck in my mind: to my question of whether he thought capitalism can really be overcome, he answered, after a short reflection, that he thinks capitalism is in a way indestructible, that somehow, today, every social situation re-engenders it. I am not mentioning this as part of a cheap argument to demonstrate Critchley's 'lack of radicality', but as a profound (although, for me, problematic) insight. The lesson of the last decades, if there is one, is about a kind of indestructibility of capitalism – when (already) Marx compared it to a vampire, we should bear in mind the living-dead aspect of vampires: they always rise up again after being stabbed to death. Even the radical Maoist attempt, in the Cultural Revolution, to wipe out the traces of capitalism, ended up in its triumphant return.

This, however, is not the whole story. There is another, no less surprising, lesson of the last decades, the lesson not only of the Chinese communists presiding over what is arguably the most explosive development of capitalism in its entire history, but also the lesson of the Western European Third Way social democracy. It is, in

short: *we can do it better*. It is as if the logic of 'obstacle as a positive condition' which underlay the failure of the socialist attempts
to overcome capitalism, is now returning with a vengeance in capitalism itself. That is to say, what if, in a way symmetrical to this
logic, an obstacle to the unencumbered reign of free-market capitalism can be its ultimate impetus. As many a perspicuous commentator observed, in the UK, the Thatcher revolution was in itself
chaotic, impulsive, marked by unforeseeable contingencies, and it
was only the Third Way Blair who was able to *institutionalize* it, to
stabilize it into new institutional forms, or, to put it in Hegelese, to
raise (what first appeared as) a contingency, a historical accident,
into necessity. In this sense, Blair *repeated* Thatcherism, elevating it
into a concept, in the same way that, for Hegel, Augustus *repeated*
Caesar, transforming–sublating a (contingent) personal name into
a concept, a title. Thatcher was not a Thatcherite, she was just
herself – it was only Blair (more than Major) who truly formed
Thatcherism as a notion. The dialectical irony of history is that only
a (nominal) ideologico-political enemy can do this to you, can
elevate you into a concept – the empirical instigator has to be
knocked off (Julius Caesar had to be murdered, Thatcher had to be
ignominiously deposed).

A reference to Marx enables us to throw a new light on this strange
necessity. In his brilliant analysis of the political *imbroglio* of the
French Revolution of 1848, Marx pointed out the paradoxical status
of the ruling Party of the Order. It was the coalition of the two royalist wings (Bourbons and Orleanists). However, since the two parties
were, by definition, not able to find a common denominator at the
level of royalism (one cannot be a royalist in general, since one should
support a certain determinate royal house), the only way for the two
to unite was under the banner of the 'anonymous kingdom of the
Republic': the only way to be a royalist in general is to be a republican (see Marx 1978: 95). And, *mutatis mutandis*, is not something
similar going on today? As we all know, capital nowadays is split into
two factions (traditional industrial capital and 'postmodern' digital-
informational-etc. capital), and the only way for the two factions to
find a common denominator is under the banner of the 'anonymous
capitalism of social-democracy': today, the only way to be a capitalist *in general* is to be a (Third Way) social democrat. This is how the
opposition Left–Right works now: it is the new Third Way Left
which stands for the interests of capital as such, in its totality (i.e., in

relative independence from its particular factions), while today's Right, as a rule, advocates the interests of some particular section of capital in contrast to other sections – which is why, paradoxically, in order to win the majority, it has to augment its electoral base by directly appealing to select parts of the working class as well. No wonder, then, that it is mostly in the modern Right parties that we find explicit references to the interests of the working class (protectionist measures against cheap foreign labor and cheap imports, etc.). The old Hegelian lesson imposes itself here yet again: an obstacle can be its own solution, the condition of impossibility is the condition of possibility.

And we should take this necessity very seriously, leaving behind all moralistic reproaches on how the Third Way social democracy 'betrayed' its historical legacy. The reason it can do it better is precisely because the inner antagonisms of global capitalism would explode (or, at least, give rise to tensions) without the Third Way minimal safety network and regulatory interventions. Orthodox neo-liberals are here victims of the same illusion as the classic Marxists: when they see the new social democrats (or Chinese communists) successfully managing capitalist growth, their reaction is: 'If they can do it, can you imagine how much more explosive the growth would have been under full conditions of liberal capitalism!', and it is here that they are wrong, unable to perceive the positive role of what appear to them as obstacles. In the case of China, it is clear that, if communists were to lose power, we would get social chaos and probably even civil war (let us go to the end: the Tien-An-Mien massacre was a blessing in disguise.)[2] The Third Way social democracy in all its versions, from Blair to Clinton, is thus a genuine option, not merely a desperate compromise attempt at finding a balance between the inherent demands of capitalism and the demands of the welfare state: they can genuinely claim that their model ultimately works better for capitalism itself. And it is the highest irony of twentieth-century history that this outcome was outlined by none other than Lenin himself, who, two years before his death, when it became clear that there would be no all-European revolution, and that the idea of building socialism in one country was nonsense, already envisaged a similar option:

What if the complete hopelessness of the situation, by stimulating the efforts of the workers and peasants tenfold, offered us the opportunity to create the fundamental requisites of civilization in a different way from that of the West European countries? (Lenin 1965: 479)

One should take note of how Lenin uses here a class-neutral term 'to create the fundamental requisites of civilization', which, as the continuation indicates, even smacks of what today some call 'alternate modernity' – no wonder his vision in his last years was simply that of a more efficient and modernizing state capitalism! This, realistically, is what would have happened if – the old Trotskyite dream – Lenin were to stay alive and operative for a couple of years more: a society somewhere in the middle between the Third Way UK and today's China.

There is nothing dishonourable in this task – the big question is just: does this solution work in the long term? Can in this way the antagonisms be kept under control (or, rather, indefinitely postponed)? This is the practical deadlock that is bothering me, and one definitely cannot get rid of it by means of a 'characterological' analysis of authors who raise these issues – as La Berge does in her opening text, which aims at no less than a 'characterological portrait of Žižek':

> Žižek, through his transference, is revealing to us his symptom: namely that the ascent of identity politics and the symbolic redress of grievances from the white-male establishment is in fact sustaining his very own subjectivity. This is the fantasy that Žižek must traverse for the writing cure to be salutary. Žižek keeps obsessively, repetitively, desperately writing of the various problems of political correctness precisely to make sure that they will still be thought of as problems, problems designed for him to address – exactly what he accuses its proponents of doing, which is the surest indication of a symptom. (above, p. 22)

My first reaction to these lines is a common-sense one: I consider this kind of 'characterological' analysis, if not supported by a close 'symptomal reading', a rather cheap trick of enabling the writer to disqualify the analysed author without really engaging with the inherent truth value of the theory in question. This kind of disqualification has a long history: Marx himself was often accused that his critique of political economy masked his deep fascination with capitalism; many Third World critics of imperialism were accused that their 'obsessive' anti-imperialism displays how the object of their critique sustains their own subjectivity, how they would have been lost if deprived of it; feminists are often mocked for relying on 'patriarchal phallogocentrism', etc. My reply is that I write a lot about the politically correct multiculturalist liberal stance simply because, in my view, it *is* today's predominant ideology. And the irony of the situation is that, if La Berge were to read my texts a little bit more carefully, she would have soon discovered that there is *another* ideological field which fits much better her accusation: if there really is an ideology about which I write 'obsessively, repetitively, desperately', it is Stalinism, to which I return all the time, although, for all practical purposes, it disappeared from the face of the earth. Apart from this main argument, suffice it to mention her critique of my thesis that 'there is no sex without an element of "harassment" ':

> From his reading of Lacan's claim that 'there is no sexual relationship', or no sex without a third term, Žižek argues that we can find a logical fallacy in sexual-harassment legislation, for 'there is no sex without an element of "harassment"' (1999: 285). We can fairly easily deconstruct any one of Žižek's complaints. To take the last one, Žižek conflates sexual harassment (unwanted sexual attention) with the impossible desire for a love object, a distance that can never be entirely subsumed and thus creates a space for the desire itself (sexual tension). Thus, there can be no sex without desire manifest as tension, but no sex without harassment?[3] (above, pp. 20–21)

La Berge's diagnosis is simply wrong: I do *not* conflate harassment with 'impossible desire for a love object, a distance that can never be entirely subsumed and thus creates a space for the desire itself'; quite on the contrary, I see the moment of harassment in the *over-proximity* of the Other *qua* neighbour/thing which I experience when I find myself occupying the position of the focus of the other's desire. It is for this reason that finding oneself in the position of the beloved is so violent, traumatic even: being loved makes me feel directly the gap between what I am as a determinate being and the unfathomable X in me which causes love. Lacan's definition of love ('Love is giving something one does not have. . .') has to be supplemented with: '. . . to someone who does not want it'. Is this not confirmed by our most elementary experience when somebody unexpectedly declares passionate love to us? Is not the first reaction, preceding the possible positive reply, that something obscene, intrusive, is being forced upon us? In the middle of Alejandro Inarritu's film *21 Grams*, Paul, who is dying of a weakened heart, gently declares his love to Cristina, who is traumatized by the recent death of her husband and two young children; when they meet the next time, Cristina explodes into a complaint about the violent nature of declaring love:

> You know, you kept me thinking all day. I haven't spoken to anyone for months and I barely know you and I already need to talk to you. . . And there's something the more I think about the less I understand: why the hell did you tell me you liked me?. . . Answer me, because I didn't like you saying that at all. . . You can't just walk up to a woman you barely know and tell her you like her. Y-o-u-c-a-n't. You don't know what she's going through, what she's feeling. . . I'm not married, you know. I'm not anything in this world. I'm just not anything. (Arriaga 2003: 107)

Upon this, Cristina looks at Paul, raises her hands and desperately starts kissing him on the mouth; so it is not that she did not like him and did not desire carnal contact with him. The problem for her was, on the contrary, that she *did* want it – the point of her complaint was: what right does he have to stir up her desire? Indeed, are we aware that Yeats' well-known lines describe one of the most claustrophobic constellations that one can imagine?

> Had I the heavens' embroidered cloths,
> Enwrought with golden and silver light,
> The blue and the dim and the dark cloths
> Of night and light and the half-light,
> I would spread the cloths under your feet:
> But I, being poor, have only my dreams;
> I have spread my dreams under your feet,
> Tread softly because you tread on my dreams.
>   (Yeats, 'He wishes for the Cloths of Heaven')

In short, as Deleuze put it, *si vous etes pris dans le reve de l'autre, vous etez foutu.*

So let us move to Bowman's contribution, whose central reproach is a Laclauian one: my notion of the 'Tao of postmodern capitalism', of Western Buddhism as the ideal ideological form of today's global capitalism, relies on the naïve-realist notion of ideology which is directly generated by the objective socio-economic process and, as such, not the result of contingent discursive struggles for hegemony; such a notion of ideology forgets the fundamental lesson of discourse theory. Since this reproach raises a fundamental issue on which also some other contributions focus, I will leave it to the end, and just add a brief remark on Buddhism: the present image of Western Buddhism is, of course, a discursive construct, the result of a series of contingent encounters (see Paine 2004). But there is a limit to this undecided game – not a limit in the sense of pre-existing reality that the predominant ideology should 'reflect', but a limit in the sense of the capitalist set of social relations which are in themselves not a pre-discursive fact but involve their own 'ideology', that of commodity fetishism. So let me pass to Devenney, who starts his essay with the claim that, 'if traversing the fundamental fantasy is a requirement for an authentic act, then this act will have to treat what Žižek terms the "real of capital". I contend in this chapter that Žižek fails to give an adequate account of capital or of political economy' (above, pp. 46–47). Here is the first salvo in elaborating this critique:

> [Žižek] makes two essential points: first that the limit of capital is capital itself, not some outside to capital. Second, this limit will be reached when capitalism finally erodes the 'last resistant spheres of non-reflected substantial being'.
> Yet the logic of this account differs from that of Marx who argues that capital generates a revolutionary class: the proletariat. For Žižek capitalism's only limit is capitalism itself. (above, p. 48)

The first point is breathtaking: in a volume in which my lack of precise knowledge and quoting is one of the main reproaches that reappears again and again, the thesis (attributed to *me*) that the limit of capitalism is capital itself is confronted with the allegedly truly Marxist thesis according to which the true limit of capitalism is that it generates proletariat as a revolutionary class – while all I was doing in the thesis attributed to me was to refer *verbatim* to one of the most famous passages in *Capital* III:

The *true barrier* to capitalist production is *capital itself*. It is that capital and its self-valorization appear as the starting and the finishing point, as the motive and purpose of the production. (Marx 1981: 358)[4]

Really, 'a level of scholarship which would be considered pitiable in the work of an undergraduate student'! Here, then, is how, after this not very promising beginning, the story goes on:

> If capitalism is viewed as an overdetermined totality, a totality which is a contingent articulation of a series of medical, economic, political, legal and other discourses, the theorist can begin to account for both the relative fixity of relations of power and economic organization, as well as their points of vulnerability. In this sense there is no object 'the economy', other than as a theoretical abstraction. Taking the abstraction seriously means precisely that other aspects of the social totality would not be seen. This blindness is then a consequence of Žižek's theoretical claims, rather than anything to do with the real abstraction: capital. (above, p. 50)

I must confess that my first reaction to this reproach was: yes, I agree, but my point is precisely that I do *not* view capitalism 'as an overdetermined totality, a totality which is a contingent articulation of a series of medical, economic, political, legal and other discourses', and this is why, for me, there definitely is an 'object "the economy"', other than as a theoretical abstraction' – the object of what Marx called the 'critique of political economy', the object whose inner logic can be deployed through the immanent analysis of its notional structure. My (Marxist) thesis remains that if one does *not* take this abstraction seriously, then 'other aspects of the social totality would not be seen' in their concrete role within social totality. Capitalism is *not* just the outcome of multiple discursive strategies and struggles for hegemony – the 'logic of the capital' is a singular matrix which designates its real. This brings us back to the Laclauian reproach formulated already by Bowman, with which I will deal later; let me state here only that the crucial point is to conceive this matrix as a 'concrete universality': it is not the question of isolating what all particular forms of capitalism have in common, their shared universal features, but of grasping this matrix as a positive force in itself, as something which all actual particular forms try to counteract, to contain its destructive effects. In this sense, truly, 'there is no capitalism': the universal matrix of capitalism is virtual-real, with all actual forms reactions to it.

The most reliable sign of capitalism's ideological triumph is the virtual disappearance of the very term in the last two or three decades: from the 1980s, 'virtually no one, with the exception of a few allegedly archaic Marxists (an "endangered species"), referred to capitalism any longer. The term was simply struck from the vocabulary of politicians, trade unionists, writers and journalists – not to mention social scientists, who had consigned it to historical oblivion' (Boltanski & Chiapello 2005: ix). So what about the upsurge of the anti-globalization movement in the last years? Does it not clearly contradict this diagnostic? No: a close look quickly shows how this movement also succumbs to 'the temptation to transform a critique of capitalism itself (centred on economic mechanisms, forms of work organization, and profit extraction) into a critique of "imperialism"' (Boltanski & Chiapello 2005: xvii). In this way, when one talks about 'globalization and its agents', the enemy is externalized (usually in the form of vulgar anti-Americanism). From this perspective, where the main task today is to fight 'the American empire', any ally is good if it is anti-American, and so the unbridled Chinese 'communist' capitalism, violent Islamic anti-modernists, as well as the obscene Lukashenko regime in Belarus (see Chavez's visit to Belarus in July 2006), may appear as progressive anti-globalist comrades-in-arms. What we have here is thus another version of the ill-famed notion of 'alternate modernity': instead of the critique of capitalism as such, of confronting its basic mechanism, we get the critique of the imperialist 'excess', with the (silent) notion of mobilizing capitalist mechanisms within another, more 'progressive', frame. However, back to Devenney, who raises here the common sense question: what arguments do I give for this central structural role of capitalism?

> This argument is extraordinary. The only evidence Žižek offers for class playing this role is that it is never directly expressed, yet despite this inherent negativity it structures the whole field.[5] (above, p. 54)

What I myself find extraordinary is the faked ignorance that sustains these lines: Devenney behaves as if, in insisting on the structuring role of class struggle, I propose an extravagant, unheard-of notion, while his own notion that capitalism is 'an overdetermined totality, a totality which is a contingent articulation of a series of medical, economic, political, legal and other discourses', is treated as a self-evident truth that needs no further evidence – as if these two opposed positions are not (each of them) grounded in detailed theoretical elaborations! What I try to do in the passage referred to by Devenney is not to provide some fresh 'evidence' for my thesis: all I do is to offer a description (which, again, is nothing new, just a recapitulation of what Althusser, Deleuze and others elaborated long ago) of how this structural role is exerted. After claiming that I fail to 'give an adequate account of capital or of political economy', Devenney finally provides a sketch of his own view on how these matters stand today:

Reproduction has now become a means of generating capital and surplus. This overlap of production and reproduction (so that for example the sciences of life both create and privatize a new territory termed genetic life through intellectual-property law) quite literally rearticulates a new understanding of life. Life itself (so called natural life) is characterized as an overdetermined code (this is how the new functional genomics considers life: genetic function depends upon unpredictable interactions between different genes, their environment and their external environment) and this code is a key object of capitalization on global markets. (above, p. 50)

Who would not agree with this – with the proviso that this direct encroachment of capitalist production onto life's reproduction, *one of* the aspects of today's new stage of capitalism, is as such a simple fact on which we can read reports in any news magazine; what is still missing is the conceptual description of how this encroachment affects the form of capitalist reproduction. Not to mention an even more interesting philosophical question (about which I have already written): how does all this affect our notion of life itself? Is the technologically reproducible life still 'life' in the way we experience it as part of our life-world? Is it this shift that accounts for the new popularity of the topic of the 'undead', the 'living dead', of a spectral life which insists beyond (biological) death.

Devenney's parting shot concerns my notion of the act which, according to him:

> Entails a subjective destitution which means that the subject cannot even evaluate whether or not the act is in line with its basic requirements, noted above. Contrast this with the psychoanalytic act which relies precisely upon an analytic encounter in which the subject of knowledge does not have its imaginary coherence verified by the analyst. Yet the presence of the other is a crucial component of the analysis, of the passage through the act. Such conditions simply do not apply in relation to the notion of the act defended by Žižek in political terms. (above, p. 58)

Basically, these lines contain two separate (although interconnected) reproaches. The first one varies a constant motif in the present volume: my notion of act is that of an 'irrational' rupture which explodes from nowhere, it is not grounded in its concrete circumstances, so that there are no criteria to distinguish a true act from a false one. (To this, I sufficiently reply elsewhere in the present text.) The second reproach concerns the difference between my notion of act and (Lacan's) notion of the psychoanalytic act: my act is a solitary gesture, what is missing in it is the encounter with the Other. This reproach also misses the point: what, for Lacan, happens at the end of the psychoanalytic cure is that, in 'traversing the fantasy', the analysand assumes the 'non-existence of the big Other', i.e., the lack of any external guarantee of his/her act (which is why, for Lacan, an analyst *ne s'autorise que de lui-même*). The analyst is not a stand-in for the big Other, but, on the contrary, the impenetrable obstacle that signals the inconsistency and the failure of the big Other. This is also why the conclusion of the analysis coincides with the 'fall of the subject supposed to know' (with the disintegration of the transferential illusion). Furthermore, Lacan's first great analysis of the act (that of Antigone's 'no' to Creon in his seminar on the ethics of psychoanalysis), concerns precisely a lone political decision (the decision to defy an edict of power) with no relation to the figure of the analyst.

Gilbert 'defends' me by way of raising against me two main reproaches: my books 'display a level of scholarship which would be considered pitiable in the work of an undergraduate student' (above, p. 62); and, I am 'a writer whose main stock-in-trade is demonstrably ill-informed and frequently inaccurate diatribes against the legacies of the New Lefts' (above, p. 63). Proofs? Here is Gilbert's reaction to my claim: 'If at a Cultural Studies colloquium in the 1970s, one was asked innocently "Is your line of argumentation not similar to that of Arendt?" this was a sure sign that one was in deep trouble' (above, pp. 63–4):

> What the hell is Žižek talking about? How on earth would Žižek *know* what 'would have happened' (with enough certainty to know that anything would have been a '*sure sign*' of anything else) at a 'cultural studies colloquium in the 1970s'. There was only one place in the world where one might have attended a 'cultural studies colloquium in the 1970s': at the University of Birmingham – and to the best of anyone's recollection (I have asked a number of people who were there), Slavoj Žižek never made it along to one. (above, p. 64)

Well, Birmingham definitely was not the only place 'in the world' – being born in 1949, I am old enough to have followed the scene around Europe from the early 1970s, where, in the aftermath of the 1968 events, a leftist critical analysis of cultural products was flourishing, especially in Germany and France, but also in Latin America. And, unfortunately, from that time, I remember clearly incidents where stating similarity to Arendt functioned as an act of ominous accusation. Gilbert's reaction to my claim that cultural studies often display a lack of proper knowledge of 'hard' sciences is even harsher:

> The hypocrisy is breathtaking, even if we limit ourselves to this passage alone, in and of itself. First, let us ask: how do we know, or claim the authority to decide, what constitutes 'proper knowledge'? Well, at the present time such authority can be conferred by institutions and their mechanisms of legitimation (degrees, titles, etc.), or by the charisma which accrues to individuals within the circuits of celebrity. However, in the 'academic world' of which Žižek is so routinely disparaging, there is another, more democratic mechanism: the established conventions of citation and reference. As tedious as these conventions no doubt appear to a jet-setting star such as Žižek, it is essential to bear in mind that this is their primary purpose: to allow any reader whatsoever, if they want to, to go and check a writer's sources, and make their

own judgments as to that writer's uses of them. The lack of such an apparatus immediately renders it impossible for such an open process of verification and potential challenge to take place. (above, p. 65)

Can one really take these lines seriously? In the wake of the so-called 'Sokal affair', my remark on the lack of proper knowledge of 'hard sciences' in cultural studies, as well as my remark on the change in the status of Hannah Arendt, are simply cases of 'stating the obvious': they do not need a detailed bibliographical support in the same sense that, say, the statement 'Sartre's existentialism was very popular in the years after World War II' or a statement 'there is a great resistance to the Derridean deconstructionist style of writing among many Anglo-Saxon analytically oriented philosophers' needs no verification through quotes.

My basic position here is a rather old-fashioned one: in philosophy, we do not need any 'authority to decide what constitutes "proper knowledge" ' – the only thing that really matters is the inherent strength and quality of the line of thought. I can well imagine (and not only imagine) a text written by an author sustained by extraordinary charisma and institutional power, which is worthless; I can well imagine (and not only imagine – a glance at the present volume is sufficient) authors who supplement their texts with a detailed apparatus of quotes and references, which merely covers up the poverty of the line of thought. And, on the contrary, philosophy abounds with authors who lacked institutional power and more or less ignored the quotes and references conventions, but nonetheless made a substantial contribution to modern thought (recall Sartre's proverbial laxity in these matters). The irony here is that what I was never accused of is committing a true offence at this level: misquoting, or manipulating with quotes, in order to make the criticized author say something he did not say – something which precisely *is* the case in the present volume!

The machine goes rolling on: I reach 'a pitch of absurdity when [I] write. . . that "Althusser is often dismissed as a proto-Stalinist" ' (above, p. 71) – Really? Again, I am old enough to remember, among other things, the reactions to Althusser from E.P. Thompson in the UK (recall his *The Poverty of Theory*, 1978), from some representatives of the younger generation of the Frankfurt School (like Alfred Schmidt's *Geschichte und Struktur*, 1978) in Germany, from

Jacques Rancière in France (see his *La leçon d'Althusser* (1974) his impassioned break with Althusser), where the accusation of 'Stalinism' was in the air all the time. The story goes on with Lenin:

> Žižek almost invariably presents Lenin's break as an example of pure volition, unmediated will, a fundamental act in the most metaphysical and individualistic sense. . .
> To the contrary, I would argue that Lenin's decision to push the revolution to its logical conclusion was *not* some miraculous accession to grace, but the product of a careful strategic calculation and a willingness to recalibrate the terms of that calculation in the face of emergent events. (above, pp. 73–74)

What follows is then the already described mechanism: when Gilbert has to admit that this ridiculous image of Lenin's break as 'a fundamental act in the most metaphysical and individualistic sense' does not fit, that I do take into account the 'conjecturalist' aspect of Lenin's politics, he reads this as *my* contradiction:

> It was a willingness to accept the fact that his actions were always already caught up in a destabilizing network of causes and effects which forced Lenin to act as he did, not some pure moment of revelation. Žižek does seem to acknowledge this much when he describes Lenin's attitude as one of 'authentic historical openness' (Žižek 2001b). But let us be clear: this undermines his entire position. (above, p. 74)

This series culminates in an accusation whose hypocrisy is really breathtaking, as Gilbert himself put it: 'What is most extraordinary about all of Žižek's polemic against critics of Leninism, is that he writes now as if the entire history of Leninism and its consequences were not deeply problematic' (above, p. 75). Here, I really cannot believe my eyes! Of course I am aware that the predominant view considers Leninism 'deeply problematic': the main thrust of my book on Lenin is precisely to counter this view. Furthermore, not only did I write extensively about Stalinism; in my book on Lenin, I also explicitly pointed out how Stalinism was a consequence of Leninism – here is an unambiguous passage from it:

> One cannot separate the unique constellation which enabled the revolutionary takeover in October 1917 from its later 'Stalinist'

turn: the very constellation that rendered the revolution possible (peasants' dissatisfaction, a well-organized revolutionary elite, etc.) led to the 'Stalinist' turn in its aftermath – therein resides the proper Leninist tragedy. Rosa Luxembourg's famous alternative 'socialism or barbarism' ended up as the ultimate infinite judgment, asserting the speculative identity of the two opposed terms: the 'really existing' socialism *was* barbarism.

Gilbert's final *coup de grace* is his earth-shaking insight that 'there already *is* an emerging coherent movement against neo-liberal capitalism to which the Western intellectual Left could ally itself in a new spirit of anti-capitalist partisanship' (above, p. 77) – as if I did not analyse this movement, trying to demonstrate that, precisely, it is not coherent!

Hamilton Grant begins in a well-known style: 'Žižek is not simply erroneous, but *exemplarily* so. Incompleteness, that is, is not self-evidently the index of "materialism" Žižek takes it to be' (above, p. 83). Again, I cannot believe my eyes: where do I claim that incompleteness is 'self-evidently the index of "materialism"'? It should be evident even to a superficial reader of my texts that I consider the notion of materialism that I propose counter-intuitive, running against the standard notion of materialism as asserting the full objective reality of nature. Does, however, this really mean that it is '*nature* – which Žižek, with Fichte, rules out from the first' (above, p. 84)? Here is Hamilton Grant's main argument:

> The striving to eliminate nature, disregarding for the moment whether the implied incompleteness of the 'striving' is indeed a hallmark of 'critical materialism', extends the morphology of Fichtean Idealism beyond philosophy into every theoretical architecture premised on incomplete constructivism, in those, that is, in which grounds for appeal are short-circuited by the assertion of a discursive, semiotic, or economic dependency of 'the real', and where 'nature' therefore emerges as the *product of freedom* (a social/historical/political construct). (above, p. 89)

There are so many obvious replies to these lines that I do not even know where to begin. First, one of the standard criticisms of my work, from Ernesto Laclau and Judith Butler up to some texts in the present volume, is that I do not grasp how (what appears as) reality is a contingent socio-symbolic construct, that I 'essentialize' an aspect of social reality (class struggle, sexual difference) into a pre-discursive real. What these critics did get right is that I effectively *reject* the 'total' socio-symbolic constructivism, asserting the real as its limitation – here, however, I am accused precisely of advocating such constructivism! The further irony here is that, for the Schelling of *Weltalter*, nature effectively *is* a 'product of freedom': the result of the primordial 'contraction' of the abyss of pure Freedom.

When, in order to prove his point, Hamilton Grant writes: 'Žižek prepares the *Weltalter* to become the metaphysics of subjectivity once it has been "rid of. . . material inertia" (1997b: 77)' (above, p. 86), the manipulation with my quote is, again, truly breathtaking. The passage from which Hamilton Grant quotes four words describes the cyberspace 'posthumanist' utopia of transforming our identity into a software that can be downloaded into different material supports and thus acquire a free-floating status: 'the fantasy of the humanity that overcomes the egotism of the con-traction-into-self and thus gets rid of the material inertia, changing the bodily reality into a transparent medium of spiritual commu-nion'. My point is thus that this idealist fantasy echoes Schelling's notion of the third 'divine age' – and, on the very next page, I explic-itly problematize such a reading of Schelling: 'Is, however, this reading of the Schellingian Third Age – the Future, the return to the Divine Bliss – as simply another version of the fantasmatic sim-ulation of the real, the only one possible?'

Since my central thesis effectively is the link between materialism and the ontological incompleteness of reality, let me quickly specify this point. How are we to interpret the so-called 'principle of uncer-tainty' which prohibits us from attaining full knowledge of particles at the quantum level (to determine the velocity *and* the position of a particle)? For Einstein, this principle of uncertainty proves that quantum physics does not provide a full description of reality, that there must be some unknown features missed by its conceptual apparatus. Heisenberg, Bohr and others, on the contrary, insisted that this incompleteness of our knowledge of quantum reality points towards a strange incompleteness of quantum reality itself, a claim which leads to a breathtakingly weird ontology. When we want to simulate reality within an artificial (virtual, digital) medium, we do not have to go to the end: we just have to reproduce features which make the image realistic for the spectator's point of view. Say, if there is a house in the background, we do not have to construct through the program the house's entire interior, since we expect that the participant will not want to enter the house; or, the construction of a virtual person in this space can be limited to his exterior – no need to bother with inner organs, bones, etc. We just need to install a program which will promptly fill in this gap if the participant's activity necessitates it (say, if he were to cut with a knife deep into the virtual person's body). It is like when we scroll down a long text on a computer screen: earlier and later pages do not pre-exist our viewing them; in the same way, when we simulate a virtual universe, the microscopic structure of objects can be left blank, and if stars on the horizon appear hazy, we need not bother to construct the way they would appear to a closer look, since nobody will go up there to take such a look at them. The truly interesting idea here is that the quantum indeterminacy which we encounter when we inquire into the tiniest components of our universe can read in exactly the same way, as a feature of the limited resolution of our simulated world, that is, as the sign of the ontological incompleteness of (what we experience as) reality itself. The idea is that God who created/'programmed' our universe was too lazy (or, rather, he underestimated our – human – intelligence): he thought that we, humans, will not succeed in probing into the structure of nature beyond the level of atoms, so he programmed the matrix of our universe only to the level of its atomic structure – beyond it, he simply left things fuzzy, like a house whose interior is not programmed in a PC game. Is, however, the theologico-digital way the only way to read this paradox? We can read it as a sign that we already live in a simulated universe, but also as a signal of the ontological incompleteness of reality itself. In the first case, the ontological incompleteness is transposed into an epistemological one, that is, the incompleteness is perceived as the effect of the fact that another (secret, but fully real) agency constructed our reality as a simulated universe. The truly difficult thing is to accept the second choice, the ontological incompleteness of reality itself. That is to say, what immediately arises is a massive common-sense reproach: but how can this ontological incompleteness hold for reality itself? Is not reality *defined* by its ontological complete-ness? If reality 'really exists out there', it *has* to be complete 'all the way down', otherwise we are dealing with a fiction which just 'hangs in the air', like appearances which are not appearances of a substantial something. Here, precisely, quantum physics enters, offering a model of how to think (or imagine, at least) such 'open' ontology.

It is here that one should apply yet again the Kantian distinction between negative and infinite judgment: the statement 'material reality is all there is' can be negated in two ways, in the form of 'material reality *is not all there is*' and 'material reality *is non-all*'. The first negation (of a predicate) leads to the standard metaphysics: material reality is not everything, there is another, higher, spiritual reality. As such, this negation is, in accordance with Lacan's formulas of sexuation, inherent to the positive statement 'material reality is all there is': as its constitutive exception, it grounds its universality. If, however, we assert a non-predicate and say 'material reality *is non-all*', this merely asserts the non-all of reality without implying any exception – paradoxically, one should thus claim that 'material reality is non-all', *not* 'material reality is all there is', is the true formula of materialism.

Marchart's basic reproach again concerns my alleged notion of 'a purely abyssal and decisionist act that is to be achieved without any strategic considerations of circumstances' (above, p. 102):

> There will be, without doubt, *an aspect* of adventurism in all acting, otherwise we would stay at home paralysed, but from the premise that in our acts we cannot rely on 'objective laws' that would guarantee success it does not follow that acts occur in a vacuum where all strategic considerations are suspended. . . But to sustain the idea of a clear-cut and total break, it is necessary for this order to be conceived as a homogeneous and self-sufficient block in the first place. Again the all-or-nothing logic of the argument leaves no room for any strategic and thus political negotiation between a counter-hegemonic project and the established order. Either the break is total, or no act has occurred. (above, pp. 102–103)[6]

Marchart then links these two opposed dimensions to the ontological difference: 'the idea of an "authentic act", achievable in its ontological purity, is as phantasmatic as the opposite idea of a total ontic obliteration of the act' (above, p. 108). Perhaps the best way to answer this reproach is *by* answering Marchart's weird claim that I miss or disavow the proximity of Hannah Arendt to Badiou: weird, because I *repeatedly* made this point – here is one of these cases, from my *On Belief*, where I also answer Marchart's other reproach (that I, following Badiou, posit an exclusive choice between act and ontic activity). I draw attention to:

The fatal limitation of the standard historicist criticism of Alain Badiou's work, according to which, the intervention *ex nihilo* of the Event into the historicity of Being is a laicized version of the religious Revelation through which Eternity directly intervenes into the temporal unfolding: is it not that Badiou himself emphasizes how one cannot derive the Event from the order of Being, since all we have in the order of Being is *la site evenementielle*, the site of the potential emergence of the Event of Truth? The first problem with this reproach is that it knocks on an open door: Badiou himself repeatedly refers to the Event as the laicized Grace.[7] More fundamentally, what these reproaches fail to see is, again, the gap that forever separates history (in the sense of a simple dynamic evolutionary unfolding) from historicity proper whose site is none other than the very tension between Eternity and History, the unique moments of their short-circuit. Which is why, against occasional misleading formulations by Badiou himself, one should assert that there is no ultimate 'synthesis' between Event and Being: *this 'synthesis' is already the Event itself*, the 'magic' appearance of the 'noumenal' dimension of Truth in the order of Being. No wonder, then, that, in his notion of the Event of Truth as external and irreducible to the process of Being, Badiou gets involved with some strange bedfellows whom he otherwise violently disavows. In her 'What is Freedom?', Hannah Arendt asserts that, far from being controllable and predictable, an act of freedom is closer to the nature of a miracle: freedom is displayed in a capacity 'to begin something new and. . .not being able to control or even foretell its consequences' (Arendt 1968: 151). A free act thus involves the

abyss of nothingness that opens up before any deed that cannot be accounted for by a reliable chain of cause and effect and is inexplicable in Aristotelian categories of potentiality and actuality. (Arendt 1968: 165)

For Arendt, and in a strict homology to Badiou, freedom is thus opposed to the whole domain of the provision of services and goods, of the maintenance of households and the exercise of administration, which do not belong to politics proper: the only place for freedom is the communal political space. What thereby gets lost is no less than Marx's fundamental insight into how 'the problem of freedom is contained in the social relations implicitly declared "unpolitical" – that is, naturalized – in liberal discourse'.

So when Marchart claims that 'only by way of this tensional relation between the ontic and the ontological, between the politico-historical situation in which we act and the quasi-transcendental conditions of all acting, action is made possible in the first place' (above, pp. 107–108), where is here the critical edge against me? I clearly repeatedly state that act is only act *with regard to* a situation: when a moment passes, act is no longer act. In this sense, there is no problem for me in what Marchart calls the ontic-ontological unity: 'one should assert that there is no ultimate "synthesis" between Event and Being: *this "synthesis" is already the Event itself*'.

Furthermore, I am well aware that Arendt was not *simply* a liberal. What is at stake in the difficult relationship between Heidegger and Arendt is Heidegger's much-decried aversion to liberalism and (liberal) democracy, which he continuously, to his end, rejected as 'inauthentic', not the idiosyncrasies of their personal liaisons. Arendt was not only opposed to Heidegger along the double axis of woman versus man and a 'worldly' Jew versus a 'provincial' German, she was (which is much more important) *the first liberal Heideggerian*, the first who tried to reunite Heidegger's insights with the liberal-democratic universe. In a closer reading, of course, it is easy to discern what enabled Arendt to support liberalism while maintaining her basic fidelity to Heidegger's insights: her anti-bourgeois stance, her critical dismissal of politics as 'interest groups' politics, as the expression of the competitive and acquisitive society of the bourgeoisie. She shared the great conservatives' dissatisfaction with the lack of heroism and the pragmatic-utilitarian orientation of the bourgeois society: 'Simply to brand as outbursts of nihilism this violent dissatisfaction with the prewar age and subsequent attempts at restoring it (from Nietzsche to Sorel to Pareto, from Rimbaud and T.E. Lawrence to Juenger, Brecht and Malraux, from Bakunin and Nechayev to Aleksander Blok) is to overlook how justified disgust can be in a society wholly permeated with the ideological outlook and moral standards of the bourgeoisie' (Arendt 1973: 328). The opposition Arendt mobilizes here is the one between *citoyen* and *bourgeois*: the first lives in the political sphere of public engagement for the common good, of the participation in running public affairs, while the second is the egotistic utilitarian fully immersed in the production process and reducing all other dimensions of life to their role in enabling the smooth running of this process. In Aristotelian terms, this opposition is the one between *praxis* and *poiesis*, between the 'high' exercise of virtues in public life, and the 'low' instrumentality of labour – the opposition whose echoes reverberate not only in Habermas' distinction between communicative action and instrumental activity, but even in Badiou's notion of Event (and in his concomitant denial that an Event can take place in the domain of production). Recall how Arendt describes, in Badiouian terms, the suspension of temporality as the defining ontological characteristic of ontic political action: acting, as men's capacity to begin something new, 'out of nothing', not reducible to a calculated strategic reaction to a given situation, takes place in the non-temporal *gap* between past and future, in the hiatus between the end of the old order and the beginning of the new which in history is precisely the moment of revolution (Arendt 1990: 205). Such an opposition, of course, raises a fundamental question formulated by Robert Pippin:

> How can Arendt separate out what she admires in bourgeois culture – its constitutionalism, its assertion of fundamental human rights, its equality before the law, its insistence on a private zone in human life, exempt from the political, its religious tolerance – and condemn what she disagrees with – its secularism, its cynical assumption of the pervasiveness of self-interest, the perverting influence of money on human value, its depoliticizing tendencies, and the menace it poses for tradition and a sense of place? (Pippin 2005: 165)

In other words, are these two sides not the two sides of the same phenomenon? No wonder then, that, when Arendt is pressed to provide the outline of the authentic 'care of the world' as a political practice that would not be contaminated by utilitarian pragmatic calculation of interests, all she can evoke are self-organizations in revolutionary situations, from the early American tradition of town-hall meetings of all citizens to revolutionary councils in the German revolution. Not that she is not politically justified in evoking these examples – the problem is that they are 'utopian', that they cannot be reconciled with the liberal-democratic political order to which she remains faithful. In other words, is Arendt with regard to liberal democracy not the victim of the same illusion as the democratic communists who, within the Really Existing Socialism, were fighting for its truly democratic version? Arendt is also right when (implicitly against Heidegger) she points out that fascism, although a reaction to bourgeois banality, remains its inherent negation, that is, within the horizon of bourgeois society: the true problem of Nazism is not that it 'went too far' in its subjectivist–nihilist hubris of exerting total power, but that it did *not* go far enough, that is, that its violence was an impotent acting out which, ultimately, remained in the service of the very order it despised. (However, Heidegger would also have been right in rejecting Arendt's Aristotelian politics as not radical enough to break out of the nihilist space of European modernity.)

Let us now pass to Mowitt, whose text engages in a more low-key version of La Berge's 'characterological' analysis:

> Throughout Žižek's work one finds him engaged in a low intensity but nevertheless steady conflict with post-structuralism. When this conflict rises above the quick and dirty thrills of caricature, it seems clear that it is driven by Žižek's desire to cast post-structuralism as the thief of his (or perhaps psychoanalysis') enjoyment. (above, p. 133)

While I find this kind of analysis problematic for reasons which I already explained in my reaction to La Berge's text, Mowitt's text does raise a series of important issues on the interconnected topics of trauma, resentment and envy; so let me add some remarks on each of these three concepts. Apropos trauma, it seems to me that Mowitt misses my central point about the *secondary* character of trauma – here is yet another quote from myself:

> For Lacan, the Real, at its most radical, has to be totally de-substantialized. It is not an external thing that resists being caught in the symbolic network, but the crack within the symbolic network itself. The Real as the monstrous Thing behind the veil of appearances is precisely the ultimate lure. . . What is the lure here? Apropos the notion of the Real as the substantial Thing, Lacan accomplishes a reversal which is ultimately the

same as the passage from the special to the general theory of relativity in Einstein. While the special theory already introduces the notion of the curved space, it conceives of this curvature as the effect of matter: it is the presence of matter which curves the space, i.e. only an empty space would have been non-curved. With the passage to the general theory, the causality is reversed: far from *causing* the curvature of the space, matter is its *effect*, i.e., the presence of matter signals that the space is curved. What can all this have to do with psychoanalysis? Much more than it may appear: in a way exactly homologous to Einstein, for Lacan, the Real – the Thing – is not so much the inert presence which curves the symbolic space (introducing gaps and inconsistencies in it), but, rather, an effect of these gaps and inconsistencies.

This brings us back to Freud himself who, in the development of his theory of trauma, changed his position in a way strangely homologous to Einstein's above-described shift. Freud started with the notion of trauma as something that, from outside, intrudes into our psychic life and disturbs its balance, throwing it out of joint with the symbolic coordinates which organize our experience – think about a brutal rape or about witnessing (or even being submitted to) a torture. From this perspective, the problem is how to symbolize the trauma, how to integrate it into our universe of meaning and thus cancel its disorienting impact. Later, Freud opted for the opposite approach. His analysis of 'Wolfman', his famous Russian patient, isolated as the early traumatic event that marked his life the fact that, as a child of 1½ years, he witnessed the parental *coitus a tergo*. However, originally, when this scene took place, there was nothing traumatic in it: far from shattering the child, he just inscribed it into his memory as an event the sense of which was not clear at all to him. Only years later, when the child became obsessed with the question 'where do children come from' and started to develop infantile sexual theories, did he draw out this memory in order to use it as a traumatic scene embodying the mystery of sexuality. The scene was thus traumatized, elevated into a traumatic Real, only retroactively, in order to help the child to cope with the impasse of his symbolic universe (his inability to find answers to the enigma of sexuality). In exact homology to Einstein's shift, the original fact is here the symbolic deadlock, and the traumatic event is resuscitated to fill in the gaps in the universe of meaning.

Does exactly the same not hold also for the Real of a social antagonism? Anti-Semitism 'reifies' (embodies in a particular group of people) the inherent social antagonism: it treats Jew as the Thing which, from outside, intrudes into the social body and disturbs its balance. What happens in the passage from the position of strict class struggle to the Fascist anti-Semitism is not just a simple replacement of one figure of the enemy (bourgeoisie, the ruling class) with another (Jews); the logic of the struggle is totally different. In the class struggle, classes themselves are caught in the antagonism which is inherent to social structure, while the Jew is a foreign intruder which causes social antagonism, so that all we need in order to restore social harmony is to annihilate Jews. That is to say, in exactly the same way Wolfman as a child resuscitated the scene of the parental coitus in order to organize his infantile sexual theories, a Fascist anti-Semite elevates the Jew into the monstrous Thing that causes social decadence.

With regard to resentment, I think it is a concept which should not be dismissed in a Nietzschean way – recall what W.G. Sebald wrote about Jean Amery's confrontation with the trauma of the Nazi concentration camps:

> The energy behind Amery's polemics derived from implacable resentment. A large number of his essays are concerned with justifying this emotion (commonly regarded as a warped need for revenge) as essential to a truly critical view of the past. Resentment, writes Amery in full awareness of the illogicality of his attempt at a definition, 'nails every one of us unto the cross of his ruined past. Absurdly, it demands that the irreversible be turned around, that the event be undone'. . . The issue, then, is not to resolve but to reveal the conflict. The spur of resentment which Amery conveys to us in his polemic demands recognition of the *right* to resentment, entailing no less than a programmatic attempt to sensitize the consciousness of a people 'already rehabilitated by time'. (Sebald 2003: 160–62)

When a subject is hurt in such a devastating way that the very idea of revenge according to *jus talionis* is no less ridiculous than the promise of the reconciliation with the perpetrator after the perpetrator's atonement, the only thing that remains is to persist in the 'unremitting denunciation of injustice'. One should give to this stance the whole anti-Nietzschean weight: here, resentment has nothing to do with the slave morality. It rather stands for the refusal to 'normalize' the crime, to make it part of a normal/explainable/accountable flow of things; after all possible explanations, it returns with its question: 'Yes, I got all this, but, nonetheless, *how could you have done it?*' In other words, the resentment for which Sebald pleads is a Nietzschean heroic resentment, a refusal to compromise, an insistence 'against all odds'.

And, finally, with regard to envy, its deadlock is grounded in the fact that human desire, as Lacan put it, is always 'desire of the Other' in both *genitivus subjectivus* and *genitivus objectivus*: desire for the Other, desire to be desired by the Other, and, especially, desire for what the Other desires – envy and *ressentiment* are thus a constitutive component of human desire, as already Augustine knew it so well – recall the passage from his *Confessions*, often quoted by Lacan, the scene of a baby jealous for his brother sucking the mother's breast ('I myself have seen and known an infant to be jealous though it could not speak. It became pale, and cast bitter looks on its foster-brother'.)

Based on this insight, Jean-Pierre Dupuy recently proposed a convincing critique of John Rawls' theory of justice: in Rawls' model of a just society, social inequalities are tolerated only insofar as they also help those at the bottom of the social ladder, and insofar as they are not based on inherited hierarchies, but on natural inequalities, which are considered contingent, not merits (Rawls 1971/1999). What Rawls does not see is how such a society would create conditions for an uncontrolled explosion of *ressentiment*: in it, I would know that my lower status is fully 'justified', and would thus be deprived of excusing my failure as the result of social injustice. Rawls thus proposes a terrifying model of a society in which hierarchy is directly legitimized in natural properties, thereby missing the simple lesson of an anecdote about a Slovene peasant who is given a choice by a good witch: she will either give him one cow, and to his neighbour two cows, or take from him one cow, and from his neighbour two cows – the peasant immediately chooses the second option. (In a more morbid version, the witch tells him: 'I will do to you whatever you want, but I warn you, I will do it to your neighbour twice!' The peasant, with a cunning smile, asks her: 'Take one of my eyes!')

No wonder that even today's Conservatives are ready to endorse Rawls' notion of justice: in December 2005, David Cameron, the newly elected leader of the British Conservative Party, signalled his intention to turn the Conservative Party into a defender of the underprivileged, declaring that: 'I think the test of all our policies should be: what does it do for the people who have the least, the people on the bottom rung of the ladder?'

Or, as Gore Vidal put it succinctly: 'It is not enough for me to win – the other must lose'. The catch of resentment is that it not only endorses the zero-sum-game principle where my victory equals the other's loss; it even implies a gap between the two, not the positive gap (we can all win with no losers at all), but a negative one: if I have to choose between my victory and my opponent's loss, I prefer the opponent's loss, even if it means also my own loss. It is as if my eventual gain from the opponent's loss functions as a kind of pathological element that stains the purity of my victory.

Friedrich Hayek (1994) knew that it is much easier to accept inequalities if one can claim that they result from an impersonal blind force, so the good thing about 'irrationality' of the market success or failure in capitalism (recall the old motif of market as the modern version of the imponderable fate) is that it allows me precisely to perceive my failure (or success) as 'undeserved', contingent. The fact that capitalism is not 'just' is thus a key feature that makes it palpable to the majority (I can accept much more easily my failure if I know that it is not due to my inferior qualities, but to chance).

What Nietzsche and Freud share is the idea that justice as equality is founded on envy – on the envy of the Other who has what we do not have, and who enjoys it; the demand for justice is thus ultimately the demand that the excessive enjoyment of the Other should be curtailed, so that everyone's access to *jouissance* should be equal. The necessary outcome of this demand, of course, is asceticism: since it is not possible to impose equal *jouissance*, what one *can* impose is only the equally shared *prohibition*. However, one should not forget that today, in our allegedly permissive society, this asceticism assumes precisely the form of its opposite, of the *generalized* super-ego injunction: 'Enjoy!'. We are all under the spell of this injunction, with the outcome that our enjoyment is more hindered than ever – recall the yuppie who combines narcissistic 'self-fulfilment' with utter ascetic discipline of jogging, eating health food, etc. This, perhaps, is what Nietzsche had in mind with his notion of the Last Man – it is only today that we can really discern the contours of the Last Man, in the guise of the hedonistic asceticism of yuppies. Nietzsche thus does not simply urge life-assertion against asceticism: he is well aware how a certain asceticism is the obverse of the decadent excessive sensuality – therein resides his criticism of Wagner's *Parsifal*, and, more generally, of the late Romantic decadence oscillating between damp sensuality and obscure spiritualism.

So what *is* envy? Recall again the Augustinian scene of a sibling envying his brother who is sucking the mother's breast: the subject does not envy the Other's possession of the prized object as such, but rather the way the Other is able to *enjoy* this object – which is why it is not enough for him simply to steal and thus gain possession of the object: his true aim is to destroy the Other's ability/capacity to enjoy the object. As such, envy is to be located into the triad of envy, thrift and melancholy, the three forms of not being able to enjoy the object (and, of course, reflexively enjoying this very impossibility). In contrast to the subject of envy, who envies the other's possession and/or *jouissance* of the object, the miser possesses the object, but cannot enjoy/consume it – his satisfaction derives from just possessing it, elevating it into a sacred, untouchable/prohibited, entity which should under no conditions be consumed (recall the proverbial figure of the lone miser who, upon returning home, safely locks the doors, opens up his chest and then takes the secret peek at his prized object, observing it in awe); this very hindrance that prevents the consummation of the object guarantees its status of the object of desire. The melancholic subject, like the miser, possesses the object, but loses the cause that made him desire it: this figure, most tragic of them all, has free access to all he wants, but finds no satisfaction in it. This excess of envy is the base of Rousseau's well-known, but nonetheless not fully exploited, distinction between egotism, *amour-de-soi* (which is natural), and *amour-propre*, the perverted preferring of oneself to others in which I focus not on achieving the goal, but on destroying the obstacle to it – here is the famous passage from the first dialogue of *Rousseau juge de Jean-Jacques*:

The primitive passions, which all directly tend towards our happiness, make us deal only with objects which relate to them, and whose principle is only *amour de soi*, are all in their essence lovable and tender; however, when, *diverted from their objects by obstacles, they are more occupied with the obstacle they try to get rid of, than with the object they try to reach,* they change their nature and become irascible and hateful. This is how *amour de soi,* which is a noble and absolute feeling, becomes *amour-propre,* that is to say, a relative feeling by means of which one compares oneself, a feeling which demands preferences, *whose enjoyment is purely negative and which does not strive to find satisfaction in our own well-being, but only in the misfortune of others.*

For Rousseau, an evil person is *not* an egotist, 'thinking only about his own interests': a true egotist is all too busy with taking care of his own good to have time to cause misfortunes to others, while the primary vice of a bad person is precisely that he is more occupied with others than with himself. Rousseau describes here a precise libidinal mechanism: the inversion which generates the shift of the libidinal investment from the object to the obstacle itself. This is why egalitarianism itself should never be accepted at its face value: the notion (and practice) of egalitarian justice, insofar as it is sustained by envy, relies on the inversion of the standard renunciation accomplished to benefit others: 'I am ready to renounce it, *so that others will (also)* not *(be able to) have it!*' Far from being opposed to the spirit of sacrifice, evil is thus the very spirit of sacrifice, ready to ignore one's own well-being – if, through my sacrifice, I can deprive the Other of his jouissance. Is this sad fact that the opposition to the system cannot articulate itself in the guise of a realistic alternative, or at least a meaningful utopian project, but only as a meaningless outburst, not the strongest indictment of our predicament? Where is here the celebrated freedom of choice, when the only choice is the one between playing by the rules and (self-)destructive violence, a violence which is almost exclusively directed against one's own – the cars burned and the schools torched were not from rich neighbourhoods, but were part of the hard-won acquisitions of the very strata from which protesters originated.

What bothers me in Ian Parker's contribution is a series of directly deceiving insinuations, like the following one: 'When Slovenia joined the European Union in 2004, Žižek wrote a brief newspaper article to explain to readers what these 2 million or so people might have to offer the new Europe' (above, p. 158). The passage, of course, insinuates that I was praising Slovene contribution from the nationalist standpoint – however, here is the very first phrase of the article to which Parker refers: 'In the months before Slovenia's entry to the

European Union, whenever a foreign journalist asked me what new dimension Slovenia would contribute to Europe, my answer was: nothing'.[8] Another totally misleading passage:

> At a moment when NSK 'State in Time' could provide an antidote to the pretensions of Europe and each national component, Žižek neglected even to mention his former comrades. One conclusion would be that too close identification with state power, or an 'over-identification' that is bewitched with access to power has taken the place of resistant subversive over-identification. (above, p. 159)

Well, I admit it, I not only 'neglected even to mention' them – for political reasons, I now actively *oppose* them. Why? Two years or so ago, members of the NSK started to complain that their role in the struggle for Slovene independence is not sufficiently recognized (i.e., that they are not properly included into the nationalist narrative of the origins of the Slovene state that is now being written). To set the record straight, they organized a collective volume celebrating their contribution, to which they invited even some rightist nationalists – anyone ready to praise them. Of course, I refused to have anything to do with this turn of NSK into state-artists. If there is a 'too close identification with state power', it is *theirs*, which is why I cut links with them.

Stamp's contribution follows the predominant rule of the volume, beginning with a disqualification: 'And yet Žižek does not *read* Derrida's text at all' (above, p. 171). Why? The point is the 'extent to which the repeated denunciations of Derrida and deconstruction . . .effectively install the "unexpected continuity" of Žižek with the very thing he fights so hard against: the thing he names "deconstructionism"' (above, p. 172) – in short, my open struggle against deconstructionism is a lure covering up my 'almost absolute proximity to those "Derridean" or "deconstructionist" readings of Hegel', so that one should read me as a 'deconstructionist-in-disavowal' (above, p. 174). There are two things that I find problematic in this diagnosis. First, the least one can say is that the parasitic attitude of being one's opponent-in-disavowal goes also for the opposite side, for Derrideans and Derrida himself. That is to say, I have no problem to admit that I am in some sense Derridean – in what sense? In the sense of identifying with the disavowed side of

Derrida's own edifice: as a Hegelian, I claim that it is Derrida who is a 'Hegelian-in-disavowal'. The main thrust of my readings of Derrida is that, in spite of his detailed interpretations of Hegel, he 'does not *read* Hegel's text at all' – a claim which can be substantiated by a close reading of one of Derrida's key late texts, his long review of Catherine Malabou's path-breaking *The Future of Hegel* (published as a foreword to the English translation), where he finally *did* start to read Hegel. Malabou's book is a Derridean reading and thorough *defence* of Hegel, and it is almost painful to observe how Derrida, deeply impressed, shattered even, by the book, in an exemplary case of intellectual honesty concedes point by point her insights which implicitly overturn the standard 'Derridean' interpretation of Hegel.

Second point: after asserting my 'almost absolute proximity' to Derrideans, Stamp goes on to formulate the difference between Derridean and my theory in the most traditional terms of 'binary logic', as a clear opposition of two externally opposed positions: in my practice, I really do not need examples, I merely use them as mere examples, as secondary illustrations of pre-established universal concepts, while deconstruction mobilizes examples in their 'aporetic singularity' which resists being subsumed under any conceptual universality:

> For all the quasi-Hegelian bluster about 'concrete universality', he *does not need* the examples he proclaims as his symptom/ *sinthome*. In a certain sense, nothing need be added for it to work. This peculiar theoretical self-sufficiency might be contrasted to deconstruction, which is nothing without an '*and*', almost nothing but its examples in their aporetic singularity. (above, pp. 173–74)

So where is here the 'almost absolute proximity'? However, the main point ignored by Stamp is that I am tempted to raise exactly the same reproach to Derrida himself: although the stated strategy of his reading is to demonstrate how examples 'resist their subsumptive incorporation by concepts', in the predominant practice of his texts, he does exactly that – the 'deconstructive reading' much too often leaves in the reader a bitter taste of utter predictability, of an inexorable machine which can subsume all texts, locating in them always the same tension between logocentric metaphysics-of-presence and

the traces that 'supplement' the metaphysical edifice, that is, that function simultaneously as its conditions of possibility and conditions of
impossibility. As for my own practice, and if I treat Stamp's reproach
somewhat naïvely, as an empirical claim, it would have been easy to
falsify it by a long list of cases where my own example led me to overturn the notion this example was meant to 'illustrate'. This is why I
effectively often do what I am accused of: repeating the same examples – what changes is their interpretation. (Just one case: see how, in
The Parallax View, I return to the 'Say "Fuck me!"' scene from David
Lynch's *Wild at Heart*, giving it a totally different interpretive twist.)

After asking a series of rhetorical questions ('What would an
example that was not subsumable under such a general law [of the
concept] look like? Is it even possible for examples to resist their subsumptive incorporation by concepts? What thinking of singularity
would this exemplary resistance [if there is any] produce?'), Stamp
concludes: 'Yet Žižek asks none of these questions. Nor could he,
since he already has his answers' (above, p. 174). This claim (that I
'ask none of these questions') is literally *not true*: asking them is the
central part of my notion of what an example is. The difference
between the Idealist and the materialist use of examples is that, in
the Platonic-Idealist approach, examples are always imperfect, they
never perfectly render what they are supposed to exemplify, so that
we should take care not to take them too literally, while, for a materialist, there is always more in the example than in what it exemplifies: that is, an example always threatens to undermine what it is
supposed to exemplify since it gives body to what the exemplified
notion itself represses, is unable to cope with. (Therein resides
Hegel's materialist procedure in his *Phenomenology*: each 'figure of
consciousness' is first staged/exemplified and then undermined
through its own example.) This is why the Idealist approach always
demands a multitude of examples – since no single example is fully
fitting, one has to enumerate them to indicate the transcendent
wealth of the Idea they exemplify, the Idea being the fixed point of
reference of the floating examples. A materialist, on the contrary,
tends to repeat one and the same example, to return to it obsessively:
it is the particular example which remains the same in all symbolic
universes, while the universal notion it is supposed to exemplify
continually changes its shape, so that we get a multitude of universal notions circulating, like flies around the light, around a single
example. Is this not what Lacan is doing, returning to the same

exemplary cases (the guessing-game with five hats, the dream of Irma's injection), each time providing a new interpretation? Such an example is the *universal Singular*: a singular entity which persists as the universal in the multitude of its interpretations.[9]

This, finally, brings us to Valentine's contribution, which, quite appropriately, closes the volume: it is *exemplary* of all other contributions, in the sense that it self-reflexively mirrors their basic procedure. Here is how Valentine announces his programme: 'So let's just sit back and have a laugh at the way that Žižek invents the necessity of an ethical position through which everyone will be constrained' (above, p. 181). Unfortunately, I cannot say the same: beneath the surface of light jokes and obscenities there is a very poor and sloppy line of argumentation: nothing to laugh at. As usual, it begins with a rather primitive misquote: the claim that I want to invent 'the necessity of an ethical position through which everyone will be constrained' (and thus 'Žižek's notion of revolution is essentially conservative since it aims to replace something that capitalism has destroyed' (above, p. 181)), is based on a misreading of the last lines of my Deleuze book, where I wrote that the logic of carnivalesque suspension:

Is limited to traditional hierarchical societies: with the full deployment of capitalism, especially today's 'late capitalism', it is the predominant 'normal' life itself which, in a way, gets 'carnivalized', with its constant self-revolutionizing, with its reversals, crises, reinventions, so that it is the critique of capitalism, from a 'stable' ethical position, which, today, more and more appears as an exception.

How, then, are we to revolutionize an order whose very principle is constant self-revolutionizing? This, perhaps, is *the* question today.

Is it not clear, from the final question that I raise, that, for me, the way to proceed is not to criticize capitalism from a ' "stable" ethical position', but, precisely, to invent an even more radical transformation than capitalism's own constant self-revolutionizing? My remark makes a point which was already made by perspicuous Deleuzians like Brian Massumi:

The more varied, and even erratic, the better. Normalcy starts to lose its hold. The regularities start to loosen. This loosening of normalcy is part of capitalism's dynamic. It's not a simple liberation. It's capitalism's own form of power. It's no longer disciplinary institutional power that defines everything, it's capitalism's power to produce variety – because markets get saturated. Produce variety and you produce a niche market. The oddest of affective tendencies are okay – as long as they pay. Capitalism starts intensifying or diversifying affect, but only in order to extract surplus-value. It hijacks affect in order to intensify profit potential. It literally valorises affect. The capitalist logic of surplus-value production starts to take over the relational field that is also the domain of political ecology, the ethical field of resistance to identity and predictable paths. It's very troubling and confusing, because it seems to me that there's been a certain kind of convergence between the dynamic of capitalist power and the dynamic of resistance. (Massumi 2002: 224)

What then follows is another standard reproach: I have not even read *Anti-Oedipus* – if I were to do it, I would soon discover that the target of Deleuze and Guattari is not Lacan, but the Oedipal logic of psychoanalysis, and that Deleuze and Guattari point out how Lacan himself, in contrast to his followers, was fully aware of the limitations of the Oedipal logic: 'Perhaps if [Žižek] had bothered to read the bloody book, or just looked up "Lacan" in the index, he might have found out that his "discoveries" – through which he claims to demonstrate both the explanatory relevance of Lacan for reading Deleuze and Guattari, and their indebted opposition to him – are already there, fully acknowledged, in *Anti-Oedipus*' (above, p. 188). Are they really? Is Valentine aware what he is saying when he claims 'There is no opposition to Lacan in *Anti-Oedipus*' (above, p. 189)? It is Valentine who should do his homework here and read *Difference and Repetition* and *The Logic of Sense*, where one finds a reference to psychoanalysis which is substantially different from its critique in *Anti-Oedipus*. In the 'real genesis' part of *The Logic of Sense*, Oedipus is conceptualized as the very agent of *de*territorialization, in clear contrast to *Anti-Oedipus*. Even more importantly, *Difference and Repetition* provides an excellent account of the Freudian 'death-drive' and compulsion-to-repeat, in clear contrast to the dismissal of the death-drive in *Anti-Oedipus*. So the least one can say is that, between *Difference and Repetition* and *Anti-Oedipus*, Deleuze radically changed his view of psychoanalysis.

Therein resides the core of my reading of Deleuze in *Organs Without Bodies*: that the accentuated opposition to psychoanalysis in *Anti-Oedipus* is to be read as an indication of the crucial shift in Deleuze's own theory. My further claim is that this shift also has catastrophic political consequences: what underlies *Anti-Oedipus* is an anarchic–wild anti-capitalism which provides no space for concrete social transformation: each such attempt is disqualified as co-opted by capitalism.[10] Valentine takes this position much further than Deleuze and Guattari themselves, ending in a paroxysm of irrational violence:

> Deleuze and Guattari recognize that all revolutionary acts and positions are immediately co-opted, if not today then tomorrow, by virtue of the fact that they are merely representations, entities, and as such interruptions of the aimless revolutionary process (1977: 341), a 'rupture with causality' (1977: 377). The point is to have a go, to simply enjoy the buzz of violence. It is for this reason that the schizophrenic is not a revolutionary. (above, p. 194)

One should then not be surprised when, quite consequently, Valentine's text ends with a thought that can well serve as the motto of any liberal hedonist – and, besides, a thought which is breathtakingly anti-Deleuzian: 'Life is too short to worry about being right. It only leads to the downward spiral of self-deception. Just grab what you can' (above, p. 195). This, so it seems to me, is exactly what most of the contributors to the present volume were doing: just grabbing what they could to hit me with, not worrying about being right. A couple of years ago, the *Premiere* magazine reported on an ingenious inquiry: they looked into how the most famous endings of Hollywood films were translated in major non-English languages. The Chinese rendered 'This is the beginning of a beautiful friendship!' from *Casablanca* as: 'The two of us will now constitute a cell of anti-Fascist struggle!' – struggle against the enemy being the top priority, way above personal relations. In contrast to it, in Japan, Clark Gable's 'Frankly, my dear, I don't give a damn!' to Vivien Leigh from *Gone With the Wind* was rendered as: 'I fear, my darling, that there is a slight misunderstanding between the two of us' – a bow to Japanese proverbial courtesy and etiquette. So, unfortunately, I cannot say that I and other contributors to this volume will join hands to constitute a new cell of anti-fascist struggle: there is a slight misunderstanding between us.

There are two exceptions to this 'grab-what-you-can' attitude, two reproaches which run through different contributions and which deserve a more detailed reply. The first one concerns my notion of act as – so the critique goes – an 'irrational' self-grounded gesture, a metaphysical free act cut off from all strategic considerations that locate it within a specific socio-political situation. The second one is that I miss the fundamental lesson of discourse-theory: every totality, every order, is the result of the contingent struggle for hegemony; there is no agency within the political space which automatically assumes the principal role, since playing a central role is always the outcome of the struggle for hegemony; there is no 'central' antagonism or level of struggle 'expressed' or 'reflected' in other struggles in a distorted/displaced way, since distortion/displacement is 'original'. Another aspect of this second reproach is Laclau's rejection of the Marxist notion of fetishism: it relies on the opposition between direct expression of an idea (or a subject) and its distorted metaphoric representation: instead of being experienced directly as what they are, relations between people are represented as relations between objects. The underlying structure is that of inversion: instead of directly expressing their social essence, individuals express it in a mystified way, as relations between things – underlying this notion of inversion is a goal to undo it and to reinstate the proper relationship. The same goes for Marx (and the young Lukàcs) when they assert the proletariat as the universal class: while all other classes represent universality in a distorted way, the proletariat effectively is in its very being the universal class. Laclau's predictable reproach is that, precisely, there is no class (no political agent) which is directly universal, in which universality is directly embodied. Or, at the level of class consciousness: the proletarian class-consciousness is the only adequate one, while the consciousness of all other classes involves a structurally necessary mystification, a short-circuit between one's own particular class position and universality – against which, again, Laclau asserts that there simply is no 'true' class consciousness as opposed to a 'false' one, since every universality is sustained ('coloured') by a particular content.

Let me begin with the first reproach: it simply misrepresents my position. It was already Badiou who elaborated the notion of the 'evental site' as the crack in the existing situation, the opening for the possible intervention of an act. The link between the situation and the act is thus clear: far from being determined by the situation (or from intervening into it from a mysterious outside), acts are possible on account of the ontological non-closure, inconsistency, gaps in a situation. To make this point clear, let me resort again to self-quoting – here is a passage from my reading of Lukàcs where I address this point in detail:

Postmodern political thinkers reject Lukàcs's *History and Class Consciousness* as the purest version of the Hegelian Marxism, asserting proletariat as the universal class, the embodied Subject-Object of History whose role as the agent of revolutionary change is inscribed into its very objective social position; plus, Lukàcs's topic of 'reification' as 'false consciousness' presupposes the possibility of 'true consciousness', the proletarian class consciousness in which historical process becomes totally transparent to itself. . . However, there is a fundamental feature of Lukàcs's theory which does not fit this image of the Hegelian historicist-determinist Lukàcs: his insistence on the utter undecidability and contingency of the revolutionary process. This is why *History and Class Consciousness* is profoundly *Leninist*. When, in his 'April Theses' from 1917, Lenin discerned the *Augenblick*, the unique chance of a revolution, his proposals were first met with stupor or contempt by a large majority of his party colleagues. Within the Bolshevik party, no prominent leader supported his call to revolution, and *Pravda* took the extraordinary step of dissociating the party, and the editorial board as a whole, from Lenin's 'April Theses' – far from being an opportunist flattering and exploiting the prevailing mood of the populace, Lenin's views were highly idiosyncratic. Bogdanov characterized 'April Theses' as 'the delirium of a madman', and Nadezhda Krupskaya herself concluded that 'I am afraid it looks as if Lenin has gone crazy'. No wonder that, in his writings of 1917, Lenin saves his utmost acerbic irony for those who engage in the endless search for some kind of 'guarantee' for the revolution; this guarantee assumes two main forms: either the reified notion of social Necessity (one should not risk the revolution too early; one has to wait for the right moment, when the situation is 'mature' with regard to the laws of historical development: 'it is too early for the Socialist revolution, the working class is not yet mature') or the normative ('democratic') legitimacy ('the majority of the population is not on our side, so the revolution would not really be democratic') – as Lenin repeatedly puts it, as if, before the revolutionary agent risks the seizure of the state power, it should get the permission from some figure of the big Other (organize a referendum which will ascertain that the majority supports the revolution). With Lenin, as with Lacan, the point is that the revolution *ne s'autorise que d'elle-même*: one should assume the revolutionary *act* not covered by the big Other – the fear of taking power 'prematurely', the search for the guarantee, is the fear of the abyss of the act. Therein resides the ultimate dimension of what Lenin incessantly denounces as 'opportunism', and his wager is that 'opportunism' is a position which is in itself, inherently, false, masking the fear to accomplish the act with the protective screen of 'objective' facts, laws, or norms, which is why the first step in combating it is to announce it clearly: 'What, then, is to be done? We must *aussprechen was ist*, "state the facts", admit the truth that there is a tendency, or an opinion, in our Central Committee. . .'. Lenin's answer is not the reference to a *different* set of 'objective facts', but the repetition of the argument made a decade earlier by Rosa Luxembourg against Kautsky: those who wait for the objective conditions of the revolution to arrive will wait forever – such a position of the objective observer (and not of an engaged agent) is itself the main obstacle to the revolution.

Can Lukàcs's *History and Class Consciousness* effectively be dismissed as the caricature of Hegelian Marxism, as the assertion of the proletariat as the absolute Subject-Object of History? The art of what Lukàcs called *Augenblick* – the moment when, briefly, there is an opening for an act to intervene in a situation – confronts us with a Lukàcs who is much more Gramscian and conjecturalist/contingentian than is usually assumed – the Lukàcsian *Augenblick* is unexpectedly close to what Badiou developed as Event – an intervention that cannot be accounted for in the terms of its pre-existing 'objective conditions'. The crux of Lukàcs's argumentation is to reject the reduction of the act to its 'historical circumstances': there are no neutral 'objective conditions', or, in Hegelese, all presuppositions are already minimally posited.

Exemplary here is Lukàcs's analysis of the 'objectivist' enumeration of the causes of the failure of the Hungarian revolutionary council-dictatorship in 1919: the treason of the officers in the army, the external blockade that caused hunger. . . Although these were undoubtedly facts which played a crucial role in the defeat, it is none the less methodologically wrong to evoke them as raw facts, without taking into account the way they were 'mediated' by the specific constellation of the 'subjective' political forces. Take the blockade: why was it that, in contrast to even stronger blockade of the Russian Soviet state, the latter did not succumb to the imperialist and counter-revolutionary onslaught? Because, in Russia, the Bolshevik party made the masses aware of how this blockade is the result of foreign and domestic counter-revolutionary forces, while, in Hungary, the party was ideologically not strong enough, so the working masses succumbed to the anti-Communist propaganda which claimed that the blockade was the result of the 'anti-democratic' nature of the regime – the logic of 'let's return to democracy and the foreign aid will start to flow in. . .'. Treason of the officers? Yes, but why did the same treason not lead to the same catastrophic consequences in Soviet Russia? And when the traitors were discovered, why was it not possible to replace them with reliable cadres? Because the Hungarian Communist Party was not strong and active enough, while the Russian Bolshevik Party mobilized properly the soldiers who were ready to fight to the end to defend the revolution. Of course, one can claim that the weakness of the Communist Party was again an 'objective' component of the social situation; however, behind this 'fact', there are again other subjective decisions and acts, so that we never reach the zero level of a purely 'objective' state of things – the ultimate point is not objectivity, but social totality as the process of the global mediation between the subjective and the objective aspects.

To take an example from a different domain, the way an ideology involves 'positing its presuppositions' is also easily discernible in the standard (pseudo-) explanation of the growing acceptance of the Nazi ideology in the Germany of the 1920s by the fact that the Nazis were deftly manipulating ordinary middle-class people's fears and anxieties generated by the economic crisis and fast social changes. The problem with this explanation is that it overlooks the self-referential circularity at work here: yes, the Nazis certainly did deftly manipulate the fears and anxieties – however, far from being simple pre-ideological facts, these fears and anxieties were already the product of a certain ideological perspective. The Nazi ideology itself (co)generated 'fears and anxieties' against which it then proposed itself as a solution. . . The crucial point to bear in mind here is that there is no 'contradiction' between the Hegelian-Marxist

Lukàcs of the proletariat as the Subject-Object of history, and this 'conjecturalist' Lukàcs: these are the two sides of the same coin.

Now we can pass to the second reproach – here it is, in Marchart's version, which repeats the old Laclau point on how:

On a formal level, *every* politics is based on the articulatory logics of 'a combination and condensation of inconsistent attitudes', not only the politics of fascism. As a result, the fundamental social antagonism will always be displaced to some degree since, as we have noted earlier, the ontological level – in this case, antagonism – can never be approached directly and without political mediation. It follows that distortion is constitutive for every politics: politics as such, not only fascist politics, proceeds through 'distortion'. (above, p. 111)

This reproach remains caught in the 'binary' tension between essence and appearance: the fundamental antagonism never appears as such, directly, in a directly transparent way (in Marxist terms: the 'pure' revolutionary situation in which all social tensions would be simplified/reduced to the class struggle never takes place, it is always mediated by other – ethnic, religious, etc. – antagonisms). So: the 'essence' never appears directly, but always in a displaced/distorted way. While this statement is in principle true, there are at least two things to add to it. First, if this is the case, why even continue to talk about the 'fundamental social antagonism'? All we have is a series of antagonisms which (can) build a chain of equivalences, metaphorically 'contaminating' each other, and which antagonism emerges as 'central' is the contingent result of a struggle for hegemony. So does this mean that one should reject the very notion of 'fundamental antagonism' (as Laclau does)? Here comes my Hegelian answer – let me make this point clear by (yet again) referring to one of my standard examples: Lévi-Strauss' exemplary analysis, from his *Structural Anthropology*, of the spatial disposition of buildings in the Winnebago, one of the Great Lake tribes. The tribe is divided into two sub-groups ('moieties'), 'those who are from above' and 'those who are from below'; when we ask an individual to draw on a piece of paper or on sand, the ground-plan of his/her village (the spatial disposition of cottages), we obtain two quite different answers, depending on his/her belonging to one or the other sub-group. Both perceive the village as a circle; but for one sub-group, there is within this circle another circle of central houses, so that we have two concentric circles, while for the other sub-group, the circle is split into two by a clear dividing line. In other words, a member of the first sub-group (let us call it 'conservative–corporatist') perceives the ground-plan of the village as a ring of houses more or less symmetrically disposed around the central temple, whereas a member of the second ('revolutionary–antagonistic') sub-group perceives his/her village as two distinct heaps of houses separated by an invisible frontier (Lévi-Strauss 1963: 131–63). The point Lévi-Strauss wants to make is that this example should in no way entice us into cultural relativism, according to which the perception of social space depends on the observer's group-belonging: the very splitting into the two 'relative' perceptions implies a hidden reference to a constant – not the objective, 'actual' disposition of buildings but a traumatic kernel, a fundamental antagonism the inhabitants of the village were unable to symbolize, to account for, to 'internalize', to come to terms with, an imbalance in social relations that prevented the community from stabilizing itself into a harmonious whole. The two perceptions of the ground-plan are simply two mutually exclusive endeavours to cope with this traumatic antagonism, to heal its wound via the imposition of a balanced symbolic structure. It is here that one can see in what precise sense the real intervenes through anamorphosis. We have first the 'actual', 'objective', arrangement of the houses, and then its two different symbolizations which both distort in an anamorphic way the actual arrangement. However, the 'real' is here not the actual arrangement, but the traumatic core of the social antagonism which distorts the tribe members' view of the actual antagonism. The real is thus the disavowed X on account of which our vision of reality is anamorphically distorted. It is *simultaneously* the thing to which direct access is not possible *and* the obstacle which prevents this direct access; the thing which eludes our grasp *and* the distorting screen which makes us miss the thing. More precisely, the real is ultimately the very shift of perspective from the first to the second standpoint: the Lacanian real is not only distorted, but *the very principle of distortion* of reality.

This three-level *dispositif* is strictly homologous to Freud's three-level *dispositif* of the interpretation of dreams: for Freud also, the unconscious desire in a dream is not simply its core never appearing directly, distorted by the translation into the manifest dream-text, but the very principle of this distortion – here is a key passage from Freud's *Introductory Lectures to Psychoanalysis*:

> The latent dream-thoughts are the material which the dream-work transforms into the manifest dream. . . The only essential thing about dreams is the dream-work that has influenced the thought-material. We have no right to ignore it in our theory, even though we may disregard it in certain practical situations. Analytic observation shows further that the dream-work never restricts itself to translating these thoughts into the archaic or regressive mode of expression that is familiar to you. In addition, it regularly takes possession of something else, which is not part of the latent thoughts of the previous day, but which is the true motif force for the construction of the dream. This indispensable addition [*unentbehrliche Zutat*] is the equally unconscious wish for the fulfilment of which the content of the dream is given its new form. A dream may thus be any sort of thing in so far as you are only taking into account the thoughts it represents – a warning, an intention, a preparation, and so on; but it is always also the fulfilment of an unconscious wish and, if you are considering it as a product of the dream-work, it is only that. A dream is therefore never simply an intention, or a warning, but always an intention, etc., translated into the archaic mode of thought by the help of an unconscious wish and transformed to fulfill that wish. The one characteristic, the wish-fulfillment, is the invariable one; the other may vary. It may for its part once more be a wish, in which case the dream will, with the help of an unconscious wish, represent as fulfilled a latent wish of the previous day. (Freud 1973: 261–62)

Every detail is worth analyzing in this brilliant passage, from its implicit opening motto 'what is good enough for practice – namely the search for the meaning of dreams – is not good enough for theory', to its concluding redoubling of the wish. Its key insight is, of course, the 'triangulation' of latent dream-thought, manifest dream-content and the unconscious wish, which limits the scope of – or, rather, directly undermines – the hermeneutic model of the interpretations of dreams (the path from the manifest dream-content to its hidden meaning, the latent dream-thought), which runs backwards along the path of the formation of a dream (the transposition of the latent dream-thought into the manifest dream-content by the dream-work). The paradox is that this dream-work is not merely a process of masking the dream's 'true message': the dream's true core, its unconscious wish, inscribes itself only through and in this very process of masking, so that the moment we re-translate the dream-content back into the dream-thought expressed in it, we lose the 'true motif force' of the dream – in short, it is the process of masking itself which inscribes into the dream its true secret. One should therefore turn around the standard notion of the deeper and deeper penetration to the core of the dream: it is not that we first penetrate from the manifest dream-content to the first-level secret, the latent dream-thought, and then, in a step further, even deeper, to the dream's unconscious core, the unconscious wish. The 'deeper' wish is located into the very gap between the latent dream-thought and manifest dream-content. (A similar procedure is at work in the metaphoric dimension of everyday language. Let us say I am an editor who wants to criticize a submitted manuscript; instead of brutally saying 'the text needs to be rewritten so that at least its most stupid parts will disappear', I ironically hint that 'the text will probably need some fumigating' – does this metaphoric sub-stitution not introduce a much more ominous reference to germs and insects, to killing, etc.?)

This is how, for Deleuze, in a strict conceptual homology, economy exerts its role of determining the social structure 'in the last instance': economy in this role is never directly present as an actual causal agent, its presence is purely virtual, it is the social 'pseudo-cause', but, pre-cisely as such, absolute, non-relational, the absent cause, something that is never 'at its own place': 'that is why "the economic" is never given properly speaking, but rather designates a differential virtuality to be interpreted, always covered over by its forms of actualization' (Deleuze 1994: 186). It is the absent X which circulates between the multiple series of the social field (economic, political, ideological, legal. . .), *distributing them in their specific articulation.* One should thus insist on the radical difference between the economic as this virtual X, the absolute point of reference of the social field, and the economic in its actuality, as one of the elements ('subsystems') of the actual social totality: when they encounter each other: that is, to put it in Hegelese, when the virtual economic encounters in the guise of its actual counterpart itself in its 'oppositional determination', this identity coincides with absolute (self)contradiction.

The consequences of these conceptual elaborations for the dilemma 'direct expression of the universal or its constitutive distortion' are clear. Laclau's basic political argument against me is that, due to my rigid class-reductionist pseudo-revolutionary vision, I am condemned to 'waiting for the Martians': since the conditions I set for revolutionary agents 'are specified within such a rigid geometry of social effects that no empirical actor can fit the bill'. However, in order to sustain the appearance that I am talking about real agents, I have to have recourse to the 'process of "Martianization"': 'to attribute to actually existing subjects the most absurd features, while keeping their names so that the illusion of a contact with reality is maintained'. One cannot but take note of how close this process mockingly described by Laclau as 'Martianization' resembles his own theory of hegemony: an empirical event is 'elevated to the dignity of the Thing', it starts to function as the embodiment of the impossible fullness of society. Referring to Joan Copjec, Laclau compares hegemony to the 'breast-value' attached to partial objects: so, *mutatis mutandis*, is his thesis not that, since Martians are impossible but necessary, in the process of hegemony, an empirical social element is invested with 'Martian value' – the difference between me and him being that I (am supposed to) believe in real Martians, while he knows that the place of Martians is forever empty, so that all we can do is invest empirical agents with the 'Martian value'?[11]

It is Laclau who is here (like Kant) all too naïve in his critical stance, that is, in his assertion of the irreducible gap between empty universality and its distorted representation. From my Hegelian standpoint, this gap can be overcome – how? Not through the arrival of an adequate direct presentation of the universal, but so that *distortion as such is asserted as the site of universality*: universality *appears* as the distortion of the particular – in exact homology to Freud's logic of dreams, where the 'universal' unconscious desire (which, to put it in Marxist terms, determines the dream 'in the last instance') is not the core of the dream expressed in the dream's text in a displaced/distorted form, but the very principle of this distortion. In this precise sense, it is wrong to say that the 'central' social antagonism ('class struggle') is always expressed/articulated in a distorted/displaced way: it is the very *principle* of this distortion. Consequently, the true 'class politics' has nothing whatsoever to do with focusing exclusively on class struggle and reducing all particular struggles to secondary expressions and effects of the one and only 'true' struggle – let me clarify this point with a reference to Mao Ze-Dong's 'On Contradiction' from 1937 (although it is today no longer fashionable to refer to Mao). According to Mao, the dogmatic Marxists 'do not understand that it is precisely in the particularity of contradiction that the universality of contradiction resides':

There are many contradictions in the process of development of a complex thing, and one of them is necessarily the principal contradiction whose existence and development determines or influences the existence and development of the other contradictions.

For instance, in capitalist society the two forces in contradiction, the proletariat and the bourgeoisie, form the principal contradiction. The other contradictions, such as those between the remnant feudal class and the bourgeoisie, between the peasant petty bourgeoisie and the bourgeoisie, between the proletariat and the peasant petty bourgeoisie, between the non-monopoly capitalists and the monopoly capitalists, between bourgeois democracy and bourgeois fascism, among the capitalist countries and between imperialism and the colonies, are all determined or influenced by this principal contradiction. . .

When imperialism launches a war of aggression against such a country, all its various classes, except for some traitors, can temporarily unite in a national war against imperialism. At such a time, the contradiction between imperialism and the country concerned becomes the principal contradiction, while all the contradictions among the various classes within the country (including what was the principal contradiction, between the feudal system and the great masses of the people) are temporarily relegated to a secondary and subordinate position.[12]

This is Mao's key point: the principal (universal) contradiction does not overlap with the contradiction which should be treated as dominant in a particular situation – the universal dimension literally *resides* in this particular contradiction. In each concrete situation, a different 'particular' contradiction is the predominant one, in the precise sense that, in order to win the fight for the resolution of the principal contradiction, one should treat a particular contradiction as the predominant one, to which all other struggles should be subordinated. In China under the Japanese occupation, the patriotic unity against the Japanese was the predominant thing if the communists wanted to win the class struggle – *any direct focusing on class struggle in* these *conditions went against class struggle itself*. (Therein, perhaps, resides the main feature of 'dogmatic opportunism': to insist on the centrality of the principal contradiction at a wrong moment.)

We can see how, far from concerning only pure theory, these considerations directly reverberate in political choices: for Laclau, every 'essentialist' clinging to some central agency whose centrality is itself not the outcome of a contingent struggle for hegemony is too narrow to capture the open-ended contingent process through which universal political agents constitute themselves; it is only the notion of populism, of 'people' as hegemonically constructed political agent, which adequately renders this process. So, to conclude, I would like to add a note on populism.

I agree with Laclau's attempt to define populism in a formal-conceptual way, also taking note of how, in his last book, Laclau has clearly shifted his position from 'radical democracy' to populism (he now reduces democracy to the moment of democratic demand *within* the system); however, as it is clear to him, populism can also be very reactionary – so how are we to draw a line here? Here enters my proposal: every construction of and action on behalf of people as a political subject is not *eo ipso* populism. In the same way that Laclau claims that Society does not exist, *the People also does not exist*, and the problem with populism is that, within its horizon, people *do* exist – the People's existence is guaranteed by its constitutive exception, by the *externalization* of the enemy into a positive intruder/obstacle. The formula of the non-populist reference to the people should thus be a paraphrase of Kant's definition of beauty as *Zweckmaessigkeit ohne Zweck*: the popular without people: that is, the popular which is cut through, thwarted, by a constitutive antagonism which prevents it from acquiring the full substantial identity of a People. That is why populism, far from standing for the political as such, always involves a minimal *de-politicization*, 'naturalization', of the political.

This accounts for the fundamental paradox of authoritarian fascism: it almost symmetrically inverts what Mouffe calls the 'democratic paradox': if the wager of (institutionalized) democracy is to integrate the antagonistic struggle itself into the institutional/ differential space, transforming it into regulated agonism, fascism proceeds in the opposite direction. While fascism, in its mode of activity, brings the antagonistic logic to its extreme (talking about the 'struggle to the death' between itself and its enemies, and always maintaining – if not realizing – a minimum of an extra-institutional threat of violence, of a 'direct pressure of the people' by-passing the complex legal-institutional channels), it posits as its political goal precisely the opposite, an extremely ordered hierarchic social body (no wonder fascism always relies on organicist/corporatist metaphors). This contrast can be nicely rendered in the terms of the Lacanian opposition between the 'subject of enunciation' and the 'subject of the enunciated (content)': while democracy admits antagonistic struggle as its goal (in Lacanese: as its enunciated, its content), its procedure is regulated-systemic; fascism, on the contrary, tries to impose the goal of hierarchically structured harmony through the means of an unbridled antagonism.

In a homologous way, the ambiguity of the middle class, this contradiction embodied (as already Marx put it apropos Proudhon), is best exemplified by the way it relates to politics: on the one hand, the middle class is against politicization – they just want to sustain their way of life, to be left to work and lead their life in peace (which is why they tend to support the authoritarian coups which promise to put an end to the crazy political mobilization of society, so that everybody can return to his or her proper work). On the other hand, they – in the guise of the threatened patriotic hard-working moral majority – are the main instigators of the grass-root mass mobilization (in the guise of the rightist populism – for example, in France today, the only force truly disturbing the post-political technocratic–humanitarian administration is le Pen's National Front).

This is why the big event not only in Europe in early 2006 was that anti-immigration politics 'went mainstream': they finally cut the umbilical link that connected them to the far Right fringe parties. From France to Germany, from Austria to Holland, in the new spirit of pride at one's cultural and historical identity, the main parties now find it acceptable to stress that the immigrants are guests who have to accommodate themselves to the cultural values that define the host society – it is 'our country, love it or leave it'.

So it is not only that today's political field is polarized between the post-political administration and populist politicization; phenomena like Berlusconi demonstrate how the two opposites can even coexist in the same political force: is the Berlusconi movement *Forza Italia!* not a case of post-political populism, that is, of a mediatic–administrative government legitimizing itself in populist terms. And does the same not hold to some degree even for the Blair government in the UK, or for the Bush administration in the USA? In other words, is populism not progressively replacing the multi-culturalist tolerance as the 'spontaneous' ideological supplement to the post-political administration, as its 'pseudo-concretization', its translation into a form that can appeal to the individuals' immediate experience? The key fact here is that pure post-politics (a regime whose self-legitimization would have been thoroughly 'techno-cratic', presenting itself as competent administration) is inherently impossible: any political regime needs a supplementary 'populist' level of self-legitimization.

Populism is ultimately always sustained by the ordinary people's frustrated exasperation, by a cry of, 'I do not know what is going on, I just have had enough of it! It cannot go on! It must stop!' – an impatient outburst, a refusal to patiently understand, the exaspera-tion at the complexity, and the ensuing conviction that there must be somebody responsible for all the mess, which is why an agent who is behind and explains it all is needed. Therein, in this refusal-to-know, resides the properly *fetishist* dimension of populism. That is to say, although, at a purely formal level, fetish involves a gesture of trans-ference (on the object-fetish), it functions as an exact inversion of the standard formula of transference (with the subject supposed to know): what fetish gives body to is precisely my disavowal of knowl-edge, my refusal to subjectively assume what I know. Therein resides the contrast between fetish and symptom: a symptom embodies a repressed knowledge, the truth about the subject that the subject is not ready to assume. This is why Freud engaged in speculating on how fetish is the last object seen before stumbling upon the fact that the woman has no penis: it is the last support of the subject's ignorance. In Edith Wharton's *The Age of Innocence*, the young Newland's wife herself is his fetish: he can pursue his affair with the Countess Olenska only insofar as the wife is supposed *not* to know about it – the moment Newland learns that the wife knew about his affair all the time, he can no longer pursue his love interest in the Countess, although his wife is now dead and there is no obstacle to him marrying the Countess.

Now we can also answer the reproach that commodity fetishism relies on the opposition between direct expression of an idea (or a subject) and its distorted metaphoric representation. Let us explain this point via the reference to the thesis that, today, we live in a post-ideological world. There are two ways to understand this thesis: either we take it in a naïve post-political sense (finally liberated from the burden of great ideological narratives and causes, we can dedicate ourselves to pragmatically solving real problems), or in a more critical way, as a sign of today's predominant cynicism (today's power no longer needs a consistent ideological edifice to legitimize its rule; it can afford to directly state the obvious truth – search for profits, brutal imposition of economic interests). According to the second reading, there is no longer a need for refined procedure of *Ideologiekritik*, for a 'symptomal reading' that detects the faults in an ideological edifice: such a procedure knocks on an open door, since the thoroughly cynical power discourse concedes all this in advance, like today's analysand who calmly accepts the analyst's suggestions about his innermost obscene desire, no longer being shocked by anything.

Is, however, this effectively the case? If it is, then *Ideologiekritik* and psychoanalysis are today ultimately of no use, since the wager of their interpretive procedure is that the subject *cannot* openly admit and really assume the truth about what s/he is doing. However, psychoanalysis opens up a way to unmask this apparent proof of its uselessness, by way of detecting, beneath the deceiving openness of post-ideological cynicism, the contours of fetishism, and thus to oppose the *fetishist* mode of ideology which predominates in our allegedly 'post-ideological' era, to its traditional *symptomal* mode, in which the ideological lie which structures our perception of reality is threatened by symptoms *qua* 'returns of the repressed', cracks in the fabric of the ideological lie. Fetish is effectively a kind of *envers* of the symptom. That is to say, symptom is the exception which disturbs the surface of the false appearance, the point at which the repressed other scene erupts, while fetish is the embodiment of the lie which enables us to sustain the unbearable truth. Let us take the case of the death of a beloved person: in the case of a symptom, I 'repress' this death, I try not to think about it, but the repressed trauma returns in the symptom; in the case of a fetish, on the contrary, I 'rationally' fully accept this death, and yet I cling to the fetish, to some feature that embodies for me the disavowal of this death. In this sense, a fetish can play a very constructive role of allowing us to cope with the harsh reality: fetishists are not dreamers lost in their private worlds, they are thoroughly 'realists', able to accept the way things effectively are – since they have their fetish to which they can cling in order to cancel the full impact of reality. There is a wonderful early short story by Patricia Highsmith, 'Button', about a middle-class New Yorker who lives with a mongoloid 9-year-old son who babbles meaningless sounds all the time and smiles, while saliva is running out of his open mouth; one late evening, unable to endure the situation, he decides to take a walk on the lonely Manhattan streets where he stumbles upon a destitute homeless beggar who pleadingly extends his hand towards him; in an act of inexplicable fury, the hero beats the beggar to death and tears off from his jacket a button. Afterwards, he returns home a changed man, enduring his family nightmare without any traumas, capable of even a kind smile towards his mongoloid son; he keeps this button all the time in the pocket of his trousers – a perfect fetish, the embodied disavowal of his miserable reality, the constant reminder that, once at least, he did strike back against his miserable destiny.

So, back to the reproach that commodity fetishism relies on the opposition between direct expression of an idea (or a subject) and its distorted metaphoric representation: this reproach only holds if one sticks to the simplistic notion of fetish as an illusion obfuscating the true state of things. In psychiatric circles, there is a story told about a man whose wife was diagnosed with acute breast cancer and died 3 months afterwards; the husband survived her death unscathed, being able to talk coolly about his traumatic last moments with her – how? Was he a cold distanced monster with no feelings? Soon, his friends noticed that, while talking about his deceased wife, he always held in his hands a hamster, her pet object: his fetish, the embodied disavowal of her death. No wonder that, when, a couple of months later, the hamster died, the guy broke down and had to be hospitalized for a long period, treated for acute depression. So, when we are bombarded by claims that in our post-ideological cynical era nobody believes in the proclaimed ideals, when we encounter a person who claims he is cured of any beliefs, accepting social reality the way it really is, one should always counter such claims with the question: OK, but *where is your hamster – the fetish which enables you to (pretend to) accept reality 'the way it is'?* And does exactly the same not hold for the Marxian commodity fetishism? Here is the very beginning of the famous subdivision 4 of Chapter 1 of *Capital*, on 'The Fetishism of the Commodity and its Secret':

A commodity appears at first sight an extremely obvious, trivial thing. But its analysis brings out that it is a very strange thing, abounding in metaphysical subtleties and theological niceties. (Marx 1992: 163)

These lines should surprise us, since they turn around the standard procedure of demystifying a theological myth, of reducing it to its terrestrial base: Marx does not claim, in the usual way of Enlightenment critique, that the critical analysis should demonstrate how what appears a mysterious theological entity emerged out of the 'ordinary' real-life process; he claims, on the contrary, that the task of the critical analysis is to unearth the 'metaphysical subtleties and theological niceties' in what appears at first sight just an ordinary object. In other words, when a critical Marxist encounters a bourgeois subject immersed in commodity fetishism, the Marxist's reproach to him is not: 'The commodity may seem to you to be a magical object endowed with special powers, but it really is just a reified expression of relations between people'. The actual Marxist's reproach is, rather: 'You may think that the commodity appears to you as a simple embodiment of social relations (that, for example, money is just a kind of voucher entitling you to a part of the social product), but this is not how things really seem to you – in your social reality, by means of your participation in social exchange, you bear witness to the uncanny fact that a commodity really appears to you as a magical object endowed with special powers'. It is in this precise sense that today's era is perhaps less atheist than any prior one: we are all ready to indulge in utter scepticism, cynical distance, exploitation of others 'without any illusions', violations of all ethical constraints, extreme sexual practices, etc., etc. – protected by the silent awareness that the big Other is ignorant about it. Niels Bohr provided the perfect example of how this fetishist disavowal of belief works in ideology: seeing a horseshoe hanging above the entrance to Bohr's country-house, a surprised visitor said that he did not believe in the superstition that the horseshoe keeps the bad spirits out of the house and brings luck, to which Bohr snapped back: 'I also do not believe in it; I have it there because I was told that it works also if one does not believe in it!' Fetishism does not operate at the level of 'mystification' and 'distorted knowledge': what is literally 'displaced' in the fetish, transferred onto it, is not knowledge but *illusion itself*, the belief threatened by knowledge. Far from obfuscating 'realistic' knowledge of how things are, fetish is, on the contrary, the means that enables the subject to accept this knowledge without paying the full price for it: 'I know very well /how things really stand/, and I am able to endure this bitter truth because of a fetish (hamster, button. . .) in which the illusion to which I stick is embodied'.

At this point, where I would have to inquire into where and what my critics' hamsters are, I prefer to stop.

NOTES

1 Incidentally, this is not my term – I refer to Olivier Malnuit who coined the term 'liberal communists'.
2 Persons who were there at the time of the events informed me that what directly triggered the student demonstrations was what they perceived as preferred treatment of foreign students, especially from African countries – a racist motif, in short.
3 Note the totally jargonistic use of the term 'deconstruct': it means simply a critical analysis which shows a confusion in the opponent's reasoning!
4 The German term is '*die wahre Schranke*', which, of course, brings into play the Hegelian opposition of *Schranke* and *Grenze*, external limitation and inherent limit.
5 It is interesting to read this reproach together with Marchart's – also Laclauian – statement that 'the fundamental social antagonism will always be displaced to some degree since, as we have noted earlier, the ontological level – in this case, antagonism – can never be approached directly and without political mediation. It follows that distortion is constitutive for every politics' (above, p. 111). In short, what Marchart reproaches me with is that I do not see what, according to Devenney, is my 'only evidence', namely how the central element is never directly expressed, but always displaced.
6 Marchart briefly mentions the nineteenth-century Canudos community in Brazil as my example of a 'total break'; however, his dismissal of the Canudos community as 'a sort of forerunner of twentieth-century sects like the Davidians' (above, p. 103) is highly questionable – does he know what he is talking about?
7 And, interestingly, when, in my account of Badiou (see chapter 3 of *The Ticklish Subject*, 1999), I point out the religious paradigm of his notion of the Event of Truth, some critics of Badiou referred to me approvingly, as if I meant this as a *criticism* of Badiou. That such is not the case is amply proved by my ensuing book, *The Fragile Absolute* (2000).
8 And, to avoid the suspicion that, later in the article, I move to a more positive approach, here is its last phrase: 'This, then, is perhaps the "contribution" to Europe of Slovenia and the other accession countries: to cause us to ask the question that lies beneath the self-congratulatory

celebrations: what Europe are we joining? And when confronted with this question, we are all in the same boat, "New" and "Old" Europe' (Žižek 2004e).

9 Robert Pfaller, often a sharp critic of my work, provided a detailed analysis of my use of examples in 'Interpassivity and Misdemeanors. The Analysis of Ideology and the Žižekian Toolbox' (2006).

10 Peter Hallward (personal communication) is right in his critique of the Deleuzian politics: the poetics of resistance, of creating *lignes de fuite*, of never being where one is expected to dwell, is not enough; the time has come to start creating what one is tempted to call liberated territories, the well-defined and delineated social spaces in which the reign of the system is suspended: a religious or artistic community, a political organization. . .

11 Furthermore, Laclau only develops hegemony as the particular elevated into the embodiment/representation of the impossible thing; what is missing is how the particular element which represents all can only do it through negating the unifying feature of the all. Two worn-out examples should suffice here: for Marx, the only way to be a 'royalist in general' is to be a republican; for Hegel, man (who creates himself) in general is king (who is what he is by nature). This tension *precedes* the tension friend/enemy as reflected in hegemonic struggle.

12 I quote from the version available online at http://www.marxists.org/reference/archive/mao/selected-works/volume-1/mswv1_17.htm.

BIBLIOGRAPHY

Adorno, T.
  1974   *Minima Moralia: Reflections from Damaged Life* (trans. Edmund Jephcott; London: New Left Books).
Alliez, E.
  2004   *The Signature of the World* (trans. Eliot Albert and Alberto Toscana; London: Continuum).
Althusser, L.
  1970   *Reading Capital* (London: Verso/New Left Books).
Amis, M.
  1999   *London Fields* (London: Vintage).
  2003   'Translator's   Introduction'   in   Renzo   Novatore   (1924) *Toward the Creative Nothing* (Los Angeles: Venomous Butterfly Publications. Available at: http://www.omnipresence.mahost.org/ creativenothing.htm (accessed 6 July 2006).
Arendt, H.
  1968   *Between Past and Future* (New York: Viking Press).
  1972   *Crises of the Republic* (San Diego, New York and London: Harcourt Brace & Company).
  1973   *The Origins of Totalitarianism* (New York: Harcourt Brace Jovanovich).
  1990   *On Revolution* (London and New York: Penguin).
Armstrong, T. (ed.)
  1992   *Michel Foucault: Philosopher* (New York: Routledge).
Arriaga, Guillermo
  2003   *21 Grams* (London: Faber and Faber).
Autry, J.A. & S. Mitchell
  1998   *Real Power: Business Lessons from the Tao Te Ching* (London: Nicholas Brealey).
Badiou, A.
  2003   *Saint Paul: The Foundation of Universalism* (trans. Ray Brassier; Stanford: Stanford University Press).
Behr, E.T. & Lao, Tzu
  1997   *The Tao of Sales: The Easy Way to Sell in Tough Times* (Shaftesbury: Element).

Bennington, G.
1998   *Interrupting Derrida* (London and New York: Routledge).
Blate, M.
1978   *The Tao of Health: The Way of Total Well-Being* (Davie, Fla.:
        Falkynor Books).
Bolen, J.S.
1982   *The Tao of Psychology: Synchronicity and the Self* (San Francisco:
        Harper & Row).
Boltanski, L. & E. Chiapello
2005   *The New Spirit of Capitalism* (London: Verso Books).
Bowman, P.
2003   'Who Moved My Worth?: Management Self-Help Books and
        You!', *Signs of the Times*. Available at: <http://www.signsofthetimes.
        org.uk/bowman.html>.
Boynton, R.S.
1998   'Enjoy Your Žižek! An Excitable Slovenian Philosopher Examines
        the Obscene Practices of Everyday Life – Including His Own',
        Linguafranca: The Review of Academic Life, 7:7. Available at: http://
        www.robertboynton.com/articleDisplay.php?article_id=43   (Accessed
        29 March 2006.)
Brenner, C.
1990   'Working Alliance, Therapeutic Alliance and Transference',
        (reprinted in A.H. Esman (ed.) 1990, *Essential Papers on Transference*;
        New York: New York University Press).
Brown, W.
1995   *States of Injury: Power and Freedom in Late Modernity* (Princeton:
        Princeton University Press).
Buchanan, J.M.
2005   'Afraid to be Free: Dependency as Desideratum', *Public Choice*
        124: 19–31.
Burke, E.
1982   *Reflections on the Revolution in France* (London: Penguin).
Butler, J.
1987   *Subjects of Desire: Hegelian Reflections in Twentieth-Century
        France* (New York: Columbia University Press).
1993   *Bodies that Matter* (New York: Routledge).
1997   *Excitable Speech: A Politics of the Performative* (London and New
        York: Routledge).
Butler, J., E. Laclau & S. Žižek
2000   *Contingency, Hegemony, Universality* (London: Verso).
Butler. R.
2005   *Slavoj Žižek – Live Theory* (London: Continuum).
Butler, R. & S. Stephens
2005   'Editors' Introduction', in Slavoj Žižek 2005: 1–17.
Capra, F.
1985   *The Tao of Physics: An Exploration of the Parallels between Modern
        Physics and Eastern Mysticism* (Boston and New York: Shambhala).

Caruth, C.
  1996 *Unclaimed Experience: Trauma, Narrative and History* (London and New York: Johns Hopkins University Press).
Clarke, J.J.
  2000 *The Tao of the West: Western Transformations of Taoist Thought* (London and New York: Routledge).
Connolly, W.
  2002 *Identity/Difference: Democratic Negotiations of Political Paradox* (Minneapolis: University of Minnesota Press [originally published 1991]).
Cowen, T.
  2005 'Self-deception as the Root of Political Failure', *Public Choice*, 124: 437–51.
Critchley, S.
  2007 *Infinitely Demanding* (London and New York: Verso).
Debord, G.
  1994 *The Society of the Spectacle* (trans. Donald Nicholson-Smith; New York: Zone Books).
Deleuze, G.
  1990 *The Logic of Sense* (trans. M. Lester, with C. Stivale; [originally published 1968] New York: Columbia University Press).
  1994 *Difference and Repetition* (trans. Paul Patton; London: Athlone [originally published 1969].
Deleuze, G. & F. Guattari
  1977 *Anti–Oedipus: Capitalism and Schizophrenia* (New York: The Viking Press).
Deleuze, G. and Guattari, F. (1988) *A Thousand Plateaus: Capitalism and Schizophrenia* (Minneapolis: University of Minnesota Press).
  1994 *What is Philosophy?* (trans. G. Burchell & H. Tomlinson; London: Verso).
Derrida, J.
  1976 *Of Grammatology* (trans. Gayatri Chakravorty Spivak; Baltimore: Johns Hopkins University Press).
  1987a *The Post Card: From Socrates to Freud and Beyond* (trans. A. Bass; Chicago: University of Chicago Press).
  1987b *The Truth in Painting* (trans. G. Bennington & I. McLeod; Chicago: University of Chicago Press).
  1988 *Limited Inc* (trans. S. Weber; Evanston: Northwestern University Press).
  1992 'Mochlos; or, the Conflict of the Faculties', *Logomachia: The Conflict of the Faculties* (ed. R. Rand; Lincoln and London: University of Nebraska Press).
  1994 *Specters of Marx* (trans. Peggy Kamuf; London: Routledge).
  1995 *On the Name* (ed. T. Dutoit; trans. D. Wood, J.P. Leavey, Jr. & I. McLeod; Stanford, CA: Stanford University Press).
  1998 *Demeure – Maurice Blanchot* (Paris: Galilée).
  2000 'Et Cetera', *Deconstructions: A User's Guide* (ed. N. Royle; Basingstoke and New York: Palgrave: 282–305).

Derrida, J. & E. Roudinesco
  2004 *For What Tomorrow. . . A Dialogue* (Stanford: Stanford University Press).
D'Souza, D.
  1996 *The End of Racism: Principles for a Multiracial Society* (London: Simon & Schuster).
Dizdarević, T.
  2001 'Certain Blind Spots in Psychotherapeutic Approach to War Victims', *Zdravstvo.com*. Available at: <http://www.health-bosnia.com/radovi/tarikd.htm> (accessed 1 August 2005).
Education Commission of the States
  2005 'ECS Education Policy Issue Site: Special Education – Overidentification'. Available at: <http://www.ecs.org/html/issue.asp?issueid=112&subIssueID=199> (accessed 1 August 2005).
Esman, A.H. (ed.)
  1990 *Essential Papers on Transference* (New York: New York University Press).
Fichte, J.G.
  1962 *Fichte-Gesammtausgabe der Bayerischen Akademie der Wissenschaften* (eds R. Lauth & H. Jacob; Stuttgart-Bad Canstatt: Frommann-Holzboog).
  1971 *Fichtes Werke* (ed. Immanuel Hermann Fichte; 9 vols; Berlin: Walter de Gruyter).
  1982 *The Science of Knowledge* (trans. Peter Heath and John Lachs; Cambridge: Cambridge University Press).
  2000 *Foundations of Natural Right: According to the Principles of the Wissenschaftslehre* (ed. F. Neuhouser; Cambridge and New York: Cambridge University Press).
Fink, B.
  1995 *The Lacanian Subject* (Princeton: Princeton University Press).
Flieger, J.A.
  1999 'Overdetermined Oedipus: Mommy, Daddy and Me as Desiring-Machine', in I. Buchanan (ed.) *A Deleuzian Century?* (Durham, N.C.: Duke University Press).
Foucault, M.
  1977 *Language, Counter-Memory, Practice* (trans. Donald F. Bouchard; Ithaca: Cornell University Press).
Freud, S.
  1921 *Group Psychology and the Analysis of the Ego*, in S. Freud (1964) *The Standard Edition of the Complete Psychological Works of Sigmund Freud, Volume XVIII (1920–1922)* (London: Hogarth Press).
  1933 *New Introductory Lectures on Psychoanalysis* (Lecture XXXI: The Dissection of the Psychical Personality), in S. Freud (1964) *The Standard Edition of the Complete Psychological Works of Sigmund Freud, Volume XXII (1932–1936)* (London: Hogarth Press).
  1953 *The Complete Psychological Works of Sigmund Freud: 'A Case of Hysteria', Three Essays on the Theory of Sexuality, and other works. Volume 18* (ed. J. Strachey; London: The Hogarth Press).

1964　Analysis Terminable and Interminable. *The Standard Edition of the Complete Psychological Works of Sigmund Freud, Volume 23* (ed. J. Strachey et al.; London: Hogarth Press, 216–53).

1973　*Introductory Lectures on Psychoanalysis* (Harmondsworth: Penguin Books).

1990　'The Dynamics of Transference' (reprinted in Esman 1990: 28–36).

2001　*The Complete Psychological Works of Sigmund Freud: 'Beyond the Pleasure Principle', 'Group Psychology' and Other Works Volume 18*. (ed. J. Strachey. London: Vintage).

Gasché, R.

1994　*Inventions of Difference: On Jacques Derrida* (Cambridge, Mass. and London: Harvard University Press).

Gelley, A. (ed.)

1995　*Unruly Examples: On the Rhetoric of Exemplarity* (Stanford: Stanford University Press).

Gilbert, J.

2001　'A Certain Ethics of Openness: Radical Democratic Cultural Studies'. *Strategies*, 19 (2) November: 189–208.

2003　'Friends and Enemies: Which Side is Cultural Studies On?' *Interrogating Cultural Studies*', in P. Bowman (ed.), (London: Pluto).

Gilroy, P.

1994　*The Black Atlantic* (London: Verso).

Gordon, A.F., and Newfield, C.

1996　*Mapping Multiculturalism* (Minneapolis: University of Minnesota Press).

Gramsci, A.

1971　*Selections from the Prison Notebooks* (London: Lawrence and Wishart).

1977　'The Revolution against Capital' in David Forgacs (ed.), *A Gramsci Reader* (London: Lawrence and Wishart).

Grossberg, L.

1992　*We Gotta Get Out of this Place: Popular Conservatism and Popular Culture* (New York: Routledge).

Gržnić, M.

2004　*Situated Contemporary Art Practices: Art, Theory and Activism from (the East of) Europe* (Ljubljana: Založba ZRC).

Guiliano, M.

2005　*French Women Don't Get Fat: The Secret of Eating for Pleasure* (New York: Knopf).

Guttierez-Jones, C.

1998　'Injury by Design', *Cultural Critique* 40: 73–102.

Habermas, J.

1991　*The Structural Transformation of the Public Sphere: Inquiry into a Category of Bourgeois Society* (Cambridge, Mass.: MIT Press).

Hall, S.

1988　*The Hard Road to Renewal: Thatcherism and the Crisis of the Left* (London: Verso).

Hamilton Grant, I.
2006 *On an Artificial Earth: Philosophies of Nature after Schelling* (London: Continuum).

Hartmann, H.
1958 *Ego Psychology and the Problem of Adaptation* (New York: International Universities Press [originally published 1939]).

Harvey, D.
2005 *A Brief History of Neoliberalism* (Oxford: Oxford University Press).

Harvey, I.
1992 'Derrida and the Issues of Exemplarity', in D. Wood (ed.), *Derrida: A Critical Reader* (Oxford: Blackwell: 193–217).

Hayek, F.
1994 *The Road to Serfdom* (Chicago: University of Chicago Press).

Hegel, G.W.F.
1970 *Phänomenologie des Geistes. Werke 3* (Frankfurt am Main: Suhrkamp).
1977 *Phenomenology of Spirit* (trans. A.V. Miller; Oxford: Oxford University Press).

Heidegger, M.
1931 *Vom Wesen des Grundes* (Frankfurt am Main.: Vittorio Klostermann).
1957 *Der Satz vom Grund* (Pfullingen: Neske).
1985 *Schelling's Treatise on the Essence of Human Freedom* (trans. Joan Stambaugh; Athens, OH: Ohio University Press).

Hindmoor, A.
1999 'Rent Seeking Evaluated', *The Journal of Political Philosophy* 7(4): 434–52.

Hoff, B.
1982 *The Tao of Pooh* (New York: E.P. Dutton).

Hogrebe, W.
1989 *Prädikation und Genesis. Metaphysik als Fundamentalheuristik im Ausgang von Schellings 'Die Weltalter'* (Frankfurt am Main: Suhrkamp).

Homer, S.
2001 'It's the Political Economy Stupid!', *Radical Philosophy*, 108: 7–16.

Horney, K.
1924 On the Genesis of the Castration Complex in Women. *International Journal of Psycho-Analysis*, 5: 50–65.
1926 The Flight from Womanhood: The Masculinity-Complex in Women, as Viewed by Men and by Women. *International Journal of Psycho-Analysis*, 7: 324–39.

Jameson, F.
1978 'Imaginary and Symbolic in Lacan: Marxism, Psychoanalytic Criticism, and the Problem of Subject', *Yale French Studies* 55–56: 338–95.
1998 *The Cultural Turn* (Verso: New York).

Jeffs, N.
1995 'Transnational Dialogue in Times of War: The Peace Movement in ex-Yugoslavia', *Radical Philosophy* 73: 2–4.
Jessop, B.
1982 *The Capitalist State* (Oxford: Martin Robertson).
Johnson, S.
1998 *Who Moved My Cheese?: An Amazing Way to Deal with Change in Your Work and in Your Life* (New York: G.P. Putnam's Sons).
Kant, I.
1900 *Kants gesammelte Schriften* (ed. Königlich Preussische Akademie der Wissenschaften; [Cited *Ak.*] Berlin: Walter de Gruyter).
1958 *Critique of Pure Reason* (trans. Norman Kemp Smith; London: Macmillan).
1987 *Critique of Judgment* (trans. Werner S. Pluhar; Indianapolis: Hackett).
1993 *Opus postumum* (trans. Eckart Förster and Michael Rosen; Cambridge: Cambridge University Press).
Kay, J.
1981 'When Psychiatric Residents Treat Medical Students: Passage through Idealization and Overidentification', *General Hospital Psychiatry* 3 (2): 89–94.
Kay, S.
2003 *Žižek: A Critical Introduction* (London: Polity).
Kingsnorth, P.
2003 *One No, Many Yeses: A Journey to the Heart of the Global Resistance Movement* (London: Free Press).
Klein, M.
1957 *Envy and Gratitude: A Study of Unconscious Sources* (London: Tavistock).
1986 *The Selected Melanie Klein* (ed. Juliet Mitchell; New York: The Free Press).
Klein, N.
2002 *Fences and Windows* (London: Flamingo).
Kojève, A.
1969 *Introduction to the Reading of Hegel* (ed. A. Bloom; trans. J.H. Nichols; New York: Basic Books).
Lacan, J.
1979 *Four Fundamental Concepts of Psycho-Analysis* (trans. Alan Sheridan; Harmondsworth: Penguin [originally published 1973]).
1992 *The Ethics of Psychoanalysis 1959–1960: The Seminar of Jacques Lacan Book VII* (trans. with notes Dennis Porter; London: Routledge [originally published 1986]).
1998 *The Seminar of Jacques Lacan, Book XX. On Feminine Sexuality, The Limits of Love and Knowledge, 1972–1973 (Encore)* (trans. B. Fink; New York and London: W.W. Norton).
2002 *The Seminar of Jacques Lacan VIII: Transference, 1960–61.* (trans. C. Gallagher, from unedited French manuscripts).

2002a   *The Seminar of Jacques Lacan IX: Identification, 1961–62*. (trans. C. Gallagher, from unedited French manuscripts).

2002b   *The Seminar of Jacques Lacan X: Anxiety, 1962–63* (trans. C. Gallagher, from unedited French manuscripts).

2002c   *The Seminar of Jacques Lacan XVII: Psychoanalysis Upside Down/The Reverse Side of Psychoanalysis, 1969*–70 (trans. C. Gallagher).

LaCapra, D.

2004   *History in Transit: Experience, Identity, Critical Theory* (New York: Cornell University Press).

Laclau, E.

2000   *Contingency, Hegemony, Universality: Contemporary Dialogues on the Left* (ed. J. Butler Ernesto Laclau & Slavoj Žižek; London: Verso).

2004   'Glimpsing the Future', in S. Critchley & O. Marchart (eds), *Laclau: A Critical Reader* (London: Routledge).

2005   *On Populist Reason* (London: Verso).

Laclau, E. & C. Mouffe

1985   *Hegemony and Socialist Strategy: Towards a Radical Democratic Politics* (London: Verso).

Laibach

1996   *Jesus Christ Superstars* [CD audio recording]. Mute.

2003   *WAT* (sound recording; Mute Records).

Landsberg, M.

1996   *The Tao of Coaching: Boost Your Effectiveness at Work by Inspiring and Developing Those around You* (London: Harper Collins).

2000   *The Tao of Motivation: Inspire Yourself and Others* (London: Harper Collins Business).

Lee, B.

1975   *The Tao of Jeet Kune Do* (Santa Clarita, Calif.: Ohara Publications).

Lee, B. & J. Little

1997   *The Tao of Gung Fu: A Study in the Way of Chinese Martial Art* (Boston: C.E. Tuttle).

Lenin, V.I.

1965   *Collected Works* (vol. 33; Moscow: Progress Publishers).

Lévi-Strauss, C.

1963   'Do Dual Organizations Exist?', *Structural Anthropology* (New York: Basic Books).

Littler, J. (ed.)

2004   *Mediactive 2: Celebrity* (London: Lawrence and Wishart).

Lloyd, D.

1995   'Kant's Examples', in A. Gelley (ed.), *Unruly Examples: On the Rhetoric of Exemplarity* (Stanford, CA: Stanford University Press): 255–76.

LRE News

2003   Connecticut State Summit on Overidentification and Disproportion in Special Education'. Available at: <http://ctserc.org/.lrenews/Articles/Fall2003/ConnecticutStateSummitO.html> (accessed 1 August 2005).

Lyotard, J.F.
  1988   *The Differend* (trans. George Van Den Abbeele; Manchester: Manchester University Press).
Machiavelli, A.
  1988   *The Prince* (ed. Quentin Skinner & Russell Price; Cambridge: Cambridge University Press).
Malcolm, J.
  1981   *Psychoanalysis: The Impossible Profession* (New York: Knopf).
Mandel, E.
  1975   *Late Capitalism* (London: Verso).
Marchart, O.
  2006   *Post-foundational Political Thought: Political Difference in Nancy, Lefort, Badiou and Laclau* (Edinburgh: Edinburgh University Press).
  2006a   'Time for a New Beginning. Arendt, Benjamin, and the Messianic Conception of Political Temporality', in *Redescriptions. Yearbook of Political Thought and Conceptual History*, vol. 10 (2006).
Marx, K.
  1978   'Class Struggles in France'. *Collected Works* (vol. 10; London: Lawrence and Wishart).
  1981   *Capital* (vol. III; London: Penguin Books).
  1992   *Capital* (vol. I; London: Penguin).
Marx, K. & F. Engels
  1967   *The Communist Manifesto* (Harmondsworth: Penguin).
  1970   *The German Ideology: Introduction to a Critique of Political Economy* (London: Lawrence and Wishart).
Massumi, B.
  2002   'Navigating Movements', in Mary Zournazi (ed.), *Hope* (New York: Routledge).
Mendelsohn, E.
  2002   'The Analyst's Bad-Enough Participation', *Psychoanalytic Dialogues* 12 (3): 331–58.
Mensing, S.
  n.d.   'Learning to Feel and Integrate Your Feelings'. Available at: <http://emoclear.com/processes/feelintegrate.html> (accessed 1 August 2005).
Messing, B.
  1989   *The Tao of Management* (Aldershot: Wildwood House).
Metz, P. & J. Tobin
  1996   *The Tao of Women* (Shaftesbury: Element).
Milevska, S.
  2005   'Objects and bodies: Objectification and Over-identification in Tanja Ostojić's Art Projects', *Feminist Review* 81: 112–18.
Miller, D.
  1997   *The Tao of Muhammad Ali* (London: Vintage).
  2000   *The Tao of Bruce Lee* (London: Vintage).
Miller, J.-A.
  1989   'Jacques Lacan: Bemerkungen über sein Konzept des Passage à l'acte', in *Wo Es War* 7–8: 39–49.

Mitchell, J.
1974   *Psychoanalysis and Feminism* (London: Allen Lane).
Monroe, A.
2005   *Interrogation Machine: Laibach and the NSK State* (Cambridge, Mass.: MIT Press).
Montaigne, M. de
2004   'De l'expérience', *Essais, Livre III* (1595 edn). Available at: http://www.bribes.org/trismegiste/es 3ch13.htm (accessed 1 April 2005).
Morgan, D.
2000   *Kant Trouble: Obscurities of the Enlightened* (London: Routledge).
Mowitt, J.
1992   *Text: The Genealogy of an Antidisciplinary Object* (Durham, N.C.: Duke University Press).
1997   'Survey and Discipline: Literary Pedagogy in the Context of Cultural Studies', in A. Kumar, *Class Issues: Pedagogy, Cultural Studies and the Public Sphere* (New York: New York University Press).
2000   'Trauma Envy', *Cultural Critique* 46 (Autumn): 272–97.
2002   *Percussion: Drumming, Beating, Striking* (Durham and London: Duke University Press).
Mudrak, M.
2001   'Neue Slowenische Kunst and the Semiotics of Suprematism', in I. Arns (ed.), (2003), *IRWIN RETROPRINCIP: 1983–2003* (Frankfurt: Revolver).
Muller, J.P. & W. Richardson (eds)
1988   *The Purloined Poe: Lacan, Derrida, and Psychoanalytic Reading* (Baltimore, Mass. & London: Johns Hopkins University Press).
Murata, S.
1992   *The Tao of Islam: A Sourcebook on Gender Relationships in Islamic Thought* (Albany, N.Y.: State University of New York Press).
Myers, T.
2003   *Slavoj Žižek* (London: Routledge).
Nancy, J.-L.
1997   *Hegel: L'inquiétude du negative* (Paris: Hachette).
Nietzsche, F.
1996   *On the Genealogy of Morals: A Polemic* (trans. D. Smith; Oxford and New York: Oxford University Press).
Nobus, D. & M. Quinn
2005   *Knowing Nothing, Staying Stupid: Elements for a Psychoanalytic Epistemology* (London: Routledge).
NSK
2002   *NSK Electronic Embassy* [online]. Available at: http://www.ljudmila.org/embassy/ (accessed 8 November 2005).
O'Connor, N. & J. Ryan
1993   *Wild Desires and Mistaken Identities: Lesbianism and Psychoanalysis* (London: Virago).
Osborne, P.
2000   *Philosophy in Cultural Theory* (London: Routledge).

Paine, J.
2004   *Re-Enchantment* (New York: Norton).
Parker, I.
2004   *Slavoj Žižek: A Critical Introduction* (London: Pluto Press).
2004a   'Žižek: Ambivalence and Oscillation', *Psychology in Society* 30: 23–34.
2005   'Laibach and Enjoy: Slovenian Theory and Practice', *Psychoanalysis, Culture & Society* 10: 105–12.
Parry, B.
2004   *Postcolonial Studies: A Materialist Critique* (London: Routledge).
Pfaller, R.
2006   'Interpassivity and Misdemeanors. The Analysis of Ideology and the Žižekian Toolbox' (unpublished paper).
Pippin, R.
2005   *The Persistence of Subjectivity* (Cambridge: Cambridge University Press).
Rancière, J.
1974   *La leçon d'Althusser* (Paris: Gallimard).
Rawls, J.
1971/99   *A Theory of Justice* (Cambridge, Mass.: Harvard University Press).
Ray, I.
2000   *A Treatise on the Medical Jurisprudence of Insanity* (New York: Beard Books [originally published 1838]).
Read, J. (2003) 'A Universal History of Contingency: Deleuze and Guattari on the History of Capitalism'. *borderlands* [online], 2 (3). Available at: http://www.borderlandsejournal.adelaide.edu.au/vol2no3_2003/read_contingency.htm
Richardson, J.
2000   'NSK 2000? Irwin and Eda Cufer, Interviewed by Joanne Richardson', <http://subsol.c3.hu/subsol_2/contributors/nsktext.html> (accessed 3 January 2003).
Rioch, J.M.
1990   'The Transference Phenomenon in Psychoanalytic Theory', (reprinted in Esman 1990): 252–66.
Ronell, A.
1994   'Trauma TV', *Finitude's Score: Essays for the End of the Millennium* (Lincoln, Ill.: University of Nebraska Press).
Rousseau, J.J.
1987   'On the Social Contract', reprinted in *The Basic Political Writings* (Cambridge, Mass.: Hackett Publishing).
Sandkühler, H.-J. (ed.)
1984   *Natur und geschichtlicher Prozess. Studien zur Naturphilosophie Schellings* (Frankfurt am Main: Suhrkamp).
Sandler, J., C. Dare & A. Holder
1979   *The Patient and the Analyst* (London: Maresfield Reprints [originally published 1973]).

Schafer, R.
1990   'The Interpretation of Transference and the Conditions for
        Loving', (reprinted in A.H. Esman (ed.) 1990, *Essential Papers on
        Transference*; New York: New York University Press): 401–22.
Scheler, M.
1972   *Ressentiment* (trans. William Holdheim; New York: Schocken
        Books).
Schelling, F.W.J. von
1856–1861   *Sämmtliche Werke* (ed. K.A. Schelling; Stuttgart and
        Augsburg: J.G. Cotta'scher Verlag).
1946   *Die Weltalter. Fragmente. In den Urfassungen von 1811 und 1813*
        (ed. Manfred Schröter; Munich: Beck).
1972   *Grundlegung der positiven Philosophie. Münchener Vorlesungen
        WS 1832/3 und SS 1833* (ed. Horst Fuhrmans; Torino: Bottega
        d'Erasmo).
1986   *Philosophical Inquiries into the Nature of Human Freedom* (trans.
        James Gutmann; La Salle, Ill.: Open Court).
1994   *Philosophische Entwürfe und Tagebücher 1809–1813 Philosophie
        der Freiheit und Weltalter* (ed. Lothar Knatz, Hans-Jorg Sandkühler &
        Martin Schraven; Hamburg: Meiner).
1997   *Ages of the World* (trans. Judith Norman; Ann Arbor, Mich.:
        University of Michigan Press).
1998   *System der Weltalter* (ed. Siegbert Peetz; Frankfurt am Main.:
        Vittorio Klostermann).
2000   *The Ages of the World* (trans. Jason M. Wirth; New York: SUNY).
2002   *Weltalter-Fragmente* (ed. K. Grotsch; Stuttgart-Bad Canstatt:
        Frommann-Holzboog).
Schmidt, A.
1978   *Geschichte und Struktur. Fragen einer marxistischen Historik*
        (Münster: Ullstein Taschenbuchvlg).
Schopenhauer, A.
1974   *The Fourfold Root of the Principle of Sufficient Reason* (trans.
        E.J.F. Payne; La Salle, Ill.: Open Court).
Sebald, W.G.
2003   *On the Natural History of Destruction* (London: Penguin Books).
Sharpe, M.
2004   *Slavoj Žižek: A Little Piece of the Real* (London: Ashgate).
Simmel, G.
1983   *Philosophische Kultur: Über das Abenteuer, die Geschlechter, und
        die Krise der Moderne: Gesammelte essais* (Berlin: Verlag Klaus
        Wagenbach).
Siu, R.G.H.
1957   *The Tao of Science: An Essay on Western Knowledge and Eastern
        Wisdom* (Cambridge, Mass.: M.I.T. Press).
Sokal, A.
1999   *Fashionable Nonsense: Postmodern Intellectuals' Abuse of Science*
        (London: Saint Martin's Press).

Spivak, Gayatri Chakravorty
1999   *A Critique of Postcolonial Reason: Toward a History of the Vanishing Present* (Cambridge, MA and London: Harvard University Press).
Stamp, R.
2003   'Our Friend Žižek', *Film-Philosophy* 7 (28) (September). Available at: http://www.film-philosophy.com/vol7–2003/n29stamp (accessed 28 March 2005).
Stavrakakis, Y.
2003   'Re-Activating the Democratic Revolution: The Politics of Transformation Beyond Reoccupation and Conformism', in *Parallax*, 9 (2): 56–71.
Stein, M.H.
1990   'The Unobjectionable Part of the Transference', (reprinted in Esman 1990: 382–400).
Stengers, I.
1997   *Power and Invention* (trans. Paul Bains; Minneapolis: University of Minnesota Press).
Stepančič, L.
1994   'The Poster Scandal: New Collectivism and the 1987 Youth Day', in I. Arns (ed.), (2003), *IRWINRETROPRINCIP: 1983–2003* (Frankfurt: Revolver).
Thompson, E.P.
1978   *The Poverty of Theory and Other Essays* (London: The Merlin Press).
Valentine, J.
2004   'The Mood of Networking Culture in DATA Browser 01', *Economising Culture* (New York: Autonomedia).
2005   'Everyone's At It: Regulation and the New Rentier Economy', Available at <http://www.signsofthetimes.org.uk/>.
Virno, P.
2004   *A Grammar of the Multitude* (New York: Semiotext[e]).
Waldby, C.
2002   'Stem Cells. Tissue Cultures, and the Production of Biovalue', in *Health: An Interdisciplinary Journal for the Social Study of Health, Illness and Medicine*, July 2002; 6: 305–23, London: Sage.
Warminski, A.
1987   *Readings in Interpretation: Hölderlin, Hegel, Heidegger* (Minneapolis, Minn.: University of Minnesota Press).
Watts, A.
1995   *The Tao of Philosophy: The Edited Transcripts* (Boston: C.E. Tuttle).
Whitfield, D.
2006   *Articles of Faith. Available at:* <http://www.redpepper.org.uk/brit/x-feb06-whitfield.htm>
2006a   *Marketisation of Public Services* (London: Spokesman Books).
Williams, R.
1977   *Marxism and Literature* (Oxford: Oxford University Press).

Wolpe, H.
1990 *Race, Class and the Apartheid State* (UNESCO: Apartheid and Society Series).
Wright, E. & E. Wright (eds)
1999 *The Žižek Reader* (London: Blackwell).
Zhang, L.
1992 *The Tao and the Logos: Literary Hermeneutics, East and West* (Durham, N.C. and London: Duke University Press).
Žižek, S.
1988 *Le plus sublime des hystériques. Hegel passe* (Paris: Point Hors Ligne).
1988a 'The Object as a Limit of Discourse: Approaches to the Lacanian Real', *Prose Studies* 11(3): 94–120.
1989 *The Sublime Object of Ideology* (London: Verso).
1990 'Beyond Discourse Analysis', in Ernesto Laclau (ed.), *New Reflections on the Revolution of our Time* (London: Verso).
1991 *Looking Awry: An Introduction to Jacques Lacan through Popular Culture* (Cambridge, Mass.: MIT Press).
1991a *Enjoy Your Symptom! Jaques Lacan in Hollywood and Out* (Cambridge Mass.: MIT Press).
1991b *For They Know Not What They Do: Enjoyment as a Political Factor* (London: Verso).
1992 *Everything You Always Wanted to Know About Lacan (But Were Afraid to Ask Hitchcock)* (London: Verso).
1993 *Tarrying with the Negative: Kant, Hegel, and the Critique of Ideology* (Durham N.C.: Duke University Press).
1993a 'Es gibt keinen Staat in Europa', in I. Arns (ed.), (2003), *IRWIN-RETROPRINCIP: 1983–2003* (Frankfurt: Revolver). Also available at <http://www.nettime.org/desk-mirror/zkp 2/staat.html> (accessed 3 August 2003).
1993b 'Why are Laibach and NSK not Fascists?', in I. Arns (ed.), (2003), *IRWINRETROPRINCIP: 1983–2003* (Frankfurt: Revolver): 49–50. Also available at <http://www.nskstate.com/> (accessed 8 November 2005).
1994 *The Metastases of Enjoyment* (London: Verso).
1996 *The Indivisible Remainder: An Essay on Schelling and Related Matters* (London: Verso).
1996a 'Selfhood as Such is Spirit: F.W.J. Schelling on the Origins of Evil', in Joan Copjec (ed.), *Radical Evil* (London: Verso).
1997 *The Plague of Fantasies* (London: Verso).
1997a 'Multiculturalism, or the Logic of Multinational Capitalism', *New Left Review* 225 (September–October): 28–51.
1997b 'The Abyss of Freedom', in F.W.J. von Schelling (1997): 3–93.
2001 *The Fright of Real Tears: Krzysztof Kieslowski between Theory and Post-Theory* (London: BFI).
2003 'Not a desire to have him, but to be like him'. *London Review of Books* [online], 25 (16). Available at: http://www.lrb.co.uk/v25/n16/zize01_.html

Žižek, S. (ed.)
1998   *Cogito and the Unconscious* (Durham N.C.: Duke University Press).
1998a   'A Leftist Plea for "Eurocentrism"', *Critical Enquiry* 2: 988–1009.
1999   *The Ticklish Subject* (London: Verso).
1999a   'Human Rights and its Discontents'. Available at: <http://www.bard.edu/hrp/Žižek transcript.htm> (accessed 7 June 2002).
1999b   'Against the Double Blackmail', *New Left Review* 234: 76–82.
1999c   'The Rhetorics of Power', *Diacritics*, 31(1): 91–104.
2000   *The Fragile Absolute: Or, Why is the Christian Legacy Worth Fighting For?* (London: Verso).
2000a   *Contingency, Hegemony, Universality: Contemporary Dialogues on the Left*, in J. Butler, Ernesto Laclau and Slavoj Žižek, London, Verso.
2000b   'Foreword' to Zupančič, A., *Ethics of the Real: Kant, Lacan.* London: Verso.
2001   *Did Somebody Say Totalitarianism?: Five Interventions in the (Mis)Use of a Notion* (London, Verso).
2001a   *On Belief* (London, Routledge).
2001b   'Repeating Lenin'. Available at: <http://www.lacan.com/replenin.htm>
2002   *Welcome to the Desert of the Real* (London, Verso).
2002a   *Revolution at the Gates: A Selection of Writings from February to October 1917: V. I. Lenin* (edited with an Introduction and Afterword by Slavoj Žižek; London: Verso).
2002b   *For They Know Not What They Do: Enjoyment as a Political Factor* (London and New York: Verso, 2nd edn).
2004   *Iraq: The Borrowed Kettle* (London: Verso).
2004a   *Organs Without Bodies. On Deleuze and Consequences* (London and New York: Routledge).
2004b   'Everything You Ever Wanted to Know About Schelling (But Were Afraid to Ask Hitchcock)', in Judith Norman and Alistair Welchman (eds), *The New Schelling* (London: Continuum).
2004c   'Over the Rainbow', *London Review of Books* 26 (21): 20.
2004d   'What Lies Beneath', *The Guardian* (Saturday 1 May).
2004e   'What Does Europe Want?' *In These Times*. Available at: <http://inthesetimes.com/site/main/article/166/> (accessed 8 November 2005).
2005   *Interrogating the Real* (London and New York: Continuum).
2005a   'Žižek Live', in Butler 2005: 139–52.
2005b   'Some Politically Incorrect Reflections on Violence in France & Related Matters'. Available at: <http://www.lacan.com/zizfrance.htm> (accessed 23 November 2005).
2005c   'The Pope's Failures'. *In These Times* (8 April. Available at: <http://www.inthesetimes.com/site/main/article/2059/> (accessed 11 August 2005).
2005d   'The Act and its Vicissitudes', *The Symptom* 6. Available at: <http://www.lacan.com/symptom6_articles/zizek.html> (accessed 23 November 2005).

2005e   'The Constitution is Dead. Long Live Proper Politics', *The Guardian* (4 June).

2005f   'Foreword: They Moved the Underground', in Monroe, A., *Interrogation Machine: Laibach and the NSK State* (Cambridge, Mass.: MIT Press).

2006   *The Parallax View* (Cambridge, Mass.: The MIT Press).

2006a   *A Pervert's Guide to Cinema, Part 1* (Channel 4, 16 March).

2006b   'Nobody has to be vile'. *London Review of Books* 28 (7): 10.

Žižek, S. & G. Daly

2004   *Conversations with Žižek* (London: Polity).

Zupančič, A.

2000   *Ethics of the Real: Kant, Lacan* (London: Verso).

INDEX